REA

FRIENDS OF ACPL

INDIANA POLITICS DURING THE CIVIL WAR

INDIANA POLITICS

DURING THE

CIVIL WAR

By
KENNETH M. STAMPP

INDIANA UNIVERSITY PRESS
Bloomington / London
In Association with
THE INDIANA HISTORICAL BUREAU

Copyright © 1949 by The Indiana Historical Bureau
Copyright © 1978 for the New Preface by Kenneth M. Stampp
All rights reserved
No part of this book may be reproduced or utilized in
any form or by any means, electronic or mechanical,
including photocopying and recording, or by any information
storage and retrieval system, without permission in writing
from the publisher. The Association of American University
Presses' Resolution on Permissions constitutes the only
exception to this prohibition.

Manufactured in the United States of America
Library of Congress catalog card number: 77-23629
ISBN 0-253-37022-1

2077018

To
S. K. and K.

CONTENTS

	Preface to the New Edition	ix
	Preface	xvii
I.	The Hoosier Commonwealth	1
II.	Political Kaleidoscopics	15
III.	A Dutiful Victory	31
IV.	Unity Out of Disunion	49
V.	The Politics of Patriotism	74
VI.	Mobilizing a Sovereign State	100
VII.	Republicanism Repudiated	128
VIII.	The Collapse of Constitutional Government	158
IX.	The Backwash of War	186
X.	Voting Down the Rebellion	217
XI.	The Problems of Peace	255
	Bibliography	269
	Index	281

PREFACE TO THE NEW EDITION

This political study of Indiana during the Civil War had its inception in the late 1930s as a doctoral dissertation at the University of Wisconsin. After its completion in 1941 the manuscript was revised for publication, but the Second World War and the vicissitudes of the Indiana Historical Bureau delayed that event until 1949. I am pleased that the Indiana University Press has agreed to reprint my book in its original form, because it represents a point of view not only about certain specific historical events but about history in general. This point of view, economic determinism, is identified especially with the late Charles A. Beard,[1] and it was popular among many young historians of my generation. Economic determinism is the perspective from which I view the Hoosier experience during the Civil War era—the era that Beard labeled the Second American Revolution.

This is not precisely my perspective today, for, as always, the intervening decades seem to have changed the past as well as the present. Beard's concept of a Second American Revolution now appears to be much too narrow and simplistic, and many modern economic historians question his interpretation of the economic significance of the Civil War.[2] Nevertheless, I still believe that my earlier perspective explains a great deal and that it is by no means altogether out of date. The political and social tensions so evident in Indiana's wartime society

were the products not only of military conflict but of a
recent transportation revolution, of a decline in self-
sufficient agriculture and an unsettling growth in com-
mercialization and urbanization, and of a dramatic party
reorganization and a major shift in the political balance
of power. Viewed broadly as a political and social phe-
nomenon, not merely as a conspiracy of eastern bankers,
industrialists, and railroad magnates to wrest power from
southern planters and western farmers, the concept of a
Second American Revolution has substance to it.

When this book was published the reviews were generally favorable, and at the present time it remains the
only book-length study devoted exclusively to Indiana's
Civil War years.[3] However, much that is directly or indirectly relevant to the subject has been written since
1949, and it may be useful for me to indicate the points
at which these recent writings suggest different approaches
or revisions of my interpretations. After a book has been
in print for nearly thirty years, an author is likely to
feel somewhat disengaged from its argument and hence
no longer compelled to defend it to the last word. Actually, the purely factual side of my account has held
up reasonably well. It is about matters of emphasis and
interpretation—the more imaginative and creative aspects
of historical writing—that historians are so much affected
by changes in perspective.

No doubt if I were writing this book today I would be
influenced by recent studies of voter behavior, which indicate that American voters respond to a complex mixture of family, local, and regional traditions and to reli-
gious and ethnic loyalties, as well as to ideological appeals
and perceptions of economic self-interest. In examining
the political realignments of the 1850s and the origins of
the third American party system in Indiana I would de-
vote more space to nativism and the temperance movement, but not at the expense of economic interests or
attitudes toward slavery, slavery expansion, or the south-

ern Slave Power. In order to probe more deeply into the reasons for the shifting fortunes of Indiana Republicans and Democrats between 1856 and 1864, I would make use of county election data now available at the Survey Research Center at the University of Michigan. An analytical study of key counties that shifted from one party to the other might lead to a fuller explanation of why the Democrats carried the state in 1856 and 1862, while the Republicans carried it in 1860 and 1864.

It is unlikely that a present-day historian would undertake a study of this kind without utilizing the social science methodology of the so-called New Political History —its use of sophisticated statistical procedures and its application of computer technology to the analysis of election returns. However, I would not be satisfied with the new methodology alone, for traditional political history has by no means been entirely outmoded. There are limits to what we can learn from a computer or explain with a statistical chart. Many aspects of political behavior still can be studied most effectively from literary sources using traditional methods of historical criticism.

What I have to say about the role of Indiana Democrats, especially the peace Democrats (see chapters 8 and 9), best illustrates the way in which the concerns of the 1930s influenced my perspective. What I would now want to add to my interpretation of the Democrats doubtless illustrates the way in which the concerns of today modify my view of what is important. Most of the peace Democrats of 1863-64 called for an armistice and a renewed attempt to restore the Union through a sectional compromise. A small handful of them questioned the value of a Union held together with bayonets and claimed that the war was destroying democracy and threatening a military despotism. To them a temporary dissolution of the Union was a small price to pay for peace and for the hope that voluntary reunion would eventually come. Republicans, for partisan reasons, attached the pejorative term "Copperhead" to all peace Democrats, suggesting that they were "rebel sympathizers" who, at the very least, flirted with treason. In the heat of the political campaign of 1864 Republicans were prone to stigmatize all Democrats as Copperheads, even though the great majority of Democrats continued to support the war for the Union. Eventually this interpretation found its way into much historical writing, thus perpetuating the belief that peace Democrats were at heart southern sympathizers of questionable loyalty.[4]

My own research, reinforced by my view of what was most important in the rhetoric of the peace Democrats, caused me to see them in a rather different light. I found no evidence that the mass of peace Democrats was disloyal; rather, they had undertaken the difficult task of defending civil liberties in wartime and of criticizing the military policies of state and national Republican administrations. Doubtless the suppression of civil liberties in the United States during the First World War and the reckless charges of treason during the post-war Red Scare sensitized me to the issues of arbitrary arrests of civilians and of freedom of speech and press raised by Democrats who supported the war as well as by those who favored peace.

Moreover, I was struck by the complaints of peace Democrats that northeastern business interests were using the war emergency for their own selfish purposes—that they were promoting federal banking and fiscal policies beneficial to them but injurious to western farmers. Democrats in the Indiana legislature sounded like precursors of the post-war Grangers and Populists when they complained about discriminatory practices of the railroads and argued the need for state regulation. This suggested to me that they were not so much allies of the Confederates as champions of the principles of traditional Jacksonian Democracy and opponents of a Union dominated by eastern economic interests. In short, they were western sectionalists. On page 211, I portray Daniel W.

Voorhees, a leading peace Democrat, as the defender of a traditional agrarian way of life which he thought was being destroyed by the war. From my present perspective I still believe that this interpretation of Copperheadism is valid, and I am not inclined to modify it. Indeed, the recent researches of Frank L. Klement led him to similar conclusions about the Copperheads throughout the Midwest.[5]

However, after going back over my old notes and re-reading the propaganda of the peace Democrats, I am now impressed by another dimension of Copperheadism, one whose importance was less apparent to me at the time this book was written and to which I alluded only briefly. I should have given more attention to the fact that Copperhead propaganda was replete with the most demagogic appeals to racism—with charges that Republicans believed in racial equality, perhaps even in interracial marriages. The Copperheads were the first to use the term "miscegenation," and they tried to frighten Northerners with warnings that racial amalgamation was a likely consequence of emancipation. Democrats seldom referred to the Republican party except as the "Black Republican party," and they predicted that Lincoln's Emancipation Proclamation would cause a "black tide" to flow over the North, taking employment away from white workingmen. Not only did they exploit the widespread racial prejudices of the northern people, they were themselves obsessed with fear of the so-called Black Menace—an ill-defined but acute apprehension that their Anglo-Saxon civilization would be "Africanized." Thus the Copperhead appeal was in large measure racist.

If all of this seems clear to me now, it is not because of new evidence that was unavailable in the 1930s. What has changed is not the evidence but the world in which I live—and, as a result, my conception of what is important. In the depression years of the 1930s, racism seemed less "revelant" than the economic issues that the Copperheads raised, even though they appealed to race prejudice at least as often as to economic self-interest. Needless to say, if I were writing this book today I would put heavy stress on the racist dimension of Copperheadism, just as several other historians recently have done,[6] for the perspective of the 1970s makes me much more sensitive to the importance of racism in American society. As a historian I find this to be a sobering experience, one that increases my skepticism that even the best methodology will ever transcend our limitations of vision and produce definitive historical works.

On other subjects my perspective from the 1970s does not presently indicate the need for substantial revisions of interpretation. For example, I do not feel compelled to reevaluate the role of Indiana's war governor—the tough, efficient, pragmatic, and politically ruthless Oliver P. Morton. He was suited by talent and temperament for dealing with the practical problems confronting his state during the war years, and he disposed of his enemies inside and outside his party with great skill. Another Indiana Republican, George W. Julian, congressman from the Fifth District, played a different role which brought him into frequent conflict with Governor Morton. For a decade or more Julian was the conscience of the Indiana Republican party—a Free Soiler, political abolitionist, and Radical Republican who was determined to keep his party on the antislavery track, to expand the war for the Union into a crusade for emancipation, and, later, to win justice for the freedmen. Julian is worth more attention than he receives in this book, and, fortunately, since its publication he has become the subject of a perceptive biography.[7] Many other topics that I have dealt with have been amplified in numerous articles in the pages of the *Indiana Magazine of History*.

Kenneth M. Stampp

Berkeley, California
May, 1977

NOTES

1. See especially Charles A. and Mary R. Beard, *The Rise of American Civilization* (2 vols., New York, 1927).
2. For some of the key essays see Ralph Andreano, ed., *The Economic Impact of the American Civil War* (Cambridge, rev. ed., 1967), and David T. Gilchrist and W. David Lewis, eds., *Economic Change in the Civil War Era* (Greenville, Del., 1965).
3. Emma L. Thornbrough, *Indiana in the Civil War Era, 1850-1880* (Indianapolis, 1965), is a valuable work covering a longer span of Indiana history.
4. See, for example, Wood Gray, *The Hidden Civil War: The Story of the Copperheads* (New York, 1942), and George Fort Milton, *Abraham Lincoln and the Fifth Column* (New York, 1942).
5. See the following writings by Klement: "Middle Western Copperheadism and the Genesis of the Granger Movement," *Mississippi Valley Historical Review*, XXXVIII (1952), pp. 679-94; *The Copperheads in the Middle West* (Chicago, 1960); and "Carrington and the Golden Circle Legend in Indiana during the Civil War," *Indiana Magazine of History*, LXI (1965), pp. 31-52. For evaluations of recent writings on the Copperheads see Richard O. Curry, "The Union As It Was: A Critique of Recent Interpretations of the Copperheads," *Civil War History*, XIII (1967), pp. 25-39, and Robert H. Abzug, "The Copperheads: Historical Approaches to Civil War Dissent in the Midwest," *Indiana Magazine of History*, LXVI (1970), pp. 40-55.
6. Emma L. Thornbrough, "The Race Issue in Indiana Politics during the Civil War," *Indiana Magazine of History*, XLVII (1951), pp. 163-88; Emma L. Thornbrough, *The Negro in Indiana* (Indianapolis, 1957); V. Jacque Voegeli, *Free But Not Equal: The Midwest and the Negro during the Civil War* (Chicago, 1967); Forrest G. Wood, *Black Scare: The Racist Response to Emancipation and Reconstruction* (Berkeley and Los Angeles, 1968).
7. Patrick W. Riddleberger, *George W. Julian: Radical Republican* (Indianapolis, 1966).

PREFACE

INDIANA is one of the few states whose role in the Civil War has not been the subject of a book-length study. Yet of the states which participated in that great conflict perhaps none is more deserving of such attention. In a sense Indiana provides a case study in how the war affected a typical commonwealth of the Old Northwest. Here one can see with exceptional clarity the usual conflict between the Federal War Department and a powerful state executive. Here one can examine the sources of sectional and interstate jealousies. Here one can discover the extreme difficulty with which individualistic Americans were mobilized and regimented for war. Here one can weigh the profound influence of the Civil War upon the lives and thoughts of the people.

But the story of Indiana in this period offers more than that. Nowhere else did the war produce greater political tensions than among the Hoosiers. Nowhere else did the people debate more violently the merits of the revolutionary social changes which the war brought about. Without a doubt there has been a tendency to exaggerate immensely the number of Hoosiers who were openly prosouthern or who favored "peace at any price." Indiana's people overwhelmingly favored the prosecution of the war until the Union was restored. But there was a deep and bitter division between those who wanted "the Union as it was" and those who wanted to break with the past and build a new nation functioning upon new economic principles. It was this issue that arrayed the old Jacksonians against the Republican-dominated Union party. It was this that kept Indiana hanging on the edge of domestic violence, that made her party battles so fierce, and which, in turn, finally led to the collapse of her representative government and to the establishment of Governor Oliver P. Morton's personal dictatorship.

This study is focused upon the political aspects of Indiana's war experience, but it is hoped that politics has been interpreted in its broadest sense. It was in politics that the discords of that era found expression; it was through local politicians, close to the grass roots, that popular reactions can best be measured. One can be reasonably certain that, while political leaders like Governor Morton, George W. Julian, and Daniel W. Voorhees were expressing such clashing ideas, every shade of Indiana's public opinion somewhere found a voice. The aim of this book is to draw from the cacophony of Hoosier voices the profound meaning it actually had.

I wish to acknowledge my deep indebtedness to those who have given me aid of various kinds. Above all I am obligated to William B. Hesseltine of the University of Wisconsin who first proposed that I undertake this study, who directed my research, and who made more invaluable suggestions than I had a right to expect even from a graduate teacher. For both criticism and encouragement I am also grateful to John D. Hicks of the University of California; to Fred H. Harrington of the University of Wisconsin; to Frank Freidel of Vassar College; to Richard N. Current of Mills College; to T. Harry Williams of Louisiana State University; to George Winston Smith of the University of Illinois; and to Cedric C. Cummins of the University of South Dakota.

The staff of the Indiana State Library was more than generous in giving me access to documentary materials and in offering helpful advice. In these matters I owe special thanks to Mr. Reid Nation, former chief of the Archives Division, and to Mrs. Hazel W. Hopper, chief of the Indiana Division. The Indianapolis Public Library and the Wisconsin State Historical Society Library also gave me free use of their collections.

For his critical reading of the manuscript and for pointing out needed revisions my appreciation is due to Howard H. Peckham, director of the Indiana Historical Bureau. The editorial staff of the Historical Bureau edited the manuscript with great care and intelligence.

A few sections of the manuscript have appeared in essentially similar form in several scholarly journals. These articles are listed in the bibliography. The editors of the *Mississippi Valley Historical Review,* the *Journal of Southern History,* and the *Indiana Magazine of History* have graciously permitted me to republish portions of them.

My last debt is to my wife who gave me patient assistance at every stage in the preparation of this book.

KENNETH M. STAMPP

BERKELEY, CALIFORNIA
July, 1948

THE HOOSIER COMMONWEALTH

CHAPTER 1

THE middle years of the nineteenth century found the Old Northwest showing unmistakable signs of "growing up." By then each of its five territorial divisions had achieved statehood; squatters and brawling frontiersmen had long since departed for new lands across the Mississippi and left behind the cleared fields and peaceful communities. Institutions of culture —schools, churches, theaters, newspapers, railroads, and the telegraph—had brought in the leaven of civilization and tempered, partially at least, the bleakness of western life. The thinned ranks of old settlers might still recall the hardships of bygone days and complain of the decadence of the present, but that was a token of approaching social maturity. Most Westerners were intensely proud of the flourishing democratic society which they had created out of the American wilderness.

Western men looked expectantly to the future for even greater material rewards for their enterprise. They looked to the past only for political and economic lessons to guide them in the days ahead. But the lessons they learned from the past were as diverse as the men themselves, as rife with contradictions as was the West. The future of the Northwest could never look the same to the boat builders and merchants of the Ohio River towns, and to the investors in western railroads; to the owners

of factories, and to the tillers of the soil; to the wool
growers, and to the wheat, corn, and hog raisers; to the
incipient masters of capital, and to the propertyless
mechanics and farm hands. Most of the perplexing problems which grow out of rural versus urban interests, of
large property holders versus small property holders, had
already appeared, and their ramifications were coloring
every aspect of that section's political life. Social solidarity, if such ever existed, had given way to social
discord—to the tug of divergent economic forces. The
Northwest now held the balance of power in the nation,
but it still had to decide which way to tip the scale.

Indiana, with her wooded hills and fertile prairies
stretching from the Ohio River to Lake Michigan, lay
in the very heart of the Old Northwest and embodied all
of its interests and diversities. Her population had been
drawn from many states, but the largest numbers had
come from Ohio, Pennsylvania, Kentucky, Virginia,
North Carolina, and Tennessee. Emigrants from the
northern states had exceeded those from the South in the
later decades, but in 1860 Indiana still had more Southerners than any other state north of the Ohio. By that
time fifty-seven per cent of her population were nativeborn Hoosiers; less than ten per cent were foreign born.
There were some eleven thousand negroes in the state.[1]

The roots of the state's social attitudes lay deep in the
past, and the course of her growth had been shaped by
the accidents of natural phenomena: climate, rainfall,
soil, natural resources, and geographic location. As in
her sister states of the West, while her people had many
common interests, they also had important clashing ambitions. Never before had they felt their differences so
keenly as in the years immediately preceding the Civil
War. And these differences were at the roots of Indiana's

---

[1] U. S. Census, *Population of the United States in 1860; Compiled from . . . the Eighth Census . . .* (Washington, D. C., 1864), 111, 130.

political strife during the four years of military conflict.

The recent frontier experience, the cohesive influence of a common political organization, and the prevailing middle-class philosophy had created an abundance of common social attitudes. Local pride and sectional prejudice, for example, were almost universal and formed popular themes for political spellbinders.[2] Paradoxically, the typical Hoosier also professed a blatant nationalism and an unwavering faith in the grand future in store for the American nation. "Manifest destiny" was an article of faith and not an empty phrase to be exploited by the demagogic politician.[3] Nor was there disagreement about the wisdom and expediency of the long-agitated Homestead Act; local politicians of all parties and from every section of the state called eloquently for free farms for the homeless.[4] Finally, Hoosiers were aware that they lacked adequate capital and credit facilities and realized that this condition presented a formidable obstacle to their state's economic expansion. Farmers found it difficult to get loans or credit to tide them over until they could market their crops. The credit problem also impeded the ambitious promoters of local industry. "There is every facility here for manufacturing—means of transportation, power, and raw material," claimed

---

[2] Democrats of the Jacksonian school like Daniel W. Voorhees were especially prone to direct the passions of sectional prejudice against New England. Henry D. Jordan, "Daniel Wolsey Voorhees," in *Mississippi Valley Historical Review*, 6(1919-20):533-34, 536-37. See also New Albany *Weekly Ledger*, August 20, 1856.

[3] A typical expression of this sentiment appeared in the Indianapolis *Daily State Sentinel*, March 26, 1860: "It is plainly our destiny to extend our institutions over the whole of this continent, and the only question we have to consider is the best manner of accomplishing our great national duty."

[4] In Indiana the homestead measure was not a party issue. In 1859 the entire Congressional delegation voted in favor of the bill. Both the Democratic and Republican state platforms in 1860 endorsed the proposed law. *Ibid.*, January 13, 1860; Indianapolis *Daily Journal*, February 23, 1860.

the Indianapolis *Journal.* "All that is wanted is capital. . . ."⁵ Small wonder that a powerful group in Indiana showed interest in "cheap" money!

On all these matters Hoosiers were, for the most part, in essential agreement. But on other local and national issues—the tariff, banking, slavery, whether Indiana's economic future lay in her mills and factories, or in the exploitation of her soil—there was no such fundamental unity. These issues were fully debated in local politics. Early in the 1850's the disciples of Andrew Jackson, having dominated the state for a generation,⁶ rejoiced at the collapse of Whiggery—only to find its basic principles championed once more by a new and more vigorous political organization. The followers of Henry Clay, reanimated and strengthened by the great political upheaval of 1854, appeared, at the dawn of the campaign of 1860, more menacing than ever. This old political feud was more than a meaningless struggle for office between rival groups of politicians. Questions of far deeper significance were at stake. The leather-skinned farmers of the Wabash Valley might still have been voting for Andrew Jackson, but they were also endorsing a well-defined set of economic principles intimately associated with that magic name. And the ambitious owners of Richmond cotton mills and Indianapolis foundries had equally practical reasons for their devotion to Whig dogma.

The tariff question was always an important cause for Indiana's political divisions. Here the Democrats held a distinct advantage over their Whig and, later, Republican adversaries. The low Walker Tariff of 1846 and the still lower schedules of 1857 had the full approval of the state party. The alleged benefits of high duties

---

⁵ Indianapolis *Daily Journal,* October 3, 1860.
⁶ Except for the contests of 1836 and 1840, when William Henry Harrison was the Whig candidate, the Democrats carried Indiana in every presidential election up to 1860. Only one Whig congressman survived the election of 1852.

urged by the protectionists made few converts among Indiana Democrats. "In the West and the South the main dependence, the almost exclusive interest, is in the productions of the soil," asserted the Indianapolis *Sentinel.* "These want no protection—they demand freedom of trade to encourage them."[7] An indignant local Democrat questioned the right of tariff advocates to call their pet measure "protection for American industry." "Is not *farm labor* . . . 'American industry?' . . . If Congress should pass a high protective tariff . . . such legislation should not be 'sugar coated' over, by being styled 'Protection for American industry.' But it should be called 'discriminative legislation for the protection of manufacturing capital and labor.' "[8] Another party organ asked whether the people of Indiana were ready to give up cheap iron and coal and permit the Republican party "to tax the people of the great Northwest for the benefit of a few wealthy iron mongers in the Keystone State."[9] It also contended that the low price of iron was a distinct encouragement to the West's extensive program of railroad building.[10]

But Indiana Republicans faced a dilemma when they tried to take a stand on this issue. The difficulty lay in the heterogeneity of their constituents—in the variety of economic groups that had been attracted to the Republican standard. They found it impossible to harmonize the interests of farmers, wool growers, railroad promoters, and the manufacturers of iron and farm machinery. The Hoosier Republican organization contained both ardent protectionists and confirmed free traders. Hence party leaders found it wise to say as little as possible about the tariff.

[7] Indianapolis *Daily State Sentinel,* December 13, 1858.
[8] *Ibid.,* January 4, 1859.
[9] New Albany *Weekly Ledger,* February 22, 1860.
[10] New Albany *Daily Ledger,* quoted in Indianapolis *Daily State Sentinel,* October 29, 1851.

Unquestionably the state as a whole was strongly opposed to protection, but the clamorous minority who favored it was almost entirely within the ranks of the Republican party.[11] The result was a prolonged intraparty feud. George W. Julian, a former Free-Soil Congressman from the fifth district and now a member of the radical wing of the Republican party, classified the tariff with "certain defunct measures" of Whiggery; Caleb B. Smith, an ex-Whig conservative, was a strong protectionist.[12] Yet each of these men pretended to preach the gospel of pure Republicanism. Similarly, it was the tariff question which caused many former Whigs and Americans to distrust the anti-Nebraska Democrats who had joined the Republicans.[13] "Let not the slavery issue swallow up others equally as important," warned an old follower of Clay. "Let not too strict adherence to party defeat the endeavors of honest and patriotic men, to protect American industry."[14] But the anti-Nebraska Democrats, most of whom were farmers attracted to the fusionists by the fear of slavery expansion, were equally resentful toward the Whigs who tried to force their old principles on the new political organization. Amid such

[11] The American party, with its Whig antecedents, was decidedly partial to the principle of protection. By 1860 all but a small remnant had been absorbed by the Republicans. The Vincennes *Gazette,* a sound American party paper, declared on October 12, 1857, that the free-trade system "is the rock upon which we are splitting. It is an error that needs speedy correction."

[12] Julian to Dr. [G. C.] Starbuck, June, 1849, George W. Julian MSS., Indiana Division, Indiana State Library; Louis J. Bailey, "Caleb Blood Smith," in *Indiana Magazine of History,* 29(1933):222.

[13] Indicative of this sentiment was the refusal of many members of the American party to support Oliver P. Morton, a former Democrat, for governor in 1856 and again in 1860. "Mr. Morton is a Locofoco, except upon the slavery question," explained the American New Albany *Tribune,* February 28, 1860.

[14] Indianapolis *Daily Atlas,* December 9, 1859. John D. Defrees, a staunch old Whig, founded the *Atlas* in August, 1859, to support the candidacy of Edward Bates for the Republican nomination for president in 1860, and to preach the gospel of protection.

conflicting opinions few Republican politicians hazarded an unqualified commitment for or against protection.

If the tariff was a disturbing factor in Indiana politics, banking almost carried the state to party chaos. Disagreement was so universal, in fact, that politicians left each Hoosier free to take his own stand. No party ventured to define its position.[15] Republicans were divided between the advocates of state and national banks; Democrats ranged in their sympathies from a true Jacksonian hostility toward banks of all kinds to ultra-conservative support for the establishment of another national bank.[16] Though all could agree that credit facilities were inadequate, the proper remedy was not clear. Some debt-ridden farmers perceived their salvation in lax banking laws and an abundance of paper money, but other agrarians regarded these as the weapons of wily speculators. Men with considerable accumulations of property cherished a traditional hostility toward inflationary devices. Ambitious entrepreneurs, on the other hand, found the expansion of credit more suited to their needs. Thus the issue divided men who were desperately searching for new reservoirs of money and credit from those who felt their interests threatened by cheap money schemes.

Still, a debtor psychology clearly prevailed in Indiana, and, despite the alarming prophecies of cautious conservatives, the proponents of an abundant currency long controlled state policy. As in other parts of the West, the panic of 1837 and the ensuing depression had not put an end to loose banking practices. The operations of a State

[15] Comments concerning banking were remarkably scarce in the Republican press. The Indianapolis *Daily State Sentinel,* February 12, 1856, quoted editorials from Democratic papers to show the diversity of views within the party. "A man's opinion upon banks," it remarked, "has never been a test of his democracy, and we hope never will be made one." *Ibid.,* February 13, 1856.

[16] *Ibid.,* February 5, 1855, September 26, 1857; Logan Esarey, *State Banking in Indiana 1814-1873* (Indiana University *Studies,* No. 15, Bloomington, 1912), 282-83.

Bank, chartered for twenty-five years by the legislature in 1834,[17] were supplemented by the Banking Act of 1852 which set up a system of free banking subject to moderate government regulation. Immediately a network of free banks covered the state. By 1854 sixty-seven of these institutions were in operation and issuing a great variety of paper currency much of which circulated at various rates of discount.[18] This situation displeased both the Democrats who favored hard money and the conservative business men. Moreover, it kept state finances in a precarious condition and caused great distress among holders of Indiana securities.[19]

In the legislative session of 1855 Republicans, with the support of a few Democrats, finally rescued the exponents of sound banking. By devious methods they were able to pass a bill incorporating the Bank of the State of Indiana, even though the charter of the old State Bank still had four years to run.[20] While subject to little state regulation this institution carried on a careful, conservative banking business under the presidency of Hugh McCulloch. The direction of its branches fell into the hands of the state's most capable business men. The new State Bank did a flourishing business until the end of the Civil War when most of its branches joined the National Bank system.[21] Thanks to the Republicans the champions of sound banking had won a decisive victory.

---

[17] Esarey, *State Banking in Indiana*, 251 ff.

[18] *Ibid.*, 283; Isaac Lippincott, *A History of Manufactures in the Ohio Valley to the Year 1860* (Chicago, 1914), 152.

[19] See message of Governor Abram A. Hammond to the legislature, January 11, 1861, in Indiana *House Journal,* 1861, p. 31.

[20] In describing the tactics of the promoters of the new bank, Governor Joseph A. Wright declared: "The means and appliances brought to bear to secure the passage of this charter, would, if exposed to the public gaze, exhibit the darkest page of fraud and corruption that ever disgraced the legislature of any state." Message to the legislature, January 9, 1857, in Indiana *House Journal,* 1857, p. 23.

[21] Indianapolis *Daily State Sentinel,* November 7, 1855; Esarey, *State Banking in Indiana,* 288-97.

Negro slavery also agitated the Hoosier commonwealth. To be sure, the abolitionists won little local support, for the people overwhelmingly opposed interference with the South's "peculiar institution" and endorsed the Compromise of 1850. It was equally true that Indiana was strongly prejudiced against the Negro. The people approved, by a vote of 109,967 to 21,066, an article in the Constitution of 1850 which prohibited further Negro immigration into the state.[22] But in spite of these conservative attitudes, by the 1850's most Hoosiers were opposed to the continued expansion of slavery into the territories. In part on moral grounds and in part because they hoped to preserve the territories for free white farmers, they wanted to confine the institution to its present limits. Actually the Republicans and Douglas Democrats were not divided upon the wisdom of this objective, but only upon the question of how it could best be achieved. Buchanan Democrats who would aid the expansion of slavery found few supporters in Indiana.

Another clause in the Constitution of 1850 provided a bitter political issue for many years. This was the provision which gave the voting privilege to foreign immigrants after they had declared their intention to become citizens and resided in the United States for one year and in the state for six months. Most Hoosiers welcomed the flood of German and Irish immigrants which poured into Indiana during the forties and fifties. These newcomers made a rich cultural contribution to the state and played a substantial part in its economic progress. But inevitably the Whigs and Democrats competed with each other for their votes. Before long some of the declining Whigs, having failed to gain much support from the immigrants, were encouraging a local

---

[22] Charles Kettleborough, *Constitution Making in Indiana* (3 vols, *Indiana Historical Collections*, vols. 1, 2, 17, Indianapolis, 1916, 1930), 1:cxxxii, 222.

antiforeign movement. They helped to organize the American party which favored increasing naturalization requirements and depriving the immigrants of the suffrage. In its early years the Republican party was strongly tinged with the antiforeign "Know-Nothingism."[23]

Amid the heated debates over the tariff, banking, slavery, and immigration, still another issue clearly divided Hoosiers—one that would ultimately rock the foundations of the nation. Industrial capitalism had already begun a march to the West.[24] Men dazzled by its promises rose to espouse its cause and to dispute the control of the government with the cultivators of the soil. Jefferson's Democracy might still idealize rural virtues and envision Indiana's future in terms of prosperous farms and peaceful villages, but the dreams of others were colored by the smoke of factories and filled with humming machines. Sturdy farmers would soon feel the power of their industrial rivals as the nation passed into a new economic era.

The panic of 1857 severely checked the economic growth of Indiana, and even as late as 1860 recovery was far from complete. To meet this situation promoters of factories redoubled their efforts to attract capital and broadened their appeal in order to entice every possible group. Addressing itself to the farmers, the Richmond *Palladium* demonstrated that it took Indiana's whole agricultural surplus to pay for the manufactured goods purchased from New England and Europe. "While we

---

[23] Kettleborough, *Constitution Making in Indiana*, 1:xcv-cix, 304. The term "Know-Nothingism" in popular parlance referred to the antiforeign secret societies of the early 1850's.

[24] The census of 1860 revealed that Indiana's industrial interests had reached significant proportions. There were 5,110 establishments with a capital investment of $17,881,586, a product with an annual value of $41,840,434, and employees numbering 20,755. U. S. Census. *Manufactures of the United States in 1860; Compiled from . . . the Eighth Census* . . . (Washington, D. C., 1865), 145. See also Lippincott, *History of Manufactures,* 157 ff.

have a constantly increasing population who desire work and can get little or nothing to do, while we have cheap lands and cheap food, plenty of fuel and water power, we are told that we must fold our hands and still let people of distant States and countries amass wealth by doing our work for us—that it is not time yet for Western manufacturers to succeed."[25]

The Indianapolis *Journal* also lent its support to the industrial drive. The development of industry, it declared, "increases the value of every other business interest, as it likewise increases wealth and population. On our manufacturing interests then are we mainly to depend for our future prosperity as a city. . . ."[26] A correspondent of the *Journal* who was trying to raise capital for a cotton mill appealed to the philanthropic and Christian sentiments of men of wealth and urged them to support his movement in order to give work to needy mechanics and laborers. "Industry is as essential to the development of a virtuous community as is education," he asserted. "And the thoughts of providing employment to those seeking it . . . will afford a rich enjoyment to those who engage in any enterprise that will . . . cultivate industrious habits in the youth of our city."[27] From such beginnings there fast grew a bond that linked the destiny of one significant element in Indiana to that of the industrial East.

Despite the activities of these incipient manufacturers, in the 1850's Indiana was still chiefly a community of agriculturalists. Grazing and the harvesting of her bountiful crops were the major occupations of her citizens. The slavery issue and homestead agitation might sorely strain their political alliance with the South, but a community of interests based upon trade and mutual agrarian concerns still influenced the political attitudes

---

[25] Richmond *Palladium,* February 16, 1860.
[26] Indianapolis *Daily Journal,* February 17, 1860.
[27] *Ibid.,* March 22, 1860.

of many farmers.[28] True, the railroads had already tapped the Indiana granary and diverted most of the export trade from the Ohio and Mississippi rivers to the East; but isolated farmers were slow to understand the significance of this change. Because they had always done so, they continued to regard the river outlet as important.[29]

Nor did any sudden burst of affection replace the average Hoosier's traditional prejudices against the New England Yankee. "That will be a sorry day for the people of Indiana," wrote the New Albany *Ledger,* "when they sacrifice the friendship of their Southern neighbors for that of the cold and calculating Yankees and grasping Wall Street stockjobbers."[30] Besides, even after the diversion of the export trade to the East, a flourishing intra-valley trade still continued. Steamboating on the Mississippi and its tributaries prospered in the 1850's as it never had before, and the shipbuilders of New Albany and Evansville did a thriving business. Down this artery went the foodstuffs of the Northwest to feed the deep South, and the river boats returned with sugar, molasses, and other southern products.[31]

Governor Joseph A. Wright, looking out from Indianapolis in the winter of 1857, felt justified in attributing

[28] The origin of Indiana's population was hardly an adequate explanation of the partiality of her farmers for the South. Out of a total population of 1,350,428 in 1860, only 161,269, or barely nine per cent, were born in slaveholding states. The state of Ohio alone contributed a larger proportion (171,245) than the entire South. Indianapolis *Daily Journal,* June 27, 1863.

[29] Edward C. Smith, *The Borderland in the Civil War* (New York, 1927), 24-25.

[30] New Albany *Weekly Ledger,* August 20, 1856.

[31] Smith, *Borderland in the Civil War,* 23-24; Lippincott, *History of Manufactures,* 138 ff.; E. Merton Coulter, "Effects of Secession upon the Commerce of the Mississippi Valley," in *Mississippi Valley Historical Review,* 3(1916-17):276-78; Daniel W. Snepp, *Evansville's Channels of Trade and the Secession Movement 1850-1865* (Indiana Historical Society Publications, vol. 8, no. 7, Indianapolis, 1928); Albert L. Kohlmeier, *The Old Northwest as the Keystone of the Arch of American Federal Union* . . . (Bloomington, Ind., 1938), 116-22.

Indiana's prosperity to the operations of her railroads.[32] But had he moved south of the old National Road toward the Ohio River he would have found his assertion becoming increasingly less accurate. Here there were wide areas where railroads had not yet penetrated and where men's eyes still looked southward along the rivers. There was, in fact, between the interests of northern and southern Indiana a significant sectional cleavage which loomed large in local politics. Southern Indiana with southern Ohio and Illinois joined Missouri, Kentucky, and western Virginia to form a borderland separating North and South. In many respects it was a distinct region in itself, unified by common political and economic interests.[33] No region was more vitally interested in the preservation of the Union or more eager to compromise the outstanding differences between the two great sections. The inhabitants of the river counties often felt a warmer friendship toward their neighbors in Kentucky than toward their fellow citizens in Indiana who dwelt north of the National Road. The Ohio River, then, was far more significant as a unifying force binding together the people of the borderland than as a line bisecting the nation.[34]

Thus as the Civil War approached, the people of Indiana were far from united. They could not agree upon fundamental economic questions; they were divided in their sectional loyalties; their political parties were in a state of flux. In 1861 Hoosiers angrily debated the question of war or peace and carefully weighed their decision on the scale of personal interest. Even the four years of military conflict could not fuse the divergent elements in Indiana society, and Appomattox found the basic issues between them essentially unchanged. Yet, though the issues were the same, a revolution had

[32] Message to the legislature in Indiana *House Journal,* 1857, p. 36.
[33] Smith, *Borderland in the Civil War,* 1-7.
[34] *Ibid.,* 8.

occurred, for the balance of political power had shifted significantly. The story of the Hoosier commonwealth during the Civil War is focused upon this shift of power which marked the triumph of the principles of Clay over those of Jackson. The initial chapter was written at the ballot box in the fall of 1860.

CHAPTER 2
POLITICAL KALEIDOSCOPICS

On January 9, 1860, Senator Jesse D. Bright, accompanied by one Finley Bigger of the United States Department of the Treasury, arrived at Indianapolis from Washington. Since the Democratic state convention was scheduled to convene two days later, the visit of Indiana's senior senator to the Hoosier capital was hardly unexpected. "Looking like a business man more than a senator,"[1] with his clean-shaven face, heavy, erect figure, sartorial splendor, and imperious manner, Bright had been a familiar character at the confabulations of the Indiana Democracy for nearly a generation. Never an orator or writer, and rarely rising to the level of statesmanship, his special talent lay in the field of party management. While serving three successive terms in the United States Senate he had welded together a powerful political machine which he ruled with consummate skill. Making devotion to himself the test of party regularity, he had divided Indiana's share of the national patronage among his faithful followers and blessed the candidacy of office seekers who wore his yoke. Never before had the Democratic party of Indiana been "so nearly reduced to individual possession" as it was

---

[1] Murat Halstead, *Caucuses of 1860: A History of the National Political Conventions of the Current Presidential Campaign* . . . (Columbus, 1860), 12.

in the 1850's under Bright's control. "Doughface" was an epithet frequently hurled at him by political enemies, for he had given unqualified support to the prosouthern administrations of Pierce and Buchanan. Although he lived on the Indiana side of the Ohio River, he owned plantations and slaves in Kentucky and was at heart a Southerner.[2]

The purpose of Senator Bright's mission to Indianapolis on this particular occasion was to deal with an impending revolt against his party leadership. He was about to hazard his whole political career in a desperate effort to keep the Indiana Democracy in the Buchanan fold. He wanted to control the state delegates to the national convention at Charleston and to prevent them from being instructed to vote for Stephen A. Douglas whom he hated bitterly.[3] Bright had undertaken no easy task.

As early as 1858 the friends of Douglas who opposed Buchanan's attempt to force the proslavery Lecompton Constitution upon Kansas, after being defeated at the state convention, had called a meeting of their own to repudiate Bright and "to aid in extricating the party" from its "apparently false position." On February 23,

---

[2] Lew Wallace, *Lew Wallace, An Autobiography* (2 vols. New York, 1907), 1:236; William W. Woollen, *Biographical and Historical Sketches of Early Indiana* (Indianapolis, 1883), 223, 228; Charles B. Murphy, *The Political Career of Jesse D. Bright* (Indiana Historical Society *Publications*, vol. 10, no. 3, Indianapolis, 1931), 101-45; *Dictionary of American Biography* (20 vols. and index. New York 1928-36), 3:45-46.

[3] The enmity of these two politicians grew out of patronage difficulties and a controversy regarding Bright's re-election to the Senate in 1857. When the Senate voted on seating Bright, Douglas voted with the minority against it, and thereby incurred the everlasting hostility of Bright and his friends. William Dudley Foulke, *Life of Oliver P. Morton, Including His Important Speeches* (2 vols. Indianapolis, 1899), 1:59-60; John W. Holcombe and Hubert M. Skinner, *Life and Public Services of Thomas A. Hendricks* (Indianapolis, 1886), 195-96; David Turpie, *Sketches of My Own Times* (Indianapolis, 1903), 176 ff.; Reinhard H. Luthin, "The Democratic Split During Buchanan's Administration," in *Pennsylvania History*, 11(1944):13-14.

they perfected an organization, proclaimed Buchanan a despot, denounced Indiana's pro-Lecompton senators as "dead cocks in the pit," and adopted a ringing endorsement of Douglas.[4]

Around this nucleus during the following two years the Douglas men, proclaiming their hero as "the enlightened statesman, the tried patriot and the eloquent and fearless champion of popular rights,"[5] rallied the Democratic masses to their cause. Indiana Democrats had rebelled against the prosouthern leaders who had long dominated their party. Henceforth, they said, the wishes of the Northwest were to be considered in the party councils.[6] By the dawn of 1860 Bright and his coterie of professional politicians and officeholders had almost become leaders without followers, and the insurgents now threatened to capture the party machine.[7]

Since Douglas was obviously gaining strength in Indiana, even a majority of the old party wheelhorses deserted Bright and ranged themselves as gracefully as possible in the ranks of the new leader. Rededicating himself to the Cincinnati platform of 1856 and its doctrine of popular sovereignty, J. J. Bingham, editor of the Indianapolis *Sentinel,* finally climbed off the fence and made his paper the central organ of the Douglas forces.[8] In August, 1859, Thomas A. Hendricks, aspiring to the gubernatorial nomination, resigned his post as commissioner of the General Land Office and thus signalized his desertion of the administration.[9] Similarly the managers of the various candidates for state offices tried

[4] Indianapolis *Daily State Sentinel,* January 21, February 24, 1858.
[5] *Ibid.,* November 19, 1858.
[6] Wallace, *Autobiography,* 1:240.
[7] Charles Kettleborough, "Indiana on the Eve of the Civil War," in *Proceedings of the Tenth Annual Meeting of the Ohio Valley Historical Association* (Indiana Historical Society *Publications,* vol. 6, no. 1 [Indianapolis, n. d.]), 150-51.
[8] Indianapolis *Daily State Sentinel,* February 3, December 14, 1859.
[9] Holcombe and Skinner, *Thomas A. Hendricks,* 201-2.

to prove their man to be the genuine Douglas man and denied any friendship with Bright. "Few people worship the setting sun," wrote one observer, "and in the gray dawn of the coming Presidential olympiad, it is not difficult to foresee that the great champion of the mighty Northwest is the rising luminary of the coming day."[10]

Yet, although they controlled an overwhelming majority of the delegates to the approaching convention, the Douglas managers watched Bright closely as he held secret conferences with Governor Willard, Judge Pettit of Kansas, United States Marshal Robinson, and other friends of the administration who met him in Indianapolis.[11] Few were inclined to underestimate his resourcefulness, and some feared he might still disrupt their careful plans. "If Mr. Bright had a regard for the harmony and success of the Democracy of Indiana he would have confined his attention to his public duties in Washington," nervously opined the *Sentinel*.[12] There were also disturbing rumors of a corruption fund which allegedly had been raised in Washington to procure the defeat of Douglas at the state convention or to bribe the delegates to Charleston to ignore their instructions. Because of these reports, Bright's arrival with a member of the Treasury department seemed all the more sinister.[13]

[10] Indianapolis *Daily State Sentinel*, July 30, 1859.

[11] Indianapolis *Daily Journal*, January 11, 1860. In these men Bright had at his command some of the best brains in the Democratic party of Indiana. Governor Ashbel P. Willard, "a dashing Prince Rupert sort of leader," was a brilliant stump speaker and extremely popular among the rank and file of the party. Wallace, *Autobiography*, 1:236; Turpie, *Sketches*, 155 ff.; Woollen, *Biographical and Historical Sketches*, 105. United States Marshal John L. Robinson had long been Bright's ablest lieutenant. Robinson's influence was strengthened by his ownership of the Rushville *Jacksonian* which he had made a strong administration organ. Holcombe and Skinner, *Thomas A. Hendricks*, 194-95.

[12] Indianapolis *Daily State Sentinel*, January 10, 1860.

[13] Indianapolis *Daily Journal*, January 5, 12, 1860.

2

On January 11 the delegates to the Democratic state convention assembled at Metropolitan Hall. State committeeman Joseph W. Chapman, a special friend of Senator Bright, called the meeting to order. At once the Douglas men, led by Gordon Tanner, Lew Wallace, and John C. Walker, seized control. They elected Judge Robert Lowry to the chairmanship and captured the committee on credentials. Most of the contested election cases were ultimately settled in their favor. The other important committees, especially the one on resolutions and the one to appoint a new state central committee, were appointed by the pro-Douglas chairman. The party machinery was now in the hands of the insurgents.[14]

With the complete defeat of the administration men clearly foreshadowed, Governor Willard rose and withdrew the name of Cyrus L. Dunham who had been the Bright candidate for the gubernatorial nomination. In response to a call Dunham made a short speech in which he begged for peace in the party, promised to support the Charleston nominee, but refused to commit himself to Douglas. He then nominated Thomas A. Hendricks for the honor he had relinquished and generously praised his competitor.[15]

Hendricks, then just forty years of age, of medium height, with a large head covered with heavy brown hair, and "an oval face clean shaven like the statesmen of old," had already attained a high degree of personal popularity. His removal from the field of active politics while serving in the land office had made him the man upon whom both divisions of the party could most easily unite.[16] After his nomination had been ratified by the convention, Hendricks mounted the platform and begged

---

[14] Indianapolis *Daily Journal,* January 12, 13, 1860.
[15] *Ibid.,* January 13, 1860.
[16] Holcombe and Skinner, *Thomas A. Hendricks,* 202-4; Wallace, *Autobiography,* 1:236.

for a united state organization regardless of the action of the party elsewhere.[17]

But the futility of all the pleas for unity became apparent when the convention debated the issue of instructing the delegates to Charleston. The clause in the platform directing them to cast their ballots for Douglas as long as there was any reasonable prospect of success produced an excited discussion and determined opposition from the Bright faction. The administration men sought to forestall its adoption by counterproposals either to instruct for General Joseph Lane of Oregon (formerly of Indiana), or to send the delegates entirely uninstructed. The Douglas men rejected both amendments and passed their resolution by the decisive vote of 265 ayes to 129 nays. Then the victorious insurgents put on a wild demonstration before the assembled reporters and discomfited friends of Buchanan.[18]

After this crucial issue had been decided in their favor, the Douglas men were ready to make liberal concessions to their opponents on other matters. Despite an unqualified endorsement of the Cincinnati platform of 1856, with its clear exposition of the doctrine of popular sovereignty, the state platform defended the Supreme Court and thus, indirectly, the Dred Scott decision. It further proclaimed a high regard for the ability of President Buchanan and a readiness to defend his action "when carrying out the principles of the Democratic party."[19]

So accommodating, in fact, were the friends of Douglas on these points that the Republican press frequently taunted them with having won a barren victory.[20] Never-

[17] Indianapolis *Daily State Sentinel,* January 14, 1860.
[18] Indianapolis *Daily Journal* and *Daily State Sentinel,* January 13, 1860.
[19] Other articles in the platform denounced sectional parties and platforms, urged the peaceful acquisition of Cuba, opposed any discrimination against the foreign-born population, and advocated the passage of the homestead bill. Indianapolis *Daily State Sentinel,* January 13, 1860.

theless, revolution had swept the Hoosier Democracy, and, as one Douglas delegate aptly wrote, the Bright men discovered at the close of the convention that "the State of Indiana [was] entirely out of Jessee's Breaches Pocket."[21]

Since Bright's followers gave few signs of having been conciliated by the friendly gestures of the insurgents, the new leaders looked to the future with misgivings. "It now remains to be seen," wrote a Douglas editor, "whether our party and the State ticket is to be consolidated & strengthened, or whether bickerings and dissensions are to be introduced by the persecution and proscription of every man who dares to do what he believes to be right."[22] United States Marshal Robinson was especially cool to the plea for harmony, and he returned home immediately to pour his bitterness into the columns of the Rushville *Jacksonian*.[23] As for Bright, the fallen leader, the barrier between him and the insurgents was impassable. "Yes, the State Convention did instruct for Douglas," he remarked imperiously, "but Hendricks and . . . [the rest] consented to those instructions without consulting me."[24] Bright would make the Indiana Democrats pay dearly for their freedom.

3

Meanwhile, Indiana Republican leaders, while enjoying the disunity of their foes, were similarly occupied with the almost futile task of preserving harmony in their own ranks. For six years, since their organization as the so-called "People's party" in 1854, the jarring

---

[20] Indianapolis *Daily Atlas*, January 23, 1860.
[21] A. M. Puett to John G. Davis, January 15, 1860, in *Indiana Magazine of History*, 24(1928):209.
[22] J. B. Norman, New Albany, to William H. English, January 17, 1859 [1860], William H. English Collection, Indiana Historical Society Library.
[23] Rushville *Jacksonian*, quoted in Indianapolis *Daily State Sentinel*, January 21, 1860.
[24] Holcombe and Skinner, *Thomas A. Hendricks*, 212.

elements brought together in the fusion had vied with
each other for control of the party machinery and for
the right to dictate party policy. In consequence the
meaning of Republicanism changed continuously as one
or the other of the factions gained temporary ascendancy.
Into the original fusion had gone most of the Whigs
guided by Henry S. Lane, Caleb B. Smith, and John D.
Defrees; a substantial portion of the waxing Native
Americans under the direction of Godlove S. Orth and
Schuyler Colfax; Democrats who had opposed Douglas'
Kansas-Nebraska bill, led by Oliver P. Morton; temperance men who advocated a "Maine law" for Indiana;
and Free-Soilers under the ebullient leadership of George
W. Julian. Shrewd Whig leaders quickly seized control
of the new organization and charted for it a course of
conservatism and compromise in which their interests
and experience had made them adept.

Because of the strong southern element in Indiana's
population, the border-state interests of the section south
of the National Road, and the weakness of the local
antislavery movement,[25] the fusion platform of 1854,
besides making concessions to the temperance and Know-
Nothing elements, declared the mere restoration of the
Missouri Compromise to be the chief issue of the campaign. "Their hatred of slavery was geographical, spending its force north of the Missouri restriction," recalled
Julian. "They talked far more eloquently about the duty
of keeping covenants, and the wickedness of reviving
sectional agitation, than the evils of slavery. . . ."[26] Nor
did the surprising fusionist victory in 1854 bring unity
to these discordant elements. Democrats waited expectantly for the party of "Abolitionism, Free Soilism,
Native Americanism, Maine and Anti-Maine Liquor

---

[25] Theodore C. Smith, *The Liberty and Free Soil Parties in the Northwest* (New York, 1897), 303.

[26] George W. Julian, *Political Recollections, 1840-1872* (Chicago, 1884), 136-37.

Lawism, and all the other isms hatched in the fruitful laboratory of fanaticism" to disintegrate "just so soon as the question of the offices shall be determined."[27]

Despite the formation of a national Republican party at Pittsburgh in February, 1856, Indiana fusion leaders, hoping to attract timid "Americans" into at least the state organization, continued to use the "People's party" label. Again they made concessions to the Know-Nothings in the state platform, and they placed John W. Dawson, an ardent "American" and Fillmore supporter, on the state ticket. Once more the Free-Soilers were enraged by this surrender to the "dark lantern" fraternity. "A victory won upon such a platform is even worse than defeat," growled one of their organs.[28] "It was a combination of weakness," wrote Julian. "All the Fillmore Know-Nothings and Silver-Grey Whigs of the State were recognized as brethren."[29]

But the national Republican platform drawn up at Philadelphia in June, 1856, which demanded Congressional legislation to prevent the further expansion of slavery, was as pleasing to the "irrepressibles" as it was distasteful to old Whigs and Americans. To it Julian and his followers gave their enthusiastic support. They believed that they could stand on it "and without doing much violence to its language, preach the whole antislavery gospel."[30] But this radical national platform, upon which Frémont campaigned for the presidency, wrecked the work of the conservatives at the state convention. Although they garbled it in their party press and tried to keep Julian in the background and his followers out of southern Indiana during the campaign,[31]

---

[27] Indianapolis *Daily State Sentinel,* July 13, 1854.
[28] Columbus (Indiana) *Independent,* quoted in Richmond *Jeffersonian,* May 22, 1856.
[29] Julian, *Political Recollections,* 155.
[30] Letter of Julian to the Columbus *Independent,* quoted in Richmond *Jeffersonian,* August 28, 1856.
[31] Julian, *Political Recollections,* 154.

"Americans" deserted the fusionists and cast 22,000 votes for Fillmore the following November. The Fillmorites held the political balance of power, and Indiana Republicans, along with the presidential candidate, were defeated.

Two years later fusion leaders, still shying away from the name "Republican," saw an opportunity for a new alliance with Douglas Democrats in opposition to the Kansas policy of the Buchanan administration. Showing a readiness to back down from the Philadelphia platform and to make anti-Lecomptonism the sole issue of the campaign, the state central committee addressed its call for a convention "to all persons without regard to past party designations."[32] Despite the protests of Julian and the radicals, the new party platform of 1858 was a conservative document. Partial success in the fall elections rewarded the fusionists for their political accommodations, but at the end of the campaign their party was still being torn by the struggle between the conservative majority and the radical minority.

Fusion was the life blood of Indiana Republicanism, and its shrewd leaders, still searching for a catchall, were soon ready to experiment with new combinations and new issues. Having at different times both attacked and defended the principle of popular sovereignty, some were now ready to join John D. Defrees in a cry for "true and rightful 'Popular Sovereignty,' the right of the people . . . to govern themselves. . . ." That moderate principle, together with hostility to a territorial slave code, would form a platform broad enough to accommodate the entire opposition. Northern conservatives, explained Defrees, were ready to accept the *status quo* concerning slavery in the territories until the question of statehood arose. Then, however, the slavery issue was to have no bearing upon the admission of new states.[33]

[32] Indianapolis *Daily State Sentinel,* January 12, 1858.
[33] Indianapolis *Daily Atlas,* October 3, 15, 1859.

To these views Schuyler Colfax, Republican congressman from the ninth district, also lent his personal influence.[34] Others, like Oliver P. Morton, believed that the slavery issue might well be abandoned entirely and that Republicans could win support by turning to a policy of imperialism—the conquest of Mexico, for example.[35] Observing similar sentiments in a number of Republican papers, Julian's organ asserted that the fusion politicians appeared "to be laboring to superadd to the Douglas platform . . . the filibustering programme of the blessed administration of James Buchanan. . . ."[36] The old Free-Soilers branded Defrees as a "crystalized old fogy" and denounced other conservatives for coolly surrendering the vital issue of Republicanism to a policy of "crookedness and equivocation." They made it clear at once that they would not aid the "fossil Whigs" in the pursuit of such a "dishonest and self stultifying course."[37] The Republican party had been and must continue to be an antislavery party, said Julian's paper. If the party platform were to be so modified as to ignore slavery, "then we are . . . a Democrat, and such we will remain until another decent Antislavery party can be organized." Nor would it consent to be sidetracked by agitation for the "Protective Tariff, National Bank Charters and kindred exploded ideas."[38]

Inquisitive Democrats often raised the query: What is a Republican? for what great principles does he contend? The replies that came from the county assemblies, which met to choose delegates to the state convention of 1860, merely added to the confusion. These local conventions almost unanimously denounced the John Brown raid into Virginia, the interference with slavery in the

---

[34] South Bend *St. Joseph Valley Register,* April 21, 1859.
[35] Foulke, *Oliver P. Morton,* 1:64.
[36] Centreville *Indiana True Republican,* December 16, 1858.
[37] *Ibid.,* August 12, 1858, May 26, June 2, 1859.
[38] *Ibid.,* September 2, 1858.

states, the adoption of a territorial slave code, and the reopening of the foreign slave trade. They favored the homestead bill and a transcontinental railroad. But these were scarcely issues between the two parties in Indiana. On the real issues (aside from the tariff which was ignored entirely) their opinions were ludicrously diverse. Those gatherings which were dominated by old Free-Soilers reaffirmed their devotion to the Philadelphia platform, occasionally attacked the fugitive slave law, and denounced the Know-Nothings and their antiforeign program.[39]

The conservatives, however, were generally in control. They were silent on the American platform, and they retreated from the positions assumed four years previously at Philadelphia. Many of them endorsed some form of popular sovereignty. Others, while opposing the extension of slavery, said nothing about Congressional prohibition.[40] But the river counties produced the most amazing expositions of Republican doctrine. Spencer County condemned the "fanaticism of Abolitionists," and Vanderburgh recognized the right of any new state to be admitted to the Union with or without slavery as it might elect. Warrick County censured Democratic leaders for abandoning popular sovereignty. And the Republican convention in Dearborn solemnly resolved that the principle of popular sovereignty was "as old as our government, and that the Republican party now, as ever, is ready to stand and abide by it."[41] Julian's followers expressed utter disgust.

[39] Indianapolis *Daily Journal,* January 7, February 6, 8, 13, 20, 21, 1860.
[40] *Ibid.,* February 6, 11, 16, 17, 20, 1860.
[41] *Ibid.,* February 15, 18, 19, 21, 1860.

4

With the issue thus squarely joined between "accommodators" and "irrepressibles," both factions attended the state convention in force. Before the formal proceedings had even begun, however, it was apparent that the conservatives had matters well in hand and that party policy would be shaped according to their wishes. For the gubernatorial nomination Morton, the candidate in 1856, was to be discarded out of deference to the Whig and American prejudice against a former Democrat, and Henry S. Lane, the steadfast disciple of Henry Clay, was to be selected in his place. Of all the Indiana Republican leaders none had been more active than Lane in organizing the new party, none was more popular with the rank and file, and none matched his proficiency as a stump speaker.[42] His nomination, the party managers believed, would supply the ideal leadership for a campaign in which every element of the opposition would have to be united in order to insure success.

Before the use of Lane's magnetic name could be secured, however, several problems had to be settled. Eying a senatorial seat which was to become vacant the following year, Lane showed little enthusiasm for the proffered nomination, and there were rumors that he would not accept.[43] Moreover, Morton counted many friends who were ready to back his claim, and he made no secret of his own candidacy.[44] This impasse was finally adjusted by an arrangement between the friends of the two candidates whereby Lane, while running for governor, was to be elected to the senatorship if the

---

[42] Walter R. Sharp, "Henry S. Lane and the Formation of the Republican Party in Indiana," in *Mississippi Valley Historical Review*, 7(1920-21):93-112.

[43] Indianapolis *Daily State Sentinel*, February 21, 1860.

[44] Morton to Lane, November 17, 1859, in Morton MSS., Indiana Division, Indiana State Library; Centreville *Indiana True Republican*, January 26, 1860; Indianapolis *Indiana American*, March 11, 1859.

Republicans should gain control of the new legislature. Morton, who was to be candidate for lieutenant governor, would then automatically become governor.⁴⁵

The convention proceedings ran more smoothly than the most optimistic of the political managers had hoped. The "rugged issue" wing found itself in a hopeless minority and gained scant representation on the various committees. The conservatives were in complete control.⁴⁶ Lane and Morton were quickly nominated by acclamation, and the remainder of the slate was filled with due consideration for geographical distribution, national origins, and party derivations.⁴⁷

Before the adoption of the platform, the old Whigs who favored the presidential candidacy of Edward Bates of Missouri tried every device to get the delegates to the national Republican convention instructed for their favorite. A delegation from St. Louis held a levee at the Bates House, and an "abundance of Bates brandy and wine" graced the sideboard of that popular hostelry. A "leader" from the New York *Tribune* favorable to Bates as the most available candidate was republished in circular form and widely scattered through the crowd.⁴⁸ But the minority of anti-Bates men still appeared too formidable for the adoption of formal instructions. The friends of Bates had to be content with the fact that a majority of the delegates to Chicago favored their

---

⁴⁵ Foulke, *Oliver P. Morton*, 1:66-67; Indianapolis *Daily State Sentinel*, February 22, 1860. Democratic papers professed indignation at this bargain, but a similar agreement had been made between the two Democratic candidates, Hendricks and Turpie. Turpie, *Sketches of My Own Times*, 183-84.

⁴⁶ Indianapolis *Daily State Sentinel*, February 23, 1860.

⁴⁷ Indianapolis *Daily Journal*, February 23, 1860.

⁴⁸ Indianapolis *Daily State Sentinel*, February 23, 1860; Indianapolis *Indiana American*, February 25, 1860; Centreville *Indiana True Republican*, March 1, 1860. For a general discussion of the Bates movement, see Reinhard H. Luthin, "Edward Bates's Presidential Candidacy in 1860," in *Missouri Historical Review*, 38(1944):138-61.

candidate.⁴⁹ A resolution aimed at Bates which instructed the delegates to vote for no candidate who had not been a good Republican in 1856, was laid on the table.⁵⁰ The platform retreated from the advanced positions on slavery extension reached at Philadelphia four years earlier. It was another bitter disappointment to the "irrepressibles." Far from reaffirming the power and duty of Congress to exclude slavery from all the territories, it merely denounced the doctrine that the constitution by itself carried slavery into the territories and vaguely promised to oppose slavery extension by all constitutional means. Julian and the Germans were partially appeased, however, by a resolution favoring equal rights to all citizens and opposing any change in existing naturalization laws. But the declining Americans were correspondingly chagrined, and some left the convention in a huff. The rest of the platform aroused no opposition. It demanded the immediate admission of Kansas as a free state, a homestead law, and the construction of a transcontinental railroad. It also proclaimed Republican devotion to the Union. After the completion of the business before the convention, much time was given to speechmaking. Reverend J. W. T. McMullen, who felt it his duty to "preach the devil out of politics," put the festivities on high plane by pronouncing the Republican cause "just, holy and good."⁵¹

The "accommodators" who had dominated the convention departed well pleased with their handiwork. The "irrepressibles," they were confident, would have to stay with them because they had nowhere else to go. True, some Americans were not entirely satisfied. One of their

---

⁴⁹ Howard K. Beale (ed.), *The Diary of Edward Bates 1859-1866* (vol. 4 of the American Historical Association *Annual Report*, 1930 [Washington, D. C., 1933]), 102.

⁵⁰ Indianapolis *Daily State Sentinel*, February 27, 1860; Indianapolis *Daily Journal*, February 23, 1860; Centreville *Indiana True Republican*, March 1, 1860.

⁵¹ Indianapolis *Daily Journal*, February 23, 1860.

papers acridly declared that the convention had been "a sham and a cheat . . . designed to 'rope in' Americans to a Republican convention."[52] But Republican leaders had every reason to believe that the majority of old Whigs would join them in the campaign. The only remaining danger was the possibility that a radical presidential candidate would be nominated at Chicago. Indiana leaders were ready to apply every possible device to prevent that from happening. The old political managers who now had complete control of the new party machinery saw victory within their grasp as they scanned the political skies in the spring of 1860.

[52] New Albany *Tribune*, February 28, 1860.

CHAPTER 3 — A DUTIFUL VICTORY

INDIANA politicians did not wait for the national conventions of 1860 to define party policy before launching their campaigns. As early as March the candidates for state offices were on the hustings bidding for the support of vacillating voters, political strategists were deciding which issues to stress and which to ignore, and local leaders were mobilizing the party faithful in county and township clubs. In the hotels and on the muddy streets of the Hoosier capital, in the busy river towns, in isolated hamlets, and in countless farmhouses politics quickly became the all-absorbing topic of conversation. The political battle reached a crescendo unusually early, and the air of early spring was charged with the excitement of portentous events. Few men foresaw the magnitude of the impending crisis and few possessed more that a vague concept of the underlying issues at stake, but all seemed to understand that uncommon significance would be attached to the verdict rendered at the polls that fall. Certainly there was no apathy among the electorate to trouble the politicians in that momentous campaign.

On March 10, Lane and Morton were at Terre Haute to open the Republican canvass with speeches before a Vigo County ratification meeting. Morton read a carefully prepared address, "a very solid, compact, logically constructed declaration of Republican opinion" which was later printed as a campaign document. His pride had been pricked by Democratic jests at his demotion on the Republican ticket, and, partially in self-vindication, he resolved here to assume the honor of party keynoter. The Republican press responded with high praise. Doubtless Morton derived much satisfaction from the fact that Republicans regarded his, rather than Lane's address as a political textbook for the campaign.[1]

A few weeks after the Terre Haute meeting Lane and Morton resumed their political peregrinations, and were joined by other Republican speakers. Among them was Caleb B. Smith, a delegate-at-large to the Chicago convention, an accomplished orator, and a sound Whig of the old school.[2] The flexible slavery plank in the party platform enabled these prudent partisans to adjust their views to popular sentiment in different parts of the state. But the general tone of their speeches was conservative. Lane, who had earlier branded Hinton R. Helper's *Impending Crisis* as incendiary, renounced slavery agitation and turned to themes more appealing to his Whig friends.[3] Caleb Smith scoffed at those who believed Republicans favored abolitionism or Negro equality.[4] These revitalized Whigs could not resist the temptation to compare the current crusade with the "log cabin" campaign of 1840. They recalled its color and

[1] Indianapolis *Daily Journal*, March 13, 16, 1860.
[2] *Ibid.*, March 31, 1860; Indianapolis *Daily State Sentinel*, March 16, 1860.
[3] Indianapolis *Daily State Sentinel*, February 28, 1860; James A. Woodburn, "Henry Smith Lane," in *Indiana Magazine of History*, 27(1931):283-84. On certain occasions it was possible for Lane's position on slavery to shift remarkably. Thus while speaking at the dedication of the Republican "Wigwam" at Chicago on May 12, he made no effort to deny the charge of abolitionism. "The terror of that word is well nigh passed away," he declared, "and it is fast becoming the synonym for all that is worthy in American patriotism." Indianapolis *Daily Journal*, May 16, 1860.
[4] *Ibid.*, April 30, 1860.

enthusiasm and, above all, the fact of a Whig victory. They hoped " 'to arouse . . . the fires of 1840' and carry Indiana by storm," believed a Democratic editor.⁵

Democrats, while clearly on the defensive, were not long content to leave the initiative with the Republicans. By April Hendricks, David Turpie, and other party leaders were on the stump speaking to large and enthusiastic audiences. With the hope of restoring party harmony rapidly fading, Hendricks spoke cautiously in an effort to avoid offending either faction. He was discreetly silent about his attitude toward the candidacy of Douglas. When not defending the record of the Democratic state administration, he dwelt upon generalities and rarely mentioned the slavery issue. Turpie, meanwhile, played upon an ever-popular theme by attacking the wily merchants of Boston and Salem whose forebears had grown rich in the slave trade but who turned now to abolitionism to manufacture a little political capital.⁶

On April 17 Lane and Hendricks began a series of joint debates which carried them through the larger communities of southern Indiana. Day after day excited crowds gathered at fairgrounds or courthouses to hear each candidate prod the vulnerable spots in the record of the other party. At Jeffersonville Lane maintained that he represented not only the Republicans but the whole opposition to the "sham Democracy." "I stand upon the Republican Doctrine—non-interference with slavery in the States, and its non-extension into the Territories," he affirmed. "He denounces the abolitionists down here. He does not do it in Wayne," replied Hendricks. Lane claimed the homestead bill as a Republican measure; Hendricks asserted that the Republicans had not lifted a finger for it until distinguished Democrats like Andrew Johnson had made it popular. Hendricks denounced the Republicans as radicals; Lane retorted that he had been

---
⁵ La Porte *Times*, February 25, 1860.
⁶ Indianapolis *Daily State Sentinel*, April 30, 1860.

born in Kentucky, the home of Henry Clay, and that the name of the Great Compromiser had been inscribed upon his banner ever since he had entered Indiana politics.[7] At Rockport, wrote an auditor, Lane's eulogy upon Clay "was truly sublime, causing tears to start to the eyes of many an old Whig."[8] No allusion to the sectional conflict encumbered Lane's message to the Whigs of southern Indiana, and thus reassured, many now entered the Republican fold.

2

As the time for the national conventions approached, local candidates temporarily abandoned the forum and closeted themselves with party managers in quiet consultation. The Republican delegates to Chicago, unimpeded by formal instructions or by the ambitions of a local favorite son, and representing one of the four free states considered doubtful for their party, anticipated an important role at the convention. Although they might differ on details, they were all agreed that to carry southern Indiana the Republicans would have to adopt a moderate platform and nominate a conservative presidential candidate.

If such a policy entailed a compromise with the principles embodied in the platform of 1856, the party leaders were ready with a plausible explanation. They insisted that mere success was a virtue in itself, that its achievement, by whatever means, was a moral obligation resting upon Republicans. The Indianapolis *Journal* professed a willingness to support a non-Republican like Bates if necessary. It wanted the candidate most likely to succeed, "because it is a *duty* the Republican party owes to the cause which has created it, to stop right now the advance of slavery. . . . Unite for another four years the Executive and Judicial powers for slavery, and freedom will be

---

[7] New Albany *Weekly Ledger*, April 25, 1860.
[8] Indianapolis *Daily Journal*, May 5, 1860.

by law shut up in the free States, and existing there only by sufferance.... Wherefore we want any man for our candidate who can win, for *success is a duty.*" Certainly, it added, a chance for success should not be sacrificed "to some fanciful purity of faith." As for the claims of William H. Seward, the *Journal* avowed that if the party were "to sacrifice a reasonable hope of success with another man in order to give him his due as a 'faithful leader,' we want no part in the suicide."⁹ "Success is a duty," echoed Colfax as he pressed the candidacy of Bates. Success could be achieved only by abandoning the more radical Seward. "With a formidable third party in Pennsylvania, New York, Indiana and Illinois we are beaten," he asserted. "Seward's nomination will make just that third party, and with it certain defeat."¹⁰

The minority of vociferous "irrepressibles" expressed their usual dissent. Julian, who had gained the Congressional nomination in the fifth district, favored the radical Salmon P. Chase of Ohio. His followers questioned the value of a victory won by the abandonment of principle. "You seem to think much would be gained to 'freedom' by the mere defeat of the Democratic party," caustically wrote one radical to the *Journal*. "I admit much would be gained.... But how 'freedom' should be benefited by the filling of empty stomachs and pockets, I can't so easily see." "Better a defeat and rally, than victory and demoralization to the party," advised another.¹¹

As if to give substance to the apprehensions of the "accommodators," some Indiana Know-Nothings seemed determined to act independently again in 1860. A. H. Davidson, chairman of the American state executive committee, issued a call for a meeting to select delegates to the national convention of the newly formed Constitu-

⁹ Indianapolis *Daily Journal,* March 3, 22, 1860.
¹⁰ Colfax to Sam Bowles, March, 1860, quoted in Ovando J. Hollister, *Life of Schuyler Colfax* (New York and London, 1886), 144.
¹¹ Indianapolis *Daily Journal,* March 6, April 2, 1860.

tional Union party. These conservative ex-Whigs feared that Republican professions of support for Bates were mere efforts to "seduce" them into the Chicago Convention.[12] Hence the local Constitutional Unionists assembled at Indianapolis on April 12 and there perfected a state organization. After approving the call for a national convention at Baltimore, the delegates resolved that Judge John McLean of Ohio and John Bell of Tennessee were their first choices for president and vice-president.[13] Only two Hoosiers subsequently attended the Baltimore convention, and only Richard W. Thompson, the most prominent of the local Constitutional Union politicians, played an important role there. Nevertheless, the resulting nomination of the Bell-Everett ticket was an invitation to disunity among the Indiana foes of the Democracy.[14]

It was this action by the old-line Whigs that convinced most Indiana Republicans that conservative action at Chicago was more essential than ever. "There are thousands of good, but ignorant and prejudiced men, whose sympathies are with us, that have got it into their heads that Mr. Seward is a monster," declared the Indianapolis *American*. "Admit that they are wrong, and what of that? They will not vote for him and nothing can make them."[15] Lane and Morton both agreed that Seward's nomination meant certain defeat for Indiana Republicans.[16]

While Colfax, Defrees, and many other old Whigs continued to favor the nomination of Bates,[17] the Missourian's local strength had begun to decline before the

[12] Richard W. Thompson to A. H. Davidson, February 20, 1860, Vallette Miller Collection, Indiana Division, Indiana State Library.
[13] Indianapolis *Daily Journal*, April 13, 1860.
[14] Thompson was one of the convention's vice-presidents and a member of the committee on resolutions.
[15] Indianapolis *Indiana American*, May 9, 1860.
[16] Foulke, *Oliver P. Morton*, 1:74.
[17] Indianapolis *Daily Journal*, April 13, 1860; Charles Zimmerman, "The Origin and Rise of the Republican Party in Indiana," in *Indiana Magazine of History*, 13(1917):388-90.

Republican convention met. Chiefly responsible for this trend were the protests of influential German leaders who refused to forget Bates's co-operation with Know-Nothings in 1856.[18] Consequently many conservatives began to look about for another candidate who, while acceptable to the old Whigs, would not antagonize the Germans. Lane and the Indianapolis *Journal* regarded the ancient Judge John McLean of Ohio as the ideal choice; others favored Cassius M. Clay of Kentucky; and Pennsylvanians wooed the Indiana delegation for their favorite son, Simon Cameron.[19] The *Journal* also suggested that Abraham Lincoln would make a satisfactory candidate, and reports from local politicians in southern Indiana indicated growing approbation for Douglas' Illinois rival.[20] Lincoln realizing the importance of winning the Indiana delegation, had been doing every thing possible to encourage the growth of sentiment in his favor. At least one of the delegates, Cyrus M. Allen of Vincennes, gave Lincoln his active support.[21] There was, in fact, no great obstacle to the shifting of Bates's support to Lincoln, for the latter, too, was a former Whig and a moderate in his slavery views. But regardless of who was finally supported, the delegates apparently desired to agree beforehand and then act as a unit once the balloting commenced.[22]

[18] Fort Wayne *Republican,* quoted in Centreville *Indiana True Republican,* April 12, 1860; Goshen *Times,* quoted in Indianapolis *Daily State Sentinel,* May 12, 1860.
[19] Jeremiah Nichols, Philadelphia, to D. D. Pratt, March 8, 1860, and S. I. Levering, Leverington, Pennsylvania, to Pratt, April 26, 1860, Daniel D. Pratt MSS., Indiana Division, Indiana State Library; Indianapolis *Daily Journal,* April 19, 1860.
[20] Indianapolis *Daily Journal,* April 19, 26, May 9, 1860.
[21] Lincoln to Allen, May 1, 1860, quoted in Gilbert A. Tracy (ed.), *Uncollected Letters of Abraham Lincoln* (Boston and New York, 1917), 145. "It is represented to me by men who ought to know, that the whole of Indiana might not be difficult to get," wrote Lincoln to R. N. Corwine, May 2, 1860. *Ibid.,* 146-47.
[22] Pleasant A. Hackleman, Rushville, to D. D. Pratt, March 23, 1860, and D. C. Donnohue, Greencastle, to Pratt, March 31, 1860, Pratt MSS.

The Indianans reached Chicago on May 12, four days before the convention opened. Indiana, with twenty-six votes, was exceeded only by Ohio, with forty-six votes, among the states of the Old Northwest, and her support was coveted by the managers of the various candidates. "They are suing us and wooing us," reported one of the delegates after being addressed by the friends of Lincoln and Bates in a series of caucuses.[23] While some still favored Bates, his cause was weakening, and the arguments of the Lincoln managers combined with the Chicago atmosphere were having a decided effect. On May 15 an informal poll of the Hoosiers put Lincoln in the lead despite the work of Frank Blair of Missouri and John D. Defrees of Indiana in behalf of Bates.[24]

Yet even on the opening day of the convention the Indiana delegates were still divided between the two candidates. Not until the morning of May 17 did they make their final decision. At that time the Indiana and Pennsylvania delegations met at the courthouse to hear Blair of Missouri speak for Bates. The friends of Lincoln hurried to the gathering and presented their case after Blair had finished. They claimed that Lincoln, a former resident of southern Indiana, would certainly win the Whig vote of that region. But more impressive were the warnings of Carl Schurz of Wisconsin and Gustave Koerner of Illinois, that if Bates were nominated, the Germans would bolt the ticket.[25] After that the Indianans were solidly behind Lincoln. "We Bates men of Indiana concluded that the only way to beat Seward was to go

---

[23] Chicago *Press & Tribune,* May 16, 1860. For a detailed discussion of the work of the Indiana delegation at Chicago, see Charles Roll, "Indiana's Part in the Nomination of Abraham Lincoln for President in 1860," in *Indiana Magazine of History,* 25(1929):1-13; Reinhard H. Luthin, "Indiana and Lincoln's Rise to the Presidency," in *Indiana Magazine of History,* 38(1942):385-405.

[24] Indianapolis *Daily Journal,* May 16, 17, 1860.

[25] Beale (ed.), *Diary of Edward Bates,* 130-31; Thomas J. McCormack (ed.), *Memoirs of Gustave Koerner 1809-1896* . . . (2 vols. Torch Press, Cedar Rapids, Iowa, 1909), 2:87-89.

for Lincoln as a unit," Defrees explained to Colfax.²⁶ Meanwhile, Caleb Smith had won from Judge David Davis, Lincoln's campaign manager, a promise of a place in the cabinet for his aid to the Railsplitter's cause.²⁷

At the end of the first day, though the contest was clearly one between Lincoln and Seward, the "doubtful state" delegations were none too sanguine about the prospects. Despite their predictions of certain defeat in the fall elections, the opponents of Seward left the Wigwam that night expecting his nomination, and this sentiment still prevailed on the morning of the third day.²⁸ But Horace Greeley, Andrew Curtin of Pennsylvania, Lane, and the other anti-Seward men were not willing to give up without a struggle. "Many of them never touched a bed or closed an eye that night," wrote one reporter. Another witness saw Lane "at one o'clock, pale and haggard, with cane under his arm, walking as if for a wager, from one caucus-room to another, at the Tremont House." Pleading for "success rather than Seward," Lane told the caucuses that Seward's nomination would be death to himself, and that he might in that case just as well give up the contest. An alarming report that the Republican candidates for governor in Indiana, Illinois, and Pennsylvania would withdraw in the event of Seward's nomination, had wide circulation. Lane said repeatedly that he did not care to expend "his time and money in carrying on a hopeless campaign."²⁹

---

²⁶ Quoted in Hollister, *Schuyler Colfax*, 147-48.

²⁷ Charles Gibson, "Edward Bates," in *Missouri Historical Society Collections*, 2:no. 1(1900):55; Matilda Gresham, *Life of Walter Quintin Gresham 1832-1895* (2 vols. Chicago, 1919), 1:110-11; Roll, "Indiana's Part in the Nomination of Lincoln," in *Indiana Magazine of History*, 25:9; Reinhard H. Luthin, *The First Lincoln Campaign* (Harvard University Press, 1944), 141-42.

²⁸ Halstead, *Caucuses of 1860*, 131-32, 141-42.

²⁹ Indianapolis *Daily Journal*, May 21, 1860; Halstead, *Caucuses of 1860*, 142-43; Cincinnati *Daily Commercial*, quoted in Indianapolis *Daily State Sentinel*, May 22, 1860.

This cry of a want of availability raised against Seward had a profound effect. Amid the general chaos that followed the presentation of Lincoln's name, none howled more lustily than the rollicking delegates from Indiana. Lane "leaped upon a table, and swinging his hat and cane, performed like an acrobat." The next day Indiana cast her votes solidly for Lincoln, and her "accommodators" completed their triumph by his nomination on the third ballot. "It is not that we loved Seward less but because we loved the great Republican cause more," cried Caleb Smith in triumph, and Lane, his voice hoarse with shouting, promised a majority of ten thousand for Lincoln in Indiana. "If there was a sacrifice to timidity in it, it was the sacrifice of a man for the benefit of the cause," echoed the Indianapolis *Journal*.[30] Victory—dutiful victory—appeared closer than ever as the Hoosiers left the Wigwam at the end of that memorable day.

The Republican press responded to the proceedings at Chicago with warm approval, and party editors soon uncovered elements of greatness in "Honest Abe Lincoln" of Illinois. Most gratifying of all to party managers was the immediate promise of Julian's organ to give complete support to Lincoln and to the national platform.[31] Julian still affirmed that those who had opposed Seward represented a "superficial and only half-developed Republicanism."[32] But he accepted the shrewd suggestion of his radical friend, Joshua R. Giddings of Ohio. *"Assume* the whole movement to be anti-slavery," advised Giddings, "and *on that account* call on men to support it, and if any

---

[30] Chicago *Press & Tribune,* May 19, 1860; Indianapolis *Daily Journal,* May 21, 29, 1860; Halstead, *Caucuses of 1860,* 145. Horace Greeley wrote in the New York *Tribune*: "The candidates for Governor in the great doubtful states—Col. Curtin in Pennsylvania and Gen. Lane in Indiana—were as energetic and efficient as able men must be who felt life or death for themselves and their party hung on the issue of this struggle." Quoted in Indianapolis *Daily Journal,* May 23, 1860.

[31] Centreville *Indiana True Republican,* May 24, 1860.

[32] Julian, *Political Recollections,* 177.

man fails, after election hold him up as an apostate from the faith."³³ The issues dividing "accommodators" and "irrepressibles," then, had not been resolved but only deferred.

3

While the Republicans were closing their ranks, the Democrats continued to flounder in hopeless disunity. Defeated at the state convention, Senator Bright attended the Charleston meeting in April and vowed that he would stump Indiana county by county in opposition to Douglas should the latter be nominated.³⁴ Nevertheless, the Hoosier delegates heeded their instructions and voted faithfully for Douglas during the wearisome days of futile balloting.³⁵

When the convention reassembled at Baltimore in June, the party split was completed by the nomination of two separate tickets, each of which claimed to be the regular Democratic slate. The northern wing of the party nominated Douglas on a popular-sovereignty platform. The southern seceders nominated John C. Breckinridge of Kentucky on a platform demanding Congressional protection of slavery in the territories. With heavy hearts the Indiana delegates returned to their homes where they complained bitterly of being betrayed by their heretofore friends in the South. The party press made light of the Breckinridge movement, but the corroding effect of internal dissension was obvious to all.

None doubted that Bright had every intention of making good his threat to campaign against Douglas in Indiana, especially since the Breckinridge nomination gave him a valid excuse for such action. In July he began his

---

³³ Giddings to Julian, May 25, 1860, quoted in Grace Julian Clarke, *George W. Julian* (*Indiana Historical Collections*, vol. 11, Indianapolis, 1923), 206-7.

³⁴ Halstead, *Caucuses of 1860*, 12.

³⁵ Several Indiana delegates, however, especially Lafe Develin of the fifth district, were at heart opposed to Douglas and would have gladly joined a stampede for some other candidate. *Ibid.*, 28, 58.

tour, denouncing the Douglas politicians and press as "venal and corrupt," and promising a full list of Breckinridge electors.[36] On July 17 the Indianapolis *Old Line Guard* made its appearance as the official Breckinridge organ. Two weeks later a Breckinridge mass convention at Indianapolis selected an electoral ticket, organized a state central committee, and passed a series of resolutions endorsing the national Breckinridge platform, the Buchanan administration, and the course of Bright.[37]

Douglas leaders scarcely knew what course to pursue in dealing with the Bright faction. At times they abused the "disorganizers," but more often they begged Democrats to hold together against the common foe. They argued that a division would merely appease the personal animosities of Bright.[38] "It is not the *number of Breckinridge men*," sadly wrote one Douglas leader, "but the dispiriting effect of division among our men, & the confidence created in our opponents that is to be apprehended."[39] Certainly the Breckinridge movement was far more menacing to the Douglas Democrats than the Bell-Everett campaign was to Indiana Republicans.

4

But the activities of Bell and Breckinridge men were mere eddies in the main current of Indiana politics. Most Hoosiers were chiefly interested in the contest between Republicans and Douglas Democrats. In general the campaign oratory and literature pursued familiar themes and reverted to well-tested arguments. The tariff, internal improvements, government land policy—all the aspects of the sectional conflict—were familiar issues to the Hoosier electorate. If the Democrats found new cause

---

[36] Indianapolis *Daily State Sentinel,* July 31, 1860.
[37] *Ibid.,* August 1, 1860; Indianapolis *Old Line Guard,* August 2, 9, 1860.
[38] Indianapolis *Daily State Sentinel,* July 9, 1860.
[39] William S. Holman to Allen Hamilton, July 16, 1860, in Allen Hamilton MSS., Indiana Division, Indiana State Library.

for alarm in the growing slavery agitation, Republicans were quick to deny responsibility for it. Only an unusual intensity of feeling and a widespread impression that argument had nearly run its course—that the approaching election was to be in the nature of a showdown between the contending forces—distinguished the current campaign from those which had gone before. While recent events, particularly the panic of 1857, made some men more ready to meet issues squarely and risk a crisis, the politicians continued to rival each other in affirming their devotion to conservatism.

Upon Lane's return from Chicago he and Hendricks resumed their joint debates.[40] After touring northern Indiana together in late May or early June, each went his own way for the remainder of the canvass. But neither candidate did more than enlarge upon the arguments he had advanced in the spring. Although Lane vaguely professed to stand with the founding fathers upon the principle that "freedom is national and slavery local,"[41] neither he nor Hendricks said much about the slavery issue. Both parties were equally committed to the homestead measure, but Hendricks' past record on this point was not entirely consistent and the Republicans made the most of it.[42] Moreover, the opposition of southern Democrats and Buchanan's veto of a homestead bill in the summer of 1860 further discredited Democratic professions of sympathy.

On the tariff issue, however, it was Lane and the Republicans whose position remained anomalous, for the party was still divided in its sentiments. Democrats had no such problem, and they vigorously attacked the national Republican platform's commitment to the dogma of protection. With the assertion that higher tariffs would impose fresh burdens upon western interests, the party

[40] Indianapolis *Daily Journal,* May 23, 1860.
[41] *Ibid.,* September 4, 1860.
[42] *Ibid.,* September 14, 17, 1860.

press warned the farmers and mechanics of Indiana that Republicans would foist upon them this old Whig heresy. Such a policy, they argued, would foster monopolies "for the benefit of monied aristocracies."[43]

Neither party made its position regarding slavery extension especially clear to the confused electorate. Republicans were less than candid when they explained their intentions; Douglas Democrats, keenly aware of their own embarrassing position, chose to interpret and condemn Republican policy rather than clarify their own. While the Indianapolis *Journal* affirmed that the contest was one between Slavery and Freedom and that a Democratic or Constitutional Union victory would nationalize the South's "peculiar institution," it never elaborated upon that assertion. It merely asserted that there was no "protection against this result but the election of Lincoln" who was "pledged . . . to resist the elevation of slavery above the local position in which the Government placed it."[44] Most Republicans wanted no stock in abolitionism, and some even denied that they contemplated an attack upon slavery anywhere.[45] The party press generally emphasized Lincoln's conservatism and quoted the abolitionists to prove their opposition to him.[46] Charles Sumner's polemic, "The Barbarism of Slavery," found no favor with the *Journal* which branded it a "diatribe," a "bitter, unsparing, and not entirely just" attack upon the slaveholders.[47] If Freedom was in actual jeopardy, the Republican party of Indiana was extremely cautious in its defense.

The war of words found its complement in spectacular political demonstrations which made the campaign of

---

[43] New Albany *Weekly Ledger*, February 22, 1860; Indianapolis *Daily State Sentinel*, October 17, 1860; Indianapolis *Old Line Guard*, August 23, 1860.
[44] Indianapolis *Daily Journal*, March 1, July 28, 1860.
[45] Indianapolis *Indiana American*, June 20, 1860.
[46] Indianapolis *Daily Journal*, June 6, July 27, 1860.
[47] *Ibid.*, June 8, 1860.

1860 the most colorful in the memory of the Hoosier electorate. "Speeches, day and night, torch-light processions, and all kinds of noise and confusion are the go, with all parties," commented the "independent" Indianapolis *Locomotive*.[48] Julian too was impressed by the "contrivance and spectacular display" which prevailed in the current canvass.[49] Each party took unusual pains to mobilize its followers in disciplined political clubs, but the most remarkable of these were the Lincoln "Rail Maulers" and "Wide Awakes," whose organizations extended throughout the state. Clad in gaudy uniforms the members of these quasi-military bands participated in all Republican demonstrations. The "Wide Awakes" in particular were well drilled and served as political police in escorting party speakers and in preserving order at public meetings.[50] Party emulation made every political rally the occasion for carefully arranged parades through banner-bedecked streets, torchlight processions, elaborate floats and transparencies, blaring bands, and fireworks.

Prominent national politicians were carefully selected and imported to assist local leaders in conducting the campaign. The Democrats obtained the services of Representative Clement L. Vallandigham and Senator George Pugh of Ohio among others.[51] Late in the canvass Douglas himself made a brief visit to the state. National Republican leaders, regarding Indiana as one of the "battle-ground states," were more than generous in sending outside aid. They furnished speakers to comport with every group and shade of opinion: the Germans were accommodated by the presence of Frederick Hassaurek of Cincinnati and Carl Schurz of Wisconsin;[52] the

[48] Indianapolis *Locomotive*, September 29, 1860.
[49] Julian, *Political Recollections*, 178.
[50] Indianapolis *Daily Journal*, July 9, August 11, 1860.
[51] Indianapolis *Daily State Sentinel*, July 19, 1860. Governor Willard was also active in the campaign and vigorously defended the administration until his untimely death early in October. *Ibid.*, October 6, 1860.
[52] Indianapolis *Daily Journal*, July 17, August 2, 1860.

"irrepressibles" of Julian's district listened to the appeals of Salmon P. Chase, Joshua R. Giddings, and Cassius M. Clay;[53] and the conservatives heard the moderate views of men like Frank Blair of Missouri, Thomas Corwin of Ohio, and John C. Underwood of Virginia.[54]

During the last few weeks of the campaign Democrats, sensing the imminence of defeat, turned frantically to alarmist tactics. They portrayed vividly the terrible consequences of a Republican victory, warning that it would mean complete ruin for the interests of the Northwest. Only the success of the conservative Douglas party would produce the political stability necessary for a continuation of peaceful, economic progress.[55] A Republican triumph would inaugurate the "irrepressible conflict." It would end "either in civil war for the mastery or a peaceful division of the Union."[56]

In replying to Democratic scaremongers the Republicans pursued two opposing lines of argument. First, they accused Daniel W. Voorhees, candidate for Congress in the seventh district, and other Democrats of being disunionists, and they belligerently asserted that the issue between Slavery and Freedom "might just as well be settled now as later."[57] Second, they soothingly predicted that Lincoln's policy would be one calculated to "restore and strengthen kind and fraternal feelings between all the patriotic citizens of the several States."[58] A Republican victory would end the recent sectional struggle and begin a new era of good feeling.

Thus reassured, Indiana's inherently conservative citizens went to the polls on October 9 and gave their state

---

[53] Centreville *Indiana True Republican,* August 2, 30, 1860. The *Sentinel* reported that Seward, however, had been requested to avoid Indiana during the campaign. August 29, 1860.
[54] Indianapolis *Daily Journal,* August 30, 1860.
[55] Indianapolis *Daily State Sentinel,* August 13, September 10, 1860.
[56] *Ibid.,* August 24, October 9, 1860.
[57] Indianapolis *Daily Journal,* August 17, September 26, 1860.
[58] *Ibid.,* September 7, 1860.

A Dutiful Victory 47

to the Republicans by a substantial majority.[59] Similar results in Pennsylvania and Ohio presaged the election of Lincoln in November. While the Republicans rejoiced over their victory and waited confidently for its culmination the following month, the Democrats bitterly ascribed their defeat to election frauds and to the treason of the Breckinridge men.[60] "Fanaticism and treachery have triumphed," mourned the *Sentinel*. "The 'irrepressible conflict' of Seward and Lincoln has commenced. No human foresight can see the end. Revolutions never go backward."[61]

Democratic leaders worked desperately for a political reaction in November. A Republican victory, they cried, would make disunion inevitable. The country was threatened with a fratricidal war, with universal bankruptcy, with hunger and want. Nor was there any hope "that such a day of tribulation would pass without bringing with it fire and blood—the torch of the incendiary, the blow of the assassin, the war of the poor for food. . . ."[62] The Democratic press fortified its dismal prophecies with long quotations from the secession editorials printed in southern newspapers. Once more the Republicans replied to all these dour predictions by asserting that the disunion cry was sheer bluff, a mere party trick. "One single year of Lincoln's administration will expose it so effectually that it will never be heard of again."[63]

In November Lincoln carried Indiana by a clear majority over his three opponents and thus climaxed a political revolution of fundamental significance for the

---

[59] Lane and other Republican candidates carried the state by nearly 10,000 majority. Only four of the eleven congressmen elected were Democrats, all from the southern districts: James A. Cravens, William S. Holman, John Law, and Daniel W. Voorhees. Indianapolis *Daily Journal*, October 12, 13, 14, 1860.
[60] Indianapolis *Daily State Sentinel*, October 11, 1860.
[61] *Ibid.*, October 10, 1860.
[62] *Ibid.*, November 2, 3, 1860.
[63] Indianapolis *Daily Journal*, October 13, 16, 30, 1860.

Hoosier commonwealth.⁶⁴ Not since 1840 had the Democrats lost the state in a national election; not until 1876 would they win it again. A significant feature of this election was the swing of the German voters to Republicanism, as evidenced by the fact that seven of the eight German newspapers gave their support to the victorious party.⁶⁵ Equally important was the decision of three-fourths of the Fillmore men of 1856 to desert Bell and vote for Lincoln.⁶⁶ The "accommodators" had succeeded in their efforts to attract this conservative element.

The leaders of the young party soon had to consider how they would use their victory. Success had been a self-proclaimed duty, but the implications in that attractive formula were destined in the ensuing months to torture the minds of Republicans, and, at last, to swirl them into the vortex of civil war.

⁶⁴ The official tabulation showed the following number of votes for each candidate: Lincoln, 139,033; Douglas, 115,509; Breckinridge, 12,294; and Bell, 5,306. Indianapolis *Daily Journal,* December 14, 1860.

⁶⁵ *Ibid.,* June 30, October 18, 1860.

⁶⁶ Carl F. Brand, "History of the Know Nothing Party in Indiana," in *Indiana Magazine of History,* 18(1922):304-5.

CHAPTER 4 UNITY OUT
OF DISUNION

BEFORE the last ballots had been tallied in November southern "fire-eaters" grimly prepared to demonstrate that there was more than campaign froth in their warning that Lincoln's election would disrupt the Union. Indiana Republicans were still exulting over their triumph when the news arrived that the South Carolina legislature had summoned a convention to assemble at Charleston on December 17 to consider that state's position in the Union. In dismay they watched this movement culminate in the adoption of an ordinance of secession on December 20 and saw the Gulf states quickly follow South Carolina's lead.

For the masses of Indiana's Union-loving citizens this new crisis soon dwarfed the issues of the recent campaign, and the fate of the Union became at once the all-absorbing question. When the shadowy form of Seward's "irrepressible conflict" came suddenly into bold relief, the Hoosiers recoiled from the ominous implications of a divided nation. In the utter confusion of those dismal days men of all parties looked hopefully to their political leaders for guidance and statesmanship equal to the crisis. Too often they found neither. Instead the politicians generally plied their trade as usual and considered the issues in terms of personal profit and party advantage. In like manner Indiana's men of substance carefully calculated the economic significance of the national disaster. Indeed, bigoted partisanship and narrow self-interests loomed exceedingly large during the critical weeks before the batteries of Charleston transferred the issue from the council chamber to the battlefield.

After its political triumph the Republican party of Indiana was again gravely threatened with disintegration. Try as they might party leaders were still unable to find a set of common principles to suit all factions. Upon most questions of economic policy the Republicans continued in hopeless disagreement; upon the issue of slavery there remained the basic variance between radicals and conservatives whose co-operation during the campaign had only been a temporary truce.

Accordingly, Democrats made the most of the situation and feigned a deep concern as to what the Republican victory had really meant. "Is it Republicanism, as construed by Giddings, Wilson, Sumner, Chase & Co?" queried the *Sentinel*. "Or is it the new version announced by the *Journal*—'let slavery alone?'"[1] The Democracy found solace for its defeat in the confident expectation that the Republican organization would soon dissolve. "Never before," gloated the New Albany *Ledger*, "has a party been crushed by the very fact of its triumph, and before it had tasted either the sweets or felt the responsibilities of power."[2]

Meanwhile the repercussions of southern secession threatened to complete the disruption of the Hoosier Republican organization. At first many conservative Republican businessmen and numerous party followers in southern Indiana blenched at the very thought of coercing the South, for they were convinced that it would lead to civil war. The effects of such a policy upon the river towns and the merchants of South Bend, Fort Wayne, and Indianapolis, as well as upon the downstate farmers

[1] Indianapolis *Daily State Sentinel*, November 8, 1860.
[2] New Albany *Weekly Ledger*, December 19, 1860.

who produced for the southern market, would have obviously been disastrous.

The Indianapolis *Journal,* which had long represented the conservative wing of the Republican party, was the earliest and most influential spokesman for the anti-coercion group.³ After Editor Horace Greeley proclaimed through the New York *Tribune* his apparent (though far from consistent) willingness to let the "erring sisters" depart in peace, the *Journal* aired its views with greater frankness. "No rational man can resist the argument against secession as a constitutional proceeding," it asserted, "but any rational man may hesitate before deciding the constitution shall be preserved at the expense of civil war. . . . The main question, therefore, is not the constitutionality of secession, but the blood and horror of coercion. . . . Of what value will an union be that needs links of bayonets and bullets to hold it together?"⁴ Almost daily its editorial columns dwelt upon the frightful implications of an internecine war—the ruination of trade, a crushing national debt, rebellious slaves, and starving workers—and dismissed it as "suicidal and senseless."⁵

A number of party leaders entertained similar opinions. Walter Q. Gresham, young Republican member of the state legislature from a river county, assured Lane and Morton that he would never fight in a servile or domestic war.⁶ Early in the crisis a few radicals also professed a willingness to acquiesce in disunion. They shrewdly noted that the withdrawal of the southern members would leave the Republicans in a majority in Congress. "With that majority," vaunted one, "we would be able to admit Kansas and Nebraska as Free States and thus *enclose*

---
³ Indianapolis *Daily Journal,* August 17, October 31, November 10, 1860.
⁴ *Ibid.,* November 19, 1860.
⁵ *Ibid.,* December 21, 1860.
⁶ Gresham, *Life of Walter Q. Gresham,* 1:136.

Missouri and *slavery with it*. Therefore I once more say: Let those that will, secede. . . ."⁷

Although every radical flatly rejected all proposals for appeasing the South, some conservative Republicans were prepared to retreat from the Chicago platform and support a "reasonable" compromise that was calculated to preserve the Union. In southern Indiana, even among those who had voted for Lincoln, a political reaction set in as soon as it became apparent that the Ohio River might mark the border between two hostile nations.⁸ Few believed that compromise could hold the deep South in the Union, but many still hoped to placate the border slave states and preserve the unity of the Ohio Valley.⁹

With countless compromise proposals in circulation, Indiana's Republican "accommodators" swelled the total with plans of their own. In this matter the *Journal* again took the lead and proposed the repeal of all personal liberty laws, granting to slaveholders the right of transit with their slaves through the free states, and the settlement of the slavery question in the territories by popular sovereignty or the restoration of the Missouri Compromise line.¹⁰ Lane, during a visit to Kentucky, said that the Missouri line extended to California might be acceptable to the North.¹¹ Representative William M. Dunn of the Third Congressional District offered the House Committee of Thirty-Three a set of similar proposals.¹²

---

⁷ Thomas Hielsher, Indianapolis, to George W. Julian, November 20, 1860, Julian MSS.

⁸ Smith, *Borderland in the Civil War*, 135-36.

⁹ Indianapolis *Daily Journal*, December 5, 7, 8, 18, 1860; Madison *Courier*, quoted in *ibid.*, January 28, 1861; Gresham, *Life of Walter Q. Gresham*, 1:125.

¹⁰ Indianapolis *Daily Journal*, November 29, December 4, 21, 1860. The *Journal* denied that it favored the abandonment of the Chicago platform and asserted that restoration of the Missouri Compromise "places us just where we were before Douglas renewed the slavery agitation in 1854."

¹¹ *Ibid.*, January 11, 1861.

¹² *Ibid.*, January 3, 1861.

(Dunn and Representative David Kilgore, however, were the only ones among the seven Indiana Republicans in Congress who showed much interest in concessions to the South.) Only a few Republicans were ready to support the proposition of Senator John J. Crittenden of Kentucky not only to restore the 36° 30′ line, but also to provide a Congressional slave code to protect slavery south of that line in present territory and in that "hereafter acquired."[13] Sensitive men of property warned their Republican friends that "the barometer on the exchange . . . points to foul weather" and insisted that the present was no time for partisan rancor. "If faction rules, the Government is lost."[14]

It was the Indiana Democracy, however, which assumed during the crisis the prime role of Union saver and promised to rescue the nation from the hands of those who threatened to destroy it. Every consideration of party strategy and local economic interest drove the followers of Douglas to leadership in the movement for peace and conciliation. They shrewdly cultivated the growing rift in the Republican organization and carefully paved the way for the anticipated alliance of compromise Republicans with the Democrats. What hope had the South for protection in the Union, they asked pointedly, while a party entertaining the sentiments of the Chicago platform controlled the general government? If Lincoln planned to steer a conservative course, why did he keep his lips so tightly sealed? "Is there no pilot who can safely guide the ship of state through the dangers which surround her?"[15]

The nationwide commercial crisis which accompanied the secession movement and badly frightened the propertied interests played directly into the hands of Democratic leaders. Indiana's river counties complained of

[13] *Ibid.*, January 31, 1861.
[14] *Ibid.*, January 1, 1861.
[15] Indianapolis *Daily State Sentinel,* November 16, 19, 20, 1860.

hard times and general business stagnation.[16] Throughout the state the securities which supported the paper of free banks depreciated alarmingly.[17] With recovery from the panic of 1857 still incomplete, Democratic newspapers warned that "abolition agitation and sectional strife" presaged the renewal of economic adversity.[18]

Even more ominous were the broader implications in secession perceived especially by the farmers and businessmen south of the National Road. The possible loss of their river outlet and southern market caused such men bitterly to abuse the "malignant partizan majority" whom they blamed for their present plight.[19] Equally appalling was the prospect of a Union dominated, in the absence of the southern agrarians, by the "fanatical, abolitionized, canting, hypocritical New England States," with their odious tariff and banking doctrines.[20] When Republicans passed the Morrill Tariff in February, 1861, the Democratic press used that measure to illustrate the manner in which the producing classes of the Northwest would be treated in a Union controlled by eastern cotton spinners and iron mongers.[21]

All these factors drew southern Indiana toward some course of common action with the rest of the Union-conscious borderland. From this traditional stronghold of the Hoosier Democracy emanated the most persistent

[16] Elizabeth L. Craft, Rising Sun, to Henry C. Craft, December 22, 1860, Pratt MSS.
[17] Message of Governor Hammond to the Legislature, January 11, 1861, in Indiana *House Journal,* 1861, p. 31.
[18] New Albany *Weekly Ledger,* November 21, 1860.
[19] *Ibid.,* February 6, 1861.
[20] *Ibid.,* November 28, 1860.
[21] *Ibid.,* February 13, 20, 1861; Indianapolis *Daily State Sentinel,* March 4, 19, 1861. "The Republican tariff policy," ventured the Indianapolis *Daily Sentinel,* March 25, 1861, "will do more to create a sympathy in the North-west with the South, than anything the latter could do to effect that end." The shipbuilders in the river towns were especially incensed by the passage of this tariff because it raised the duty on nearly all materials used in their industry. Madison *Courier,* quoted in Indianapolis *Daily Journal,* March 21, 1861.

demands for compromise. Every border newspaper dwelt at length upon the horrors of a civil war that would be fought upon their soil, ravage their cities and towns, and pit them against their friends and neighbors in Kentucky.[22] Angrily these appeasers berated the foes of compromise and warned that they felt no obligation "to assist in deluging the land with blood merely to preserve the Chicago platform."[23] Congressman-elect Daniel Voorhees defiantly told a Democratic meeting in the seventh district that he would never "vote one dollar, one man, or one gun . . . to make war upon the South. . . ."[24]

The opponents of coercion expressed their conciliatory views in scores of Union meetings which assembled during the winter months in almost every community in the state. While Democrats dominated such meetings, it was not uncommon for a few Republicans to participate, and officers were usually chosen on a nonpartisan basis. Invariably their resolutions suggested that the time had come for party malignity to cease, praised the efforts of the southern Union men, confessed that Southerners probably had some cause for dissatisfaction, and urged the repeal of personal liberty laws and the granting of additional guarantees to the South. Many of them specifically endorsed the Crittenden compromise; others called instead for a national convention to settle the outstanding differences between the sections.[25]

Early in the crisis some men in southern Indiana began to speculate about the possibility that all efforts to save the Union by peace and compromise might fail. What ought their course to be in the event of permanent divi-

[22] New Albany *Weekly Ledger,* November 21, 1860.
[23] *Ibid.,* January 2, 1861.
[24] Terre Haute *Journal,* quoted in Indianapolis *Daily State Sentinel,* April 13, 1861.
[25] *Ibid.,* January 28, February 23, 1861; Indianapolis *Daily Journal,* February 23, 1861; New Albany *Weekly Ledger,* January 23, 1861; James A. Cravens, Hardinsburg, to William H. English, January 20, 1861, English Collection.

sion? Actually several policies were possible and each
had its advocates. One group, believing that the political
and economic ties with the South were too vital to be
broken, would have joined its southern friends in a reconstructed Union or formed a Northwest Confederacy in
alliance with the South.[26]

In this group was the editor of the New Albany *Ledger*
who presented a sober analysis of the choice confronting
the West. Allied with the South it would retain the use
of the great rivers, "the natural outlets for our commerce." Allied with the North it could use only "those
artificial channels, railroads, which must always be a
costly means of transportation." Moreover, he added,
the West would have to choose between the low tariff
schedules of the Confederacy and paying a heavy tax
upon the goods it consumed for the support of eastern
manufacturers.[27] Congressman-elect James A. Cravens
from the second district shared these views. In the
privacy of a personal letter he proposed a division of
Illinois and Indiana to create, from the southern portion
of each, a new state to be named "Jackson." "I cannot
obliviate the fact that our interest is with the South," he
explained, "and I cannot reconcile the separation. . . ."[28]
Public meetings in several of the river counties expressed
similar opinions.[29]

On the other hand, another group with identical interests soon advocated the opposite course of action. Equally

---

[26] See William C. Cochran, "The Dream of a Northwestern Confederacy," in the State Historical Society of Wisconsin *Proceedings,* 1916 (Madison, 1917), 227-28; Paoli *Eagle,* quoted in Indianapolis *Daily State Sentinel,* January 21, 1861. On December 13, 1860, the *Sentinel* suggested that if the whole Union could not be maintained, "other combinations could be formed, as sympathies and interests should dictate. . . ."

[27] New Albany *Weekly Ledger,* April 3, 1861.

[28] James A. Cravens, Hardinsburg, to William H. English, April 9, 1861, English Collection.

[29] New Albany *Weekly Ledger,* January 9, 23, February 27, 1861; Indianapolis *Daily Journal,* January 9, 15, 1861; Gresham, *Life of Walter Q. Gresham,* 1:122.

convinced that Indiana could not separate from the South, they felt that, compromise failing, the preservation of the Union by force was their only recourse. This sentiment increased when Confederates temporarily interfered with commerce on the Mississippi, an act which roused the ire of many Westerners.[30] Even the New Albany *Ledger* growled that by such an act Southerners might provoke a demonstration that would "speedily put an end to all such efforts on the part of . . . any . . . seceding state."[31] Democratic Representative William S. Holman of the fourth district revised his original belief that coercion was "absurd."[32] Now he hoped that Indiana would never consent to the dissolution of the Union or allow any state "to appropriate to its own use the property that belongs to the whole country."[33] Many citizens of southern Indiana vacillated from one remedy to another as unfolding events altered the situation.[34]

2

Meanwhile, as some timid Republicans and a united Democracy spoke the soft words of compromise, a strange combination of "irrepressibles" and practical Republican politicians were preparing to resist every effort toward conciliation. Many in this group were at first reluctant to commit themselves openly to a policy of coercion and called instead for the mere "enforcement of the laws." But they all were convinced that to abandon their platform would be to destroy their party. They also appreciated the overwhelming need for some principle or course

---

[30] Smith, *Borderland in the Civil War*, 134-35; Cochran, "Dream of a Northwestern Confederacy," in *op. cit.*, 226; Indiana *House Journal*, 1861, pp. 236-37, 567-68.
[31] New Albany *Weekly Ledger*, January 23, 1861.
[32] Holman to Allen Hamilton, November 18, 1860, Allen Hamilton MSS.
[33] Letter of Holman to a friend, quoted in Indianapolis *Daily Journal*, February 5, 1861.
[34] Kenneth M. Stampp, "Kentucky's Influence upon Indiana in the Crisis of 1861," in *Indiana Magazine of History*, 39(1943):265-67.

of action upon which their faltering party could unite. An abject surrender to the "Slave Power" was certainly not calculated to achieve that end, for the radicals would never have abandoned their antislavery creed.[35] Their policy was to meet the issue squarely. They believed that new concessions would be no more successful than those of the past in solving a conflict that was "irrepressible."[36] If Lincoln's policy were to be one of peace and compromise, they looked upon the Republican victory as "barren" and predicted that the battle would have "to be fought over again."[37] Julian's organ violently attacked Seward and other Republicans who were ready to concede to the "rebellious partisans of slavery some of the vital principles upon which the late . . . [victory] was achieved." It confidently predicted that from civil war "one great and glorious result at least must follow—Slavery will surely die."[38] These "rugged-issue" Republicans worked sedulously at local Union meetings to block the passage of all compromise resolutions.[39]

Thousands of Lincoln's more moderate supporters shared the antipathy of the radicals toward compromise. Many shrewd politicians realized that backing down would constitute a confession that a Republican victory was a valid excuse for southern secession. With the very life of their party at stake these leaders put great pressure upon those "weak" Republicans who would relinquish

[35] Indianapolis *Indiana American,* December 5, 1860; Centreville *Indiana True Republican,* December 6, 13, 1860; Thomas Hielsher, Indianapolis, to George W. Julian, November 30, 1860, Julian MSS.

[36] Centreville *Indiana True Republican,* December 13, 1860, January 31, 1861. "We most ardently hope that the present excitement will increase, not diminish," asserted the Indianapolis *Indiana American,* November 28, 1860. "Let it now be settled whether we be freemen or not."

[37] Indianapolis *Indiana American,* November 21, 1860.

[38] Centreville *Indiana True Republican,* January 31, February 7, 1861.

[39] See letter from six Republicans of Spring Hill, Decatur County, to George W. Julian, January 21, 1861, Julian MSS.

portions of the Chicago platform. They besieged the central organ of their party with protests against its alleged abandonment of principle and exploited every partisan prejudice and patriotic impulse to foster their cause.[40] "The Republicans," professed one, "have nothing to take back. . . . We knew the man we voted for; understood his principles, and, be the consequences what they may, are determined to give him 'aid and comfort' in carrying out those principles."[41] Another avowed that if the party retreated after its "anti-slavery bluster" in the recent campaign, "Republicanism is a dead dog."[42] Here was an ominous countercurrent in the stream of public opinion.

At this critical juncture in the affairs of Indiana Republicans there emerged a political genius whose realistic mind clearly understood his party's quandary, whose strong will, matchless energy, and boundless ambition eminently fitted him for revolutionary times. Lieutenant Governor-elect Oliver P. Morton's inherent talents were then scarcely appreciated by his contemporaries. At thirty-seven his massive frame, rugged and black-bearded countenance, piercing gray eyes, and deep sonorous voice were already familiar to the leading barristers of Indiana. His law practice, especially the lucrative emoluments of railroad litigation, afforded him a comfortable income,[43] but since 1854, when he had abandoned the Democrats to join the fusionists, politics had been his chief interest. Although he began as a conservative Republican, he was always an opportunist and never hesitated to shift his views as the occasion required. His prime concern was to discover some common ground upon which his party could make a united stand. As he watched developments in November, 1860, he soon perceived in the threatened

---

[40] Indianapolis *Daily Journal*, November 21, 23, December 18, 1860.
[41] Letter of V. B. Oden, Lebanon, in *ibid.*, December 27, 1860.
[42] Quoted in *ibid.*, December 25, 1860.
[43] Julian, *Political Recollections*, 269-70; Foulke, *Oliver P. Morton*, 1:25-26.

dissolution of the Union the long-hoped-for issue. Accordingly, he boldly scorned the appeasers in his party and quickly took command of those who would make no concessions to treason.

Morton's first opportunity to express his views came on the night of November 22 when he addressed the Lincoln Rail Maulers gathered in Indianapolis to rejoice over their recent victory. Slowly and deliberately he unfolded his position in blunt language. Denying any "right" of secession except by successful revolution, he affirmed that coercion was simply the enforcement of the laws. Once the right of secession were granted the nation would be dissolved. The West, he insisted, had more at stake in the preservation of the Union than any other section. It stood in danger of being shut up "in the interior of a continent, surrounded by independent, perhaps hostile nations, through whose territories we could obtain egress to the seaboard only upon such terms as might be agreed to by treaty." Defiantly he proposed that if South Carolina were to leave the Union it should only be "at the point of the bayonet," after every effort had been made to compel her to submit to the laws. "Shall we now surrender the nation without a struggle, and let the Union go with merely a few harsh words? . . . If it was worth a bloody struggle to establish this nation, it is worth one to preserve it."[44] Force, then, was the proper remedy!

Morton's speech at once made a profound impression throughout Indiana and neighboring states.[45] Democrats denounced it bitterly; the *Sentinel* suggested that he was trying to produce "a big smoke upon the 'coercion' question, to cover up other mooted issues in his own party," which threatened its disruption.[46] But a large portion of the Republican party, finding at last a positive program

---

[44] Indianapolis *Daily Journal*, November 27, 1860.
[45] The Cincinnati *Times* called it the ablest speech upon secession that it had seen. Quoted in Indianapolis *Daily Journal*, January 18, 1861.
[46] Indianapolis *Daily State Sentinel*, November 28, 1860.

and a dynamic leader, was captivated by its sentiments. In a short time numerous party organs were chiding the Indianapolis *Journal* for its timorous stand on coercion,[47] and eventually that paper began to yield to the pressure and assumed a more bellicose attitude.

Simultaneously the coercionists stigmatized the Union meetings as "Democratic affairs" and began to chant that Democrats were the allies of traitors.[48] To offset the work of those who still hoped for peace through compromise, they sponsored scores of war meetings which promised to support every measure calculated to defend the Union against its enemies.[49] The vigorous activities of this group eventually contributed to the defeat of the peacemakers.

3

On January 10 the Republican-controlled legislature began its regular session. After electing Lane to the United States Senate and witnessing the inauguration of Morton as governor, it turned to national and state affairs.

Aside from the chaotic condition of state finances, the gravest local problem before the General Assembly was the economic crisis resulting from disunion.[50] Conditions in southern Indiana were especially serious and led to extended discussions of proposals for debt moratoriums, the suspension of specie payments, the expansion of the

[47] *Ibid.*, December 7, 1860; Indianapolis *Daily Journal*, December 8, 1860; Indianapolis *Indiana American*, December 12, 1860; Centreville *Indiana True Republican*, December 6, 1860.

[48] Indianapolis *Daily Journal*, December 12, 1860, April 10, 12, 1861; Madison *Courier*, quoted in *ibid.*, February 13, 1861; Indianapolis *Indiana American*, November 28, 1860.

[49] Indianapolis *Daily State Sentinel*, December 24, 1860; Indianapolis *Indiana American*, December 26, 1860; Indianapolis *Daily Journal*, December 24, 31, 1860, January 5, 8, 15, 22, 1861; Indiana *Senate Journal*, 1861, pp. 58-61.

[50] Indiana *House Journal*, 1861, pp. 136-37; Indiana *Senate Journal*, 1861, p. 122; Indiana General Assembly, *Brevier Legislative Reports*, compiled by Ariel and William H. Drapier, 4(1861):29, 100-1, 176, 190, 219-20.

currency of the state bank, and an increase in the number of its branches. Delegates from the river counties complained bitterly about the suffering of their people. But the legislators consumed most of their time in endless partisan debates and in the consideration of innumerable resolutions designed primarily to turn the national emergency into party capital. By the end of the session the members had wrangled over every conceivable solution to the crisis, but their "wordy, windy, useless" discussions[51] served no better purpose than to intensify party rivalries and mutual suspicion.

At the very outset the Republicans in both houses, seeking to prevent the Democrats from profiting by their disagreements, proposed that all resolutions and petitions dealing with national affairs be referred without debate to special committees on Federal relations. Angrily the Democrats denounced such "gags" at a time when they believed that a free interchange of views was important. But after many harsh words and much disorder the majority had its way.[52] This rule, however, did not entirely prevent the discussion of sectional problems; neither did it deter partisans from baiting their opponents into rash utterances. Before long the word "treason" was being bandied about the legislative halls, and wild accusations resulted in several personal affrays between members.[53] Nor could Republicans entirely conceal their

[51] Centreville *Indiana True Republican*, February 7, 1861.
[52] *Brevier Legislative Reports*, 4(1861):4-6, 15-16; Indianapolis *Daily Journal*, January 8, 9, 11, 1861.
[53] Among others M. A. O. Packard, from Marshall and Starke counties, and Henry Feagler, from De Kalb County, almost came to blows over the latter's claim that the former vowed he would fight with the South in the event of war. The House was finally obliged to pass a resolution threatening to expel any member giving or accepting a challenge to a duel. *Brevier Legislative Reports*, 4(1861):160; Indianapolis *Daily Journal*, February 2, 1861. A few days later G. C. Moody, from Pulaski and Jasper counties, challenged Horace Heffren, from Washington and Harrison counties, to a duel because of the alleged abusive language of the latter. On February 11 they met on a field in Kentucky. Failing to agree upon weapons they finally settled their difficulty peacefully, only

Unity out of Disunion 63

own internal differences. While some voiced warlike sentiments, others persisted in favoring moderation.[54] Meanwhile the Democrats flooded the legislature with the petitions and resolutions of Union meetings, called for the abandonment of party platforms, and strove to commit that body to a policy of conciliation. On the first day of the session Horace Heffren introduced resolutions in the lower chamber which declared that the General Assembly would support no man for any office at its disposal who did not favor the preservation of the Union "at any sacrifice of partizan theories or beliefs," and that "we recognize the . . . Crittenden amendment, as presenting such a basis of settlement."[55] Other Democrats followed with similar proposals.[56] The stiff-backed Republicans parried with resolutions pledging the resources of Indiana to sustain the incoming administration in enforcing the laws and preserving the Union.[57] A similar tone characterized the majority report of the senate committee on Federal relations which relegated the problem of conciliation to the wisdom of Congress.[58]

On January 24, Governor Morton transmitted to the legislature Virginia's call for a national peace conference. Commissioners from the several states were to convene in Washington on February 4 to consider plans for compromising the national difficulties. Though Morton was cold to the project, it had the support of Union lovers throughout the state.[59] The Democratic legis-

---

to be arrested by the sheriff of Campbell County, Kentucky. The House considered a proposal to expel them but took no action. *Ibid.*, February 12, 1861; *Brevier Legislative Reports*, 4(1861):216, 228-29.

[54] *Ibid.*, 4:16, 49, 80-81, 139.
[55] *Ibid.*, 4:7-8.
[56] *Ibid.*, 4:9-12, 47-48, 56.
[57] *Ibid.*, 4:24, 28, 34-36, 46-48, 70-71.
[58] *Ibid.*, 4:58-60, 86-88, 122-23, 128-29.
[59] Indianapolis *Daily State Sentinel,* January 31, 1861; Foulke, *Oliver P. Morton,* 1:104; Congressman David Kilgore to Morton, January 25, 1861, William Dudley Foulke MSS., Indiana Division, Indiana State Library; *Brevier Legislative Reports,* 4(1861):118, 127, 139-40; Indianapolis *Daily Journal,* January 26, 1861.

lators quickly submitted resolutions for the appointment of delegates.[60] Republicans ultimately agreed to the proposition, provided that the commissioners be appointed by the Governor, that their powers be so limited as to prohibit their acting finally until nineteen states were represented, and that they try to get the conference adjourned until some later date. After unsuccessful attempts by the Democrats to take from the Governor the power to appoint delegates, both houses accepted the invitation almost unanimously.[61]

Pursuant to the instructions of the legislature Governor Morton selected five staunch Republican commissioners. From each, however, Morton first obtained a written statement that he opposed all amendments to the Constitution, all propositions by which slavery would be recognized in any of the territories of the United States, and any new guarantees to slavery. They also assured the Governor that they favored the Constitution as it was and the enforcement of the laws.[62] One delegate added that in his opinion the conference was of "doubtful propriety" and a "dangerous and mischievous" precedent.[63] "The principal good anticipated for it on the part of the North," recalled another, "was to postpone the commencement of hostilities until after the inauguration of President Lincoln."[64]

Twenty-one states were represented at the Washington conference, no representatives coming from the seceded states or from Arkansas, Wisconsin, Minnesota, Michi-

[60] *Brevier Legislative Reports,* 4(1861):121, 122, 127.
[61] Indianapolis *Daily State Sentinel,* February 1, 1861; Indianapolis *Daily Journal,* January 31, 1861; *Brevier Legislative Reports,* 4(1861): 137-39, 141-46, 163-64.
[62] The original questionnaire and replies are in the Morton MSS., Indiana Division, Indiana State Library. See also Foulke, *Oliver P. Morton,* 1:105-6.
[63] Pleasant A. Hackleman to Morton, February 1, 1861, in Morton MSS., Indiana Division.
[64] E. W. H. Ellis, "Autobiography of a Noted Pioneer," in *Indiana Magazine of History,* 10(March, 1914):70.

gan, California, or Oregon. During the secret debates in
Washington the Indiana delegates reported to Morton
that they were doing everything possible to "procras-
tinate . . . in order to remain in session until after the
4th of March" and to avoid "a departure from the
principles of the Republican party."[65] Nevertheless, late
in February this convention finally did formulate and
recommend to Congress a compromise plan resembling
the Crittenden proposals and involving certain amendments to the Constitution. Upon the first and most
important section relating to the restoration of the
36°30′ line in the territories, the Indiana delegation
declined to vote, but it gave its approval to the rest of
the plan.[66]

In the legislature Horace Heffren immediately introduced a bill to let the people of the state vote upon
the Crittenden and border states propositions on the
first Monday in April. The Republicans, arguing that
such an arrangement "might bring shame to our people,"
objected, and the bill was laid upon the table.[67] Despite
this failure, plans for compromise continued to be heard.
On the last day of the session the Republicans aided in
the passage of a senate resolution asking Congress to
call a convention of the states to consider the nation's
problems and to make necessary amendments to the Constitution.[68] Congress, however, was no longer in session.
Republicans in the Indiana legislature, as in the Federal
Congress, had defeated every significant compromise.

---

[65] E. W. H. Ellis to Morton, February 7, 1861; Pleasant A. Hackleman to Morton, February 10, 1861; Godlove S. Orth to Morton, February
21, 1861, William Dudley Foulke MSS. The letters are printed in Kenneth M. Stampp, "Letters from the Washington Peace Conference of
1861," in *Journal of Southern History,* 9(1943):395-403.

[66] Indianapolis *Daily Journal,* March 1, 1861.

[67] *Brevier Legislative Reports,* 4(1861):282, 321-22. Heffren, from
Washington County, was one of the Democrats most violently prosouthern
and most strongly opposed to war. But he supported the war when it
started and became a lieutenant colonel of an Indiana regiment.

[68] *Ibid.,* 4:371-73; Indianapolis *Daily State Sentinel,* March 12, 1861.

In its final days the General Assembly engaged in a battle which almost disrupted the session completely. The chief issue was a Republican-sponsored military bill to replace the existing nebulous militia system with one alleged to be more efficient. The Democrats, professing to see an ominous sign in such a bill at that time, asserted that there was no need for such a measure, complained of the expense involved, and charged that a military despotism would be created.[69] Another bill obnoxious to the minority party provided for the reapportionment of the state. Democrats were convinced that it was drawn in such a way as to give them but two of the eleven Congressional districts.[70]

When these two measures finally came before the legislature the Democrats resorted to the time-honored practice of bolting.[71] In past years both parties had frequently used the expedient of breaking a quorum to block offensive legislation. This device was made possible by a provision of the state constitution which defined a quorum to transact legislative business as two-thirds of the members of each house. Indignant Republicans branded this "revolutionary" action as similar in spirit to South Carolina secessionism and charged that it threatened the state with anarchy and ruin.[72] But the bolters refused to return unless these measures were postponed. Since no appropriation bill had yet been passed, the Republican caucus finally took the advice of Morton and agreed to their terms. Whereupon the Democrats returned and permitted the appropriation of

[69] *Brevier Legislative Reports*, 4(1861):24, 123, 173-74; Gresham, *Life of Walter Q. Gresham*, 1:136-37; Indianapolis *Daily State Sentinel*, January 31, 1861.

[70] *Brevier Legislative Reports*, 4(1861):345; Indianapolis *Daily State Sentinel*, March 7, 1861.

[71] Indianapolis *Daily State Sentinel*, March 6, 1861; *Brevier Legislative Reports*, 4(1861), 342, 346.

[72] *Brevier Legislative Reports*, 4(1861):347-48; Indianapolis *Daily Journal*, March 6, 1861.

funds for the state government. The legislature adjourned, however, without acting upon either the militia or the apportionment bill.[73] Early in March the delegates returned to their homes with party spirits more frayed than ever.

4

In February the people of Indiana and the rest of the nation closely watched Abraham Lincoln during his slow journey to Washington. Perhaps he would drop some clue to his contemplated policy. The President-elect had accepted an invitation to stop at Indianapolis on February 11, and on the appointed day thousands of Hoosiers poured into the city to greet him and to participate in the elaborate reception planned by local dignitaries. When Lincoln's train arrived late in the afternoon, Governor Morton was at the station to receive the party.

The Governor's speech of welcome referred to the sectional crisis and sought to draw Lincoln out by pledging Indiana's support for every measure calculated to maintain the Union. Lincoln's impromptu reply was cautious and evasive. He referred to himself as the "mere instrument . . . of a great cause" and suggested that national salvation required only "the hearts of a people like yours." Then he placed the question of preserving the Union in the hands of the people themselves: "I appeal to you . . . to constantly bear in mind that with you, and not with politicians, not with Presidents, not with office-seekers, but with you is the question: Shall the Union and shall the liberties of this country be preserved to the latest generations?"

After a procession to the Bates House, Lincoln appeared on the balcony where he delivered a second brief address to the dense throng below. But on this occasion his speech had been carefully prepared in

---

[73] Indianapolis *Daily Journal* and *Daily State Sentinel,* March 8, 1861; Foulke, *Oliver P. Morton,* 1:111.

advance, and his words were filled with ominous meaning. This was to be his most important public statement before his inaugural address. He asked suggestively whether holding the forts and other Federal property and collecting the revenues would constitute invasion or coercion; and from what source came the right of a state, a small part of the whole, to break up the nation and play tyrant over the rest. Thus he implied an endorsement of the widespread belief that there was an important difference between "coercing" a sovereign state and "enforcing the laws." When Lincoln had finished, there was a great public reception in the lobby where countless politicians and curious citizens shook his hand.[74] The following morning (his fifty-second birthday) the President-elect departed for Cincinnati. In general he had made a favorable impression upon the Hoosiers.

5

During the weeks of constant debate over compromise and later when Lincoln seemed to be inactive in Washington, Governor Morton devoted himself assiduously to state affairs and to the preparation of Indiana for the conflict he anticipated. He freely expressed his conviction that war was inevitable and that public opinion must be prepared for it.[75]

With this in mind Morton took advantage of a flag-raising ceremony at the State House on January 22 to begin the orientation of the public mind. "I came not here to argue questions of State Equality," he began,

[74] John G. Nicolay and John Hay (eds.), *Complete Works of Abraham Lincoln* (12 vols. New York, c. 1894, 1905), 6:112-13; Indianapolis *Daily Journal,* February 12, 1861; George S. Cottman, "Lincoln in Indianapolis," in *Indiana Magazine of History,* 24(1928):3 ff.; Kenneth M. Stampp, "Lincoln and the Strategy of Defense in the Crisis of 1861," in *Journal of Southern History,* 11(1945):304, 309; William E. Baringer, *A House Dividing. Lincoln as President Elect* (Abraham Lincoln Association, Springfield, 1945), 268-72.

[75] Foulke, *Oliver P. Morton,* 1:104.

"but to denounce treason and uphold the cause of the Union." He cautioned against inventing excuses for the guilt of traitors and vowed that he would know no man who would stop to prescribe the conditions upon which he would maintain the flag. He would only know the man who, when standing in the presence of treason, "then recognizes but two parties—the party of the Union, and the base faction of its foes. To that man, come from what political organization he may, . . . I give my hand as a friend and brother, and between us there shall be no strife."[76] The Governor was ready to lead the party of loyal men.

On January 17, he wrote to the War Department inquiring about the number and kinds of arms due Indiana from the general government, and how they were to be obtained under the law providing for their annual distribution to the states.[77] On January 28, he addressed circulars to the various county auditors asking for a statement regarding the location and condition of arms belonging to the state. Aside from a revelation of the earlier laxity in the distribution of state arms to militia companies, he obtained little information. The few weapons that were recovered—all of a "uniform inferiority"—were repaired and put in the best condition possible by the state quartermaster general.[78] After these unsatisfactory results Morton made further efforts to get additional arms from Washington.[79]

---

[76] Indianapolis *Daily Journal,* January 23, 1861.

[77] *The War of the Rebellion: A Compilation of the Official Records of the Union and Confederate Armies* (4 series, 70 vols. Washington, D. C., 1880-1901) (cited hereafter as *Official Records*), 3 series, 1:41. The reply of the Secretary of War revealed that Indiana had but 488 guns still due from its 1861 quota. *Ibid.,* 3 series, 1:54.

[78] Indianapolis *Daily Journal,* January 31, 1861; W. H. H. Terrell, *Report of the Adjutant General of the State of Indiana* (8 vols. Indianapolis, 1869), 1:426-29. The replies of the auditors are in the Chicago-Morton Collection, Archives Division, Indiana State Library.

[79] H. K. Craig, Ordnance Office, Washington, D. C., to Morton, March 12, 1861, in Chicago-Morton Collection.

Meanwhile companies of the state militia began to tender their services to the Governor. The Indianapolis National Guards volunteered as early as January 5. Young men attracted by a military career organized new militia units in anticipation of a Federal call.[80] By the middle of March Morton was irritated with Lincoln's apparent indecision, and he made a trip to Washington to assure the President that his state would support a vigorous policy. He pledged 6,000 troops for the enforcement of the laws.[81] At least Indiana's governor was prepared for what was to come.

6

On the night of April 12, the telegraph relayed the terse report that the Confederates had responded to Lincoln's attempt to provision Fort Sumter by opening fire upon the Federal garrison. After so many weeks of perplexing inertia the news that hostilities had actually commenced affected the people of Indiana like a potent stimulant. Never before had the state witnessed such hysteria.

On Saturday, April 13, business everywhere was suspended, the streets of the capital were thronged with anxious groups discussing the news, and the newspaper offices were crowded with men eager to learn the latest reports. A call went out for a mass meeting that night, and after two halls had been filled thousands of people still lined the streets. Leaders of all parties participated. In a martial atmosphere, amid a profusion of flags, patriotic music, and cheers for Major Anderson of Fort Sumter, excited orators rivaled each other in their

---

[80] Indianapolis *Daily Journal*, January 8, 9, February 21, 1861; H. M. Scott, secretary National Guards, Indianapolis, to Morton, January 16, 1861; T. J. Brady to Morton, January 21, 1861, and J. W. Rabb, Rising Sun, to Morton, February 25, 1861; officers of the National Rifles to Morton, January 30, 1861, in Chicago-Morton Collection.

[81] Indianapolis *Daily State Sentinel*, April 11, 1861; Indianapolis *Daily Journal*, April 15, 1861; Foulke, *Oliver P. Morton*, 1:113-14.

bellicose professions. Both assemblages enthusiastically resolved to defend the government from assault and like the signers of the Declaration of Independence, pledged their "lives, fortunes and sacred honors" to that end. At the close of the meeting the news arrived that Fort Sumter had fallen, but sleepless spirits continued to disquiet the city throughout the night. The next day was "as complete an obliteration of Sunday" as Indianapolis had ever seen; from every pulpit the preachers rallied Christians to the support of their country's cause.[82]

In the days that followed Indiana eagerly mobilized for war. On April 15, Governor Morton tendered the President 10,000 men for Federal service, and on the same day Lincoln issued a proclamation calling for 75,000 volunteers from the various state militia to serve for three months. On April 16, after being informed that the state's quota would be six regiments (4,683 men), the Governor quickly published his own call for volunteers. He appointed Lew Wallace—a Democrat and a veteran of the Mexican War—adjutant general, and the latter began to transform the fairgrounds near Indianapolis into "Camp Morton."[83]

Simultaneously Morton received tenders of troops from all parts of the state, and volunteers began to pour into the capital by train, on horseback, and on foot. Union meetings in every locality affirmed the people's loyalty to the government and promised to care for the dependents of men who enlisted. The streets of Indianapolis were ablaze with flags; large crowds welcomed

---

[82] Indianapolis *Daily State Sentinel* and *Daily Journal,* April 15, 1861; John H. Holliday, *Indianapolis and the Civil War* (Indiana Historical Society *Publications,* vol. 4, no. 9, Indianapolis, 1911), 548-49; Logan Esarey, *A History of Indiana* (2 vols. 3d ed. Fort Wayne, 1924), 2:738.

[83] Morton to Lincoln, April 15, 1861, in *Official Records,* 3 series, 1:70; Terrell, *Report,* 1:4-5; Indianapolis *Daily Journal,* April 16, 1861. For an excellent account of Camp Morton during the war, see Hattie L. Winslow and Joseph R. H. Moore, *Camp Morton, 1861-1865: Indianapolis Prison Camp* (Indiana Historical Society *Publications,* vol. 13, no. 3, Indianapolis, 1940).

the young soldiers as they arrived; all activities except war preparation were practically in abeyance. The great fear among the volunteers was that they might not be accepted or that they would arrive too late. Accordingly, within a week 12,000 troops had been tendered.[84] In no less degree the martial spirit embraced the women, who promptly organized soldiers' aid societies and presented nearly every military company with a colorful banner.[85]

In the general excitement, as the war fever infected nearly everyone, talk of peace and compromise entirely ceased. The *Sentinel's* first reaction to Sumter was to denounce Lincoln's action and to ask whether war might not yet be averted, but it soon fell into line with public sentiment and demanded a vigorous policy.[86] Most other Democratic papers took a similar stand. Hendricks and Voorhees emphatically denied that they were disloyal or that they would refuse to support the government in the preservation of the Union.[87] With the fires of patriotism burning as brightly among Democrats as Republicans the number of volunteers from the river counties equalled those from any other part of the state.[88]

Yet the feverish state of the public mind did not encourage tolerance or clear thinking. On April 15 the *Journal* bluntly accused the editors of the *Sentinel* of sympathizing with treason and assumed for the Republican party a monopoly of patriotism. The offices of the *Sentinel* were in danger of destruction, and the edi-

---

[84] Indianapolis *Daily State Sentinel,* April 16, 20, 23, 1861; Indianapolis *Daily Journal,* April 16, 18, 19, 22, 1861; Terrell, *Report,* 1:5-6; Holliday, *Indianapolis and the Civil War,* 549; Wallace, *Autobiography,* 1:266-67.

[85] Holliday, *Indianapolis and the Civil War,* 555; Esarey, *History of Indiana,* 2:739.

[86] Indianapolis *Daily State Sentinel,* April 13, 15, 18, 19, 22, 1861.

[87] Terre Haute *Journal,* quoted in *ibid.,* April 29, 1861; Indianapolis *Daily Journal,* April 25, 27, 1861.

[88] Indianapolis *Daily Journal,* April 17, 18, 19, 20, 1861; Thomas M. Browne, Winchester, Indiana, to Morton, April 18, 1861, in Chicago-Morton Collection; Smith, *Borderland in the Civil War,* 167-68.

Unity out of Disunion 73

tors, who pleaded for a free press, were threatened with violent treatment. Groups of ardent patriots seized men whose opinions were suspected and forced them to take oaths of allegiance.[89]

In the face of Douglas' open support of the administration and the obvious loyalty of the Democracy, however, the *Journal* subsequently felt obliged to retract its first rash assertions and to confess that Indiana was totally loyal. "We are no longer Republicans or Democrats," it exulted. "In this hour of our country's trial, we know no party, but that which upholds the flag of our country."[90] Julian's radical organ echoed the same sentiments. It agreed that "all differences heretofore existing are forgotten; everybody is for the country and for the Union."[91] Everyone seemed to feel that the time for the discussion of causes or consequences was past, because the nation was at war.

For the present at least the episode at Fort Sumter had cleared the air and brought unity to Indiana and to the Republican party—indeed, unity out of disunion.

---

[89] Eventually Morton was forced to place an armed guard around the *Sentinel* office. Indianapolis *Daily State Sentinel* and *Daily Journal,* April 15, 1861; Terrell, *Report,* 1:236-37; Foulke, *Oliver P. Morton,* 1:115.

[90] Indianapolis *Daily Journal,* April 16, 1861. "Party lines are completely obliterated, and the people are rallying as one man to the support of the administration," wrote J. E. Philips, of Petersburg, to Morton, on April 18, 1861, in Chicago-Morton Collection.

[91] Centreville *Indiana True Republican,* April 25, 1861.

CHAPTER 5
THE POLITICS OF PATRIOTISM

A KIND of holiday spirit permeated Indiana in the spring of 1861 as the state bustled about its war business. The people had set aside all sordid partisanship; everywhere their love for the common cause produced a singular good humor. If a few skeptics remained, they were at least quiet; certainly Republicans could not surpass the Democratic masses in devotion to the war effort. Volunteers were easy to find, and Indianapolis resounded with their boisterous mirth. The perpetual parades, the roar of cannon, and the incessant sound of martial music kept the public pulse throbbing.[1]

Meanwhile Governor Morton had begun his career as war governor by applying his vast energy to the solution of many difficult problems. He lacked guiding precedents; the state was without funds; the adjutant general, quartermaster, and commissary departments were virtually defunct. Private individuals and banks supplied temporary funds,[2] but most of the needed action required the sanction of the General Assembly. And Morton

[1] Indianapolis *Daily State Sentinel,* April 17, 23, 27, 1861.
[2] Indianapolis *Daily Journal,* April 18, 1861; Terrell, *Report,* 1:3, 6; George S. Cottman, "James F. D. Lanier," in *Indiana Magazine of History,* 22(1926):199-200.

promptly issued a call for that body to assemble in special session on April 24.³

The Governor's message to the legislature, besides reviewing recent events and outlining a legislative program, was another appeal to submerge the partisan in the patriot. Now all men would have to take one side or the other, he declared, for "in time of war there is no ground upon which a third party can stand. . . . Let us . . . inaugurate the era when there shall be but one party, and that for our country."⁴

The General Assembly demonstrated the same spirit as it proceeded to its organization. In the lower house Horace Heffren renominated the previous Republican speaker, Cyrus M. Allen, and he was elected without opposition; both houses divided the other offices between the two parties.⁵ In contrast with the ceaseless wrangling of the previous winter, the special session acted with speed and relative harmony. The members emulated one another in professions of patriotism. Heffren, who before had rabidly opposed coercion, now called for a united stand against the common foe. Most of the former champions of peaceful adjustment spoke as belligerently as the rest. Men of both parties echoed the sentiments of the Governor in urging the adjournment of politics for the duration of the war.⁶ Each house unanimously adopted a resolution which declared that Indiana was united for the defense of the Federal

---

³ Indianapolis *Daily Journal,* April 19, 1861.
⁴ *Ibid.,* April 26, 1861; *Brevier Legislative Reports,* 5(spec. sess. 1861):12-15.
⁵ *Brevier Legislative Reports,* 5(spec. sess. 1861):6-7; Indianapolis *Daily State Sentinel* and *Daily Journal,* April 25, 1861.
⁶ *Brevier Legislative Reports,* 5(spec. sess. 1861):16, 19, 66, 79, 82. "What a change from last winter," rejoiced one Republican member. "Those who said that a hundred thousand men would rise up in this state to oppose the North—now come forward and vote ten thousand men for home defence." Richard P. De Hart, Indianapolis, to D. D. Pratt, April 25, 1861, Pratt MSS.

government and proclaimed her readiness to supply all the men and money needed for that purpose.⁷

Having agreed at the outset not to consider general legislation, the delegates turned directly to the task of placing the state upon a war footing and granted most of the requests of the Governor's message. A series of measures provided Morton with ample funds. The legislators appropriated $500,000 for the purchase of arms for the state volunteers and authorized the Governor to borrow money for that purpose. They legalized the issuance of $2,000,000 of state bonds to raise money for state defense or to aid the general government. They permitted local units of government to spend money for the support of soldiers' families or for home defense. They appropriated $100,000 to the Governor's contingent fund to defray the expense of calling out the militia under the requisition of the President. Finally, they granted an additional $1,000,000 to pay the cost of "enlisting, maintaining and subsisting troops." A legislative auditing committee was created to examine regularly the expenditures of the quartermaster and commissary departments.⁸ The fact that the purposes of these various appropriations overlapped considerably caused much confusion and a great deal of future trouble. But the state expected the national government eventually to repay all of its military disbursements.

With this legislative authority Morton began at once to sell Indiana bonds through the state bank and through loan commissioners who were sent to negotiate with New York bankers. J. F. D. Lanier, of Winslow, Lanier & Company of New York, a former Hoosier and long connected with Indiana finances, agreed to help the state in these loan transactions.⁹ When the bids were opened,

---

⁷ *Brevier Legislative Reports,* 5 (spec. sess. 1861) :5-6, 10, 18.
⁸ *Ibid.,* 5:27-29, 33, 40-41, 71-72; *Laws of Indiana,* 1861 (spec. sess.), 3, 5, 13, 16-20, 22.
⁹ Indianapolis *Daily State Sentinel,* June 24, July 12, 13, 1861; James M. Ray and J. J. Brown, New York, to Morton, May 25, 1861; Ray,

however, it was found that the state's credit, due to the repudiation of the internal improvement debt of the 1840's, was still weak, and the bonds had to be sold at a substantial discount. The discovery in 1862 of gigantic frauds in the sale of huge blocks of Indiana bonds by D. C. Stover, the state agent in New York, further injured Indiana's credit standing.[10]

Another problem confronting the legislature was the disposal of the volunteers who remained in Indianapolis after the first Federal quota of six regiments had been filled. Forty-nine such companies still occupied Camp Morton and many more had tendered their services and impatiently awaited acceptance. The men who had come forward too late were bitterly disappointed, and many of them began to accuse state authorities of discriminating against them. Both houses debated the question at length, and finally, on May 4, after threats of direct action from the men at Camp Morton, they passed the Six Regiments bill. This act empowered the Governor to call into state service for one year six regiments of volunteer militia. These regiments were to be created from the surplus companies in the order in which the adjutant general had received their applications. They could be used to fill any future requisition on the state by the Federal government. A few weeks later four of

---

Brown, and J. H. O'Boyle to Morton, June 22, 1861, in copies of telegraphic correspondence relating to the administration of Governor Morton, 16 volumes, Archives Division, Indiana State Library (hereafter cited as Telegraphic Correspondence), 1:53, 91; Cottman, "James F. D. Lanier," in *Indiana Magazine of History*, 22:199-200. At the regular session the General Assembly had given Lanier valuable legislative aid in certain railroad transactions in which he was interested. Gresham, *Life of Walter Q. Gresham*, 1:137.

[10] A large correspondence concerning the Stover frauds is in the Telegraphic Correspondence and Morton MS. collections. See also Indianapolis *Daily Journal*, May 26, 29, June 10, 24, 26, 1862; Indianapolis *Daily State Sentinel*, May 28, June 5, 6, 9, 18, 20, 1862; *Report on the Indiana Stock Frauds Made by the Committee of the New York Stock Exchange* (New York, 1862), copy in Morton MSS., Indiana Division.

them entered Federal service in response to the President's call for additional volunteers.[11]

In an effort to thwart any possible disloyal opposition to the war, the General Assembly enacted a bill defining and providing penalties for treason against the state of Indiana. Similarly a Felonies Act prescribed severe punishment for any person who joined the Confederate army, aided it in securing arms and provisions, or carried on a traitorous correspondence with the enemy.[12] Some representatives from southern Indiana opposed the latter measure as an impeachment of the loyalty of their section. Others professed to see in it, and its enforcement by local officers, a potential instrument of tyranny which might subvert free speech and a free press. Both Democrats and Republicans from the hard-pressed river counties feared that it would further hamper their dwindling trade by restricting commerce with Kentucky.[13]

These protests were the direct result of the economic crisis in southern Indiana. Since the outbreak of the war conditions had been growing increasingly serious, and business in the river towns was completely stagnant.[14] When some of the merchants and farmers in that region persisted in sending goods to Louisville or southward down the river, Governor Morton acted to stop them.[15] At the same time the legislature appointed committees to investigate the matter, and members from the North denounced those whose patriotism was not strong enough

[11] Terrell, *Report*, 1:11-14; *Brevier Legislative Reports*, 5(spec. sess. 1861):5-6, 16-17, 24-25, 67-71, 73-80, 89, 186; *Laws of Indiana*, 1861 (spec. sess.), 97-98.
[12] *Laws of Indiana*, 1861 (spec. sess.), 44-45, 84-85.
[13] *Brevier Legislative Reports*, 5(spec. sess. 1861):54-57, 61-62, 93-98.
[14] Indianapolis *Daily State Sentinel*, May 9, 1861; New Albany *Weekly Ledger*, May 15, 1861.
[15] Morton to Governor Richard Yates of Illinois, April 24, 1861, and to Secretary of War Chase, May 9, 1861, in Telegraphic Correspondence, 1:8, 36; Morton to Lincoln, May 4, 1861, in *Official Records,* 3 series, 1:158; Terrell, *Report*, 1:402; Indianapolis *Daily Journal*, May 7, 1861; Smith, *Borderland in the Civil War*, 278-79.

to overcome base pecuniary considerations.[16] Indignant citizens held public meetings and organized vigilance committees to check the shipment of supplies which might fall into Confederate hands. In various towns these organizations inspected warehouses, intercepted railroad shipments, and took other summary action to stop the trade with the South. Finally the Federal Treasury department intervened and stopped boats at Cairo and other points in an effort to dry up this potential source of Confederate supplies.[17] Thus the Civil War, at its very beginning, vitally affected the normal economic habits of a large section of Indiana's population.

Because the war brought so much distress to the river interests, the Republican and Democratic legislators from that section revived at the special session their demands for measures of relief. Once more they debated all the proposals introduced at the regular session, but the most popular scheme was to provide for a one year debt moratorium. The alignment for and against this measure was almost entirely sectional. Members from the southern counties warned that "loyalty was often affected by pecuniary pressure." They complained that their section was being "treated as a step child" and hinted at possible resistance to debt collections. Northern delegates argued against the constitutionality of a law which would interfere with existing contracts, asserted that such an act would injure state credit, and insisted that other markets besides Louisville and New Orleans could be found. They also suggested that the products of southern Indiana could be shipped by railroad at a slightly higher cost and that the added expense should not be balanced against the credit of the state.[18] The

---

[16] *Brevier Legislative Reports,* 5(spec. sess. 1861):8, 17, 31-32, 33, 34, 89.
[17] Indianapolis *Daily Journal,* April 20, 24, 30, May 6, 1861; Indianapolis *Daily State Sentinel,* May 6, 9, 1861; New Albany *Weekly Ledger,* June 19, 1861; Terrell, *Report,* 1:401-2.
[18] *Brevier Legislative Reports,* 5(spec. sess. 1861):8, 18, 22, 40, 93-98,

failure of every relief bill bore striking evidence of the progressive shift of political power from southern to northern Indiana.

The war dispelled the previous Democratic opposition to the reorganization of the state militia, and a bill for that purpose was hurried through the legislature and signed by Governor Morton. It provided for the creation of the "Indiana Legion" as a voluntary active militia. The Governor was authorized to appoint all officers above the rank of major (the rest were to be elected by the men) and to issue arms obtained from the general government to regularly organized companies.[19]

The Indiana Legion had a rather up-and-down existence during the war. At the beginning companies formed quickly, but the government was not able to supply arms until September, 1861. By then many units had already dissolved. Since the Legion was on a voluntary basis, its organization, discipline, and drill was effective only where border raids were feared. Southern Indiana thus bore most of the burden of state defense; but even there interest in the Legion was sporadic and varied with the degree of the external danger. Nevertheless, the state militia served to discourage raids from Kentucky, and through it thousands of men passed into the armies of the United States.[20]

2

During the early months of military preparation the

109, 156-57. Subsequently politicians from the river counties prevailed upon the quartermaster general in Washington to alleviate the situation by purchasing horses and mules in southern Indiana.

[19] *Laws of Indiana,* 1861 (spec. sess.), 52-72; Gresham, *Life of Walter Q. Gresham,* 1:143.

[20] Indianapolis *Daily Journal,* September 12, 1861, June 19, 1863; Terrell, *Report,* 1:106-7, 113, 136, 138-40. The history of the Legion during the Civil War was summarized in a report dated February 8, 1866, Adjutant General Terrell to the Hon. G. Clay Smith, of Kentucky, chairman of the militia committee of the U. S. House of Representatives. A copy of this report is in the files of the Adjutant General's Office. Archives Division, Indiana State Library.

conservative people of Indiana showed almost as much interest in the aims of the war as in its vigorous prosecution. Before its adjournment early in June the General Assembly gave considerable attention to this matter. Some members expressed concern that the conflict might be used to abolish slavery and to "subjugate" the South. They stated frankly that they supported the war with the distinct understanding that its sole aim was to preserve the Union.[21]

On April 30, both houses resolved that it was not the intention of Indiana that any portion of her resources of either men or money should ever be employed "in any aggression upon the institution of slavery or any other constitutional right belonging to any of the states." Still not satisfied, the Democrats and a few conservative Republicans continued throughout the session to agitate for further commitments of that nature. This group insisted that it bore no hatred toward the South, and Martin M. Ray, of Hancock and Shelby counties, candidly confessed that he would not endorse a war for any other purpose than the one originally defined. Most Republicans criticized these doubters and protested against their imputing to the administration other motives than those already declared.[22] Thus a majority of the state legislators had demonstrated their opposition to a crusade against slavery.

The radical minority in Indiana at once dissented from these views and warned that there could be no permanent peace without the complete abolition of slavery.[23] In response the Democratic press insistently demanded that Congress, at its approaching special session, define clearly the national objectives in the conduct of the war. Local Democratic and Union meetings everywhere vigorously denied that they were waging a crusade against

[21] *Brevier Legislative Reports,* 5(spec. sess. 1861):24, 27.
[22] *Ibid.,* 5:34-36, 46-49, 66, 184-86, 223-27, 247.
[23] Centreville *Indiana True Republican,* May 16, 23, 1861.

"our Southern brethren," or that they contemplated the "subjugation or annihilation of any State or State rights."[24] Nothing better portrayed the overwhelming opinion of Indiana in the first year of the war than the Crittenden resolution which the United States Congress adopted on July 22. The war, it affirmed, was being prosecuted "to defend and maintain the *supremacy* of the Constitution, and to preserve the Union with all the dignity, equality, and rights of the several States unimpaired; and that as soon as these objects are accomplished the war ought to cease."[25] This embodied precisely the state's purpose in its early war effort.

3

The problem of defining war aims was but one of many signs that political factionalism and party politics would soon revive in Indiana. Though neither party assumed responsibility for disrupting the harmony that followed Fort Sumter, somehow all the moribund issues had a quick resurrection. In view of the early unity of purpose among the people and the countless pleas of party leaders that politics be shunned during the war, it was a little surprising that this should have occurred so soon.

Equally surprising was the fact that Governor Morton, despite his repeated professions of nonpartisanship, was so frequently the central figure in these renewed political conflicts. To a considerable extent this was caused by the Governor's own personality and ambition. Morton was an exceptionally able executive, but he was blunt, pugnacious, ruthless, and completely lacking in a sense of humor. He refused to tolerate opposition, and he often harassed his critics to complete distraction. The men associated with him ranked only as subordinates in his entourage. Actually the Governor, aided by William

---

[24] Indianapolis *Daily State Sentinel*, May 27, July 9, 13, August 27, 1861.
[25] *Congressional Globe*, 37 Congress, 1 session, 222-23.

R. Holloway, his devoted private secretary, and by other able lieutenants, while publicly spurning politics, was quietly forging a political machine under his complete control. The incipient "Union party" of Indiana was largely Morton's handiwork and his own personal possession.

As Morton forced his way toward leadership of his party, he inevitably antagonized many rival politicians. And these rivals fought back desperately. Before long the Republican organization was again embroiled in a factional struggle for control. Those politicians who lost out to Morton or failed to win his favor were soon making violent attacks against the "nest of political speculators in Indianapolis." The Governor's tools, they complained, were trying to make the people believe "that Oliver P. Morton is the only man in this Government who has done anything . . . to save it." No man could obtain an office "unless this clique . . . [could] use him for . . . [its] benefit."[26] Characteristically the opponents of Morton, both within and without his party, went to extremes in venting their hatred toward him.

Even a civil war failed to effect harmony between the friends of Morton and Julian. Instead it merely intensified the enmity of these two leaders. Their feud resulted partly from a clash of personalities and partly from the growing conflict between radical and conservative Republicans. Julian, despite all appeals to political expediency, could not be restrained from preaching his antislavery doctrines. Nor would his organ refrain from sniping at the Governor's "satraps" for trying to manufacture "the monstrous delusion of the greatness of O. P. Morton." The Governor on his part sought to deprive Julian of his Congressional patronage and to undermine him in his own district.[27]

[26] Letter of William Wilson to Indianapolis *Daily State Sentinel*, October 2, 1861.
[27] Morton to Lincoln, April 20, 1863, in Telegraphic Correspondence,

While Julian was Morton's most frank and persistent critic, numerous other Republican politicians opposed the Governor for one reason or another. Prominent among them was a coterie of party leaders from southern Indiana who struggled during the first year of the war for a voice in the state administration. John R. Cravens, president of the state senate, Cyrus M. Allen, speaker of the house, Lucius Bingham, and Walter Q. Gresham provided this group with competent leadership in the General Assembly. Michael C. Garber, of the Madison *Courier*, one-time Democrat turned Republican, lent his editorial support.

Their imbroglio with the Governor was at least in part a sectional struggle for control of the party.[28] It began when the special session of the legislature had the militia bill under consideration. These men loudly criticized the power of appointment which the measure gave to Morton.[29] Later in the session Bingham seized upon an obnoxious military appointment as the excuse for introducing a resolution censuring the Governor's conduct.[30] Morton's Republican foes likewise attacked him for his administration of the Six Regiments Act and for his alleged failure to provide an adequate defense for the border counties. They climaxed their campaign against the Governor by promoting the creation of a legislative auditing committee to examine the military

---

16:174; Centreville *Indiana True Republican*, July 25, 1861; Julian, *Political Recollections*, 270-71; Clarke, *George W. Julian*, 217, 243-44. Julian constantly carped at Secretary of the Interior Caleb B. Smith in an effort to secure his removal. In addition to being a conservative, Smith had acceded to Morton's wishes in dispensing his patronage. Beale (ed.), *Diary of Edward Bates*, 228, 234; Indianapolis *Daily Journal*, April 7, 1862.

[28] William S. Garber, "Concerning the Quarrel between Oliver P. Morton, Governor, and Michael C. Garber, Editor, 1861-66" (unpublished manuscript in Indiana Division, Indiana State Library), 19-25.

[29] Gresham, *Life of Walter Q. Gresham*, 1:142.

[30] The resolution received only nine favorable votes. *Ibid.*, 1:143-44; *Brevier Legislative Reports*, 5(spec. sess. 1861):243-46.

accounts of the executive department.[31] Morton made no effort to conceal his distaste for what he considered an unwarranted legislative interference with his disbursement of funds and with the powers of the state auditor. Hence he ignored the committee until the state Supreme Court finally upheld its legality.[32]

Meanwhile, Garber had entered the war against Morton through the columns of the Madison *Courier*. He abused the Governor for encamping the troops raised under the Six Regiments Act at interior cities rather than on the poorly defended border. He further charged that the state executive had awarded contracts for supplies to out-of-state bidders in preference to merchants and manufacturers in southern Indiana. Thus, complained Garber, "all the men and means put into the hands of Governor Morton will be expended in utter disregard to the wants, sacrifices, conditions and position of the border counties south of the National Road."[33]

Angrily Morton's friends came to his defense. They excused his mistakes in the rush of new executive responsibilities and asked whether those "penetrating delegates of Omniscience" could have done better. The Governor was clearly agitated. He dismissed Col. John R. Cravens from his military staff when he suspected the latter of giving editorial assistance to Garber. At length he traveled to Madison to address a war rally and to answer the charges of his Republican critics.[34] But the attacks did not cease.

[31] *Brevier Legislative Reports,* 5(spec. sess. 1861) :206-9.
[32] William R. Holloway, to Morton, July 12, 1861, and Morton to [Holloway], July 12, 17, 1861, in Telegraphic Correspondence, 1:112, 113, 115; Indianapolis *Daily State Sentinel,* July 12, 1861; Indianapolis *Daily Journal,* July 13, 1861; Madison *Courier,* August 14, 1861; Terrell, *Report,* 1:388-90.
[33] Madison *Courier,* May 9, 10, 1861. Numerous editorials followed in similar vein.
[34] Indianapolis *Daily Journal,* May 16, 30, June 1, 1861; Madison *Courier,* July 28, 1861; Foulke, *Oliver P. Morton,* 1:152; Garber, "Quarrel between Morton and Garber," 4-6.

Morton never forgave his Republican traducers and gave them few opportunities to share in the sacred task of saving the Union. With scarcely an exception he barred their way to military careers, and on several occasions he intervened to prevent them from obtaining offices from the President. Such appointments, he explained, "would be mortifying to me and regarded as an endorsement of their course . . . on the part of the administration . . . ."[35] When the Governor's hold upon the state organization became more secure, he ended the political careers of most of these antagonists and relegated them to obscurity.

4

In Indiana, as elsewhere, the soldiers did not escape the attention of patronizing politicians. These volunteers were voters or potential voters, and all of them were embarking upon a never-to-be-forgotten adventure. Shrewd political leaders saw the wisdom of identifying themselves with the patriotic cause and with all projects to give aid and comfort to the army. Soon countless politicians were winning or assuming the title of "soldiers' friend" as a result of their interest in the welfare of Indiana's volunteers.

Foremost among these "soldiers' friends" was Governor Morton who, like many other state executives, gained and cherished this much-coveted appellation. He showed unflagging interest in the fortunes of Indiana's troops and paid scrupulous attention to every detail of their wellbeing. That the Governor's efforts in the soldiers' behalf were always well publicized did not in the least detract from their genuine merit. Indeed, in the first year of the war, the Democratic press was almost as complimentary

[35] Morton to Lincoln, June 27, 1861, August 6, 1862, in Telegraphic Correspondence, 4:38, 15:60; Morton to Holloway, June 27, 1862, Holloway to Morton, June 29, 30, 1862, in *ibid.*, 4:38, 43, 45; Morton to Paymaster General B. F. Larned, August 5, 1862, and Morton to Stanton, August 6, 1862, in *ibid.*, 15:27, 58.

The Politics of Patriotism 87

as was the Republican.[36] In all his projects to aid the Indiana volunteers Morton's military staff, especially Colonel Holloway, gave him faithful assistance. Holloway, who shrewdly united his own political fortunes with those of his chief, served during the war as an ardent traveling press agent for the Governor.[37]

Morton and his secretaries carried on a voluminous correspondence with the officers of the various Indiana regiments. Through this correspondence the soldiers learned of the Governor's activities and his interest in their cause. Savory words of encouragement were frequently spiced with subtle references to state and national politics. Appropriate reading matter reached the army in abundance. Morton made regular visits to the volunteers in the training camps and often journeyed to the Union lines to inspect and address the state regiments in the field. When the terms of the three-months troops expired in July, he inaugurated an elaborate system of receptions to herald their return. After a flurry of parades, entertainments, and public dinners, the Governor extolled the achievements of each regiment and consecrated the cause they had served.[38] Consequently the Indianapolis *Journal* noted that Morton's concern for the army was so universally appreciated "that he is called the 'soldiers' friend' in every regiment from Bayou Teche to the Potomac."[39]

But Governor Morton was by no means the only Indiana politician who was solicitous about the army's

[36] Indianapolis *Daily State Sentinel*, April 23, August 5, October 3, 12, 1861; Richmond *Jeffersonian*, quoted in *ibid.*, March 1, 1862; Indianapolis *Daily Journal*, September 7, 1861.

[37] Indianapolis *Daily State Sentinel*, July 19, 1862. A correspondent of the New York *Herald* reported that in talking to Holloway one gathered "that Indiana was the only state in the Union, Governor Morton the only Governor, and the Indiana soldiers the only forces in the Union army deserving of the name of soldiers." Quoted in *ibid.*, May 5, 1862.

[38] Terrell, *Report*, 1:33; Indianapolis *Daily Journal*, July 25, 26, 27, 28, 29, 1861.

[39] *Ibid.*, June 19, 1863.

interest. Most congressmen and local leaders took every opportunity to sustain the volunteers and to demand special favors for the troops from their districts. Such efforts often vexed the Governor who protested to the War Department that they were "a source of great trouble" to him.[40] When, for example, Representative Colfax, with the support of several colonels, interposed to secure the acceptance of Indiana's three-months regiments for the three-year service, Morton vigorously denied his authority to take that action. The Congressman, he ventured, was trying "to supercede me with the men and officers."[41] Never was there a dearth of men eager to befriend the armed forces.

While some politicians served the army and their country in civil offices, many others saw through the field of active military service the road to future success. At the start of the war Democratic and Republican leaders in Indiana seemed equally anxious to exchange the comforts of home for the life of the soldier. Benjamin Harrison quickly resigned as reporter of the state Supreme Court to enlist as a private; Attorney General James G. Jones deserted his office to command a regiment. The roll of Indiana colonels was filled with such prominent politicians as Cyrus L. Dunham, Walter Q. Gresham, Sol Meredith, Robert N. Hudson, ex-Senator Graham N. Fitch, Lew Wallace, and many others. That was even more true of the state's brigadier generals, many of whom subsequently became prominent in state and national affairs. Apparently, speculated the *Sentinel,* many saw in their visions of military glory "the outlines of fame's proud temple in the shadowy distance."[42]

---

[40] Morton to Secretary of War Cameron, July 5, 1861, and to Assistant Secretary of War Thomas A. Scott, September 10, 1861, in *Official Records,* 3 series, 1:350, 496.

[41] Morton to David Kilgore, May 22, 1861, in *Official Records,* 3 series, 1:226. See also *ibid.,* 219, 220; Colfax to Calvin Fletcher, June 3, 1861, in Calvin Fletcher Papers, Indiana Historical Society Library; Indianapolis *Daily Journal,* June 12, 17, 1861.

[42] Indianapolis *Daily State Sentinel,* June 28, 1861.

Even Morton, with the encouragement of his friends, more than once betrayed an interest in a military career. In August, 1861, he wrote to Lincoln requesting authority to command an army corps in the Southwest, but the President took no action.[43] Later the Governor renewed the proposal, but with no greater success.

The attainment of these military appointments in the opening months of the war rested to a great extent in the hands of the state executive. Before July 22, 1861, state governors possessed the right to appoint all officers of the volunteer troops, and by an act of Congress of that day they received the permanent power to name the regimental and company officers. This act gave Morton a tremendous appointive power, for all in all he issued 18,884 commissions during the war.[44] Inevitably the possession of this vast patronage by a civil officer provided fertile soil for political controversy and recrimination.

At the outset Morton made a conspicuous display of his nonpartisanship by granting military appointments to numerous Democrats.[45] Before long, however, several factors exposed his policy to ever-increasing criticism. One was his refusal to limit his power by accepting a board of medical examiners to pass upon the qualifications of the army surgeons he commissioned.[46] Other

---

[43] Morton to Lincoln, August 9, 1861, Morton Letter Copybook, April 1861-September 1862, p. 71; Indianapolis *Daily State Sentinel,* September 5, 14, December 3, 1861; Foulke, *Oliver P. Morton,* 1:180-81.

[44] Cameron to Morton, May 22, 1861, in *Official Records,* 3 series, 1:227-28; Terrell, *Report,* 1:85-88; Alexander H. Meneely, *The War Department, 1861. A Study in Mobilization and Administration* (Columbia University Press, 1928), 153-54.

[45] Indianapolis *Daily State Sentinel,* April 17 1861; Indianapolis *Daily Journal,* April 25, 1861; Terrell, *Report,* 1:237-38; Foulke, *Oliver P. Morton,* 1:150-51.

[46] *Brevier Legislative Reports,* 5(spec. sess. 1861):141-42; Indianapolis *Daily Journal,* October 3, 1861. As late as June 3, 1863, Dr. R. Bosworth, director of the Indiana Military Agency at Memphis, called Morton's attention to the great number of incompetent surgeons from Indiana and again advised the creation of such a board. Letter in Chicago-Morton Collection.

attacks bore the unmistakable marks of the disappointed aspirants, "the soreheads who could neither coax nor bully the Governor into giving them high offices."[47] Democrats were soon making the more serious charge that the Governor's original liberal policy had changed, and that he was now guided solely by party considerations. "If Democrats are to be excluded from the offices of the army," vowed one critic, "then let Republicans find the privates in their own ranks."[48] Some appointees might have once been Democrats, complained the *Sentinel*, "but their claim to Executive favor is identification with Governor Morton's no party 'Union party' party."[49]

The Democrats further alleged that Morton was ignoring the claims of leading men in his own party "for fear that they may overshadow him."[50] But the anti-Morton Republicans did not rely upon Democrats to voice their discontent. They boldly accused the Governor of attempting to erect a political machine through his control of military patronage. Julian's organ gibed at the favoritism Morton showed toward his "bosom friends" and "political tools."[51] "He is willing," suggested Garber in the Madison *Courier*, "to strengthen himself by uniting as far as possible the debris of the Democratic party to his fortunes."[52]

Yet, without denying the essential validity of most of these complaints, to some extent Morton was a victim of the system itself. From the outbreak of the war he was swamped with applicants for army posts. In some measure he was obliged to consider the wishes of men with local influence, to weigh the effects of his decisions

---

[47] Indianapolis *Daily Journal*, December 2, 1861; Indianapolis *Daily State Sentinel*, September 24, 1861, January 23, 31, 1862.
[48] Indianapolis *Daily State Sentinel*, July 3, 1861.
[49] *Ibid.*, July 29, 1862.
[50] *Ibid.*, July 1, September 24, 1861.
[51] Centreville *Indiana True Republican*, July 11, 1861.
[52] Quoted in Foulke, *Oliver P. Morton*, 1:152.

upon public opinion, and to estimate the action best calculated to stimulate recruiting. It was never possible for him to know the merits of each of the innumerable suitors for military office.[53] But it was also true that Morton never gave evidence of a desire to reform this dubious system.

Many of the Governor's political friends made no effort to conceal their partisanship and advised him to use his appointive power to strengthen the party. Thus a Republican committee from the eleventh district frankly objected to the commissioning of Democratic politicians, for they did not wish to lose all the "good results" of their recent victory. They questioned Morton's right "to foist upon the public . . . men whom the *people* have laid on the shelf. . . ."[54] Similarly, one of Colfax's protégés in the quartermaster's office at Paducah reported that he appointed no one "unless his 'head' has always been 'right'." He doubted the wisdom of giving "these 11th hour men all the milk and honey, although it may be policy to provide them with a *taste*."[55] Already the Union army had become hopelessly ensnarled in politics.

5

The revival of Republican factionalism was fast restoring much of the normal intensity of Indiana politics. Meanwhile, other events presaged the early emergence of strong Democratic opposition to the policies of the majority party. In the first days of war public criticism of the conduct of the war was unwise, but as time passed the dangers from open expression abated considerably.

---

[53] Terrell, *Report,* 1:87-88. "We do not know one-third of the men we appoint," the Governor's secretary once confessed, "and have no means of finding out except through the testimonials they present. . . ." W. R. Holloway to Colonel —, November 5, 1862, in Morton Letter Press Books, 1 (June 1862-January 1863) :278-82.

[54] Nelson Kellogg, *et al.,* to Morton, n. d., in Chicago-Morton Collection.

[55] Gil Pierce to Colfax, October 30, 1862, Schuyler Colfax MSS., Indiana Division, Indiana State Library.

It soon became apparent that most Democrats, while continuing to assist the war effort, intended to maintain their constitutional right to act as an opposition party. The Republicans themselves furnished ample grounds for a suspicion that their no-party plea was not entirely sincere. Thus in May, 1861, Indianapolis Republicans refused to withdraw their ticket in the city election and support a nonpartisan slate. Instead they insisted that every organ of government ought to be in the hands "of its known and firm friends."[56] Similarly, as the *Sentinel* watched the continued retirement of Democratic officeholders it branded the no-party scheme as a "sharp Republican trick to demoralize the Democratic party."[57] Indeed, complained the New Albany *Ledger,* the Republicans "conduct themselves as though 'patriotism' in these days is exclusively designed for the benefit of their party."[58]

While the Democratic masses never wavered in their determination to preserve the Union, many soon came to dread certain other results that seemed destined to accompany the war. They voiced alarm when President Lincoln, with doubtful constitutionality, proclaimed martial law, suspended the writ of habeas corpus, and authorized arbitrary arrests in Maryland. Was it not possible that the subterfuge of military necessity would subvert the American form of democratic government? "The spirit of our institutions have been changed since the war began," cried the *Sentinel,* "and revolutions never go backwards."[59] Democrats were also plagued with the fear that the war might be perverted into an antislavery

[56] Indianapolis *Daily Journal,* April 23, May 6, 7, 8, 1861.
[57] Indianapolis *Daily State Sentinel,* June 5, August 16, 19, 1861.
[58] New Albany *Weekly Ledger,* June 19, 1861. See also Indianapolis *Daily State Sentinel,* July 22, 1861; Evansville *Weekly Gazette,* August 17, 1861.
[59] Indianapolis *Daily State Sentinel,* May 3, June 25, August 3, 28, 1861; Evansville *Weekly Gazette,* July 13, 27, September 21, 1861; Smith Jones, Jonesville, to Allen Hamilton, July 26, 1861, Allen Hamilton MSS.

crusade, that "after all we may be fighting the battles of that abolition wing and not those of the whole nation."[60]

Moreover, these ardent western Jacksonians apprehended that in the smoke of battle the Republican majority might write its obnoxious economic program into the law of the land. Thus when Congress, in August, 1861, boosted the tariff another ten per cent, they immediately denounced this as "discrimination against the patriotic people of the West, who have rushed with such wonderful alacrity to sustain the government."[61] Representative James A. Cravens, though a staunch supporter of the war, confided to a friend that he had been voting steadily against tariff bills and other odious fiscal policies of the Treasury department. He feared that it might yet become necessary to "cut loose from the New England States."[62]

By the summer of 1861 all these fears and grievances were finding expression in numerous local Democratic meetings. "The people see high taxes staring them in the face, with the markets for their produce cut off," explained the New Albany *Ledger*. This anxiety, "together with the ominous givings out of some of the Republican leaders that abolition is the great end in view, begins to alarm them for the consequences of a prolonged war."[63]

Then, on July 21, the Bull Run fiasco suddenly dispelled all hope that the conflict would be anything but "prolonged." After that disaster large gatherings assembled throughout Indiana to proclaim anew their determination to maintain the Union. But it was impossible to conceal the fact that Bull Run had a sobering effect upon the people.[64] Thereafter the reaction steadily increased.

[60] Evansville *Weekly Gazette*, August 31, 1861; Smith Jones, Jonesville, to Allen Hamilton, June 30, 1861, Allen Hamilton MSS.
[61] New Albany *Weekly Ledger*, August 14, 1861.
[62] James A. Cravens to William H. English, July 28, 1861, English Collection.
[63] New Albany *Weekly Ledger*, August 14, 1861.
[64] Indianapolis *Daily Journal*, July 23, 1861.

The response of the Republicans to this growing opposition was both fierce and partisan. Soon they were again raising the cry of treason and identifying any sort of criticism with that term. Only traitors, they inferred, would denounce President Lincoln or Governor Morton while rebels were trying to destroy the nation.[65]

These incendiary appeals and the inevitable passions of war drove many patriots, under the influence of the mob, to deeds of violence. In many places the cry went up for vigilance committees to "smoke out" the traitors. The *Journal* warned ominously that the army was watching these perpetrators of treason. A soldier vowed that "such batteries as the *Sentinel* . . . should be stormed and silenced," and before long bands of volunteers were breaking up Democratic meetings. In those days, confessed Julian, "loyalty to Republicanism was . . . accepted as the best evidence of loyalty to the country. . . ."[66]

Despite the charges of disloyalty the bulk of the Democracy insisted that there was a difference between hostility to the government and a constitutional disagreement with the policies of those who administered it. These dissenters claimed to be the guardians of free speech and a free press. "When these are struck down, no matter what may be the apology therefor," cautioned the *Sentinel*, "from that day dates the decline of American liberty."[67] Nevertheless, the opposition was always exposed to the attacks of politicians and patriots who saw in its criticism nothing but base treason.

6

During the summer and fall of 1861 Republican leaders continued to parade their pretensions of wartime non-

---

[65] Indianapolis *Daily Journal,* April 23, May 3, July 6, August 19, 20, 1861.

[66] *Ibid.*, May 4, August 9, 15, 17, 31, September 2, 1861; Indianapolis *Daily State Sentinel,* August 10, September 2, 1861; Julian, *Political Recollections,* 244.

[67] Indianapolis *Daily State Sentinel,* August 12, 1861.

partisanship. They invited all loyal Democrats to join them in abandoning party names and in the formation of a great Union organization to aid the successful prosecution of the war. "It will be time enough to revive the Republican and Democratic parties," declared the *Journal,* "when we know that we have a government."[68] A few prominent Democrats, accepting this invitation to renounce party designations, joined the Union movement. Foremost among them were Lew Wallace, James Hughes, Ebenezer Dumont, C. L. Dunham, W. S. Holman, Martin M. Ray, and Allen Hamilton.[69] The Republican leaders who always dominated this enterprise gave these "War Democrats" conspicuous parts at the numerous Union meetings. In a letter to one such gathering Colonel Wallace confessed that he was fast forgetting how to speak politically, but he was with the party "which is for the Union . . . to the last man and the last dollar." On the same occasion Martin M. Ray insisted that there could be "no neutral grounds for loyalty to occupy; an attempt to divide the North and embarrass the Government on this issue is neither good patriotism nor good politics."[70] At first a substantial minority of rank-and-file Democrats endorsed the course of these leaders. Once again their party experienced a serious internal division.

The New Albany *Ledger,* which was closely identified with the river interests, was the most influential of the newspaper spokesmen for the "War Democrats." Although it had opposed coercion and entertained the idea of joining the Confederacy before the outbreak of hostilities, the *Ledger* now favored a vigorous war policy. Always faithful to the border people, it admitted that the war brought hardships to the farmers of southern

---

[68] Indianapolis *Daily Journal,* August 20, 1861.
[69] *Ibid.,* June 22, July 11, 25, 1861; Lazarus Noble to Allen Hamilton, August 21, 1861, Allen Hamilton MSS.; H. C. Duncan, "James Hughes," in *Indiana Magazine of History,* 5(1909):90-91.
[70] Indianapolis *Daily Journal,* August 20, 1861.

Indiana. But it believed that such temporary inconveniences were better than having to pay eternal tribute to the South for the use of the Mississippi River. The *Ledger* would not permit the nation to be destroyed "because an obnoxious man has been elected President." Nor would it allow a few leaders at Indianapolis to place the Democratic party in what it considered a false position.[71] As a result these river counties furnished some of the strongholds of the "War Democrats," for they still saw total ruin in disunion.

The Union party advocates won a striking victory when the popular Democrat, ex-Governor Joseph A. Wright, late minister to Prussia, returned from Europe and at once endorsed the administration's war policy.[72] On September 7 the Republicans and "War Democrats" of Indianapolis gave him a lavish reception. Introduced by Colonel Dumont, Wright spoke of the need for crushing the rebellion and suspending party politics. The Union press responded enthusiastically, and thereafter he was lionized by the war men.[73]

A few days after the gala Union reception for Wright, party leaders called another Union meeting in Indianapolis on September 17, the anniversary of the adoption of the Constitution. They summoned "all citizens, without distinction of party," who were "in favor of the maintenance of the Constitution and Union . . . and the prosecution of the war . . . to suppress the present wicked rebellion. . . ." Special invitations were issued to Wright, Governor Morton, Henry S. Lane, David Tod, Richard W. Thompson, Martin M. Ray, Colonel Ebenezer Dumont, Albert G. Porter, and others—a good cross-

---

[71] New Albany *Weekly Ledger,* September 11, 18, 25, 1861. Similar vigorous war views appeared in the Democratic Evansville *Weekly Gazette,* November 23, 30, December 7, 1861.

[72] Indianapolis *Daily Journal,* August 10, 1861.

[73] *Ibid.,* September 9, 1861; Indianapolis *Daily State Sentinel,* September 10, 1861; New Albany *Weekly Ledger,* September 18, 1861.

section of Democrats and Republicans, and in-betweens. The meeting endorsed a resolution "that the safety of our country and its institutions, requires that the people of the loyal States should present a united front to the insurgents . . . that any proffers of peace and compromise short of disbandment of the rebels in arms, and their return to their allegiance to the Constitution, are but evidences of vacillation and weakness, and tantamount to an offer to recognize the independence of the disloyal States. . . ." Senator Lane and the famed orator and old-line Whig and Constitutional Unionist Richard W. Thompson shared the speakers' platform. They lashed out against the "peace" men of the state and riddled the arguments for "compromise." Here was ground upon which all Union men presumably could stand.[74]

A few months later, when the United States Senate voted to expel Jesse D. Bright, Governor Morton found an opportunity for a brilliant "Union" maneuver. In the early months of the war, despite the demands of the legislature that he state his position, Bright had maintained a complete silence. He was still bitter over his defeat by the Douglas Democrats the previous year,[75] and his political career would have ended with the expiration of his senatorial term in 1862. Then, in August, 1861, a letter was discovered which revealed the direction of his sympathies. Although it had been written before the war actually started, it was addressed to "His Excellency, Jefferson Davis President of the Confederation of States," and introduced a friend who had improved firearms to sell.[76] On February 5, 1862, the Senate accepted

---

[74] Indianapolis *Daily Journal*, September 14, 18, 1861.

[75] Bright to William H. English, July 7, December 27, 1861, printed in *Indiana Magazine of History*, 30(1934):386-88.

[76] Indianapolis *Daily Journal*, August 20, 1861; *Brevier Legislative Reports*, 5(spec. sess. 1861):253, 256. The Indiana Senate on May 31 passed a resolution that Bright had forfeited all claim to represent Indiana in the U. S. Senate, and requested the latter body not to permit him to retain his seat. The house refused to concur.

this letter as justification for Bright's expulsion from that body.⁷⁷

Governor Morton now had the power to name Bright's successor who would serve until the next meeting of the General Assembly. Passing over the numerous aspirants in his own party, he appointed Joseph A. Wright. While this selection annoyed some of the Republicans, no single act did more to strengthen the Union party. Thus, exulted the *Journal,* the Governor had demonstrated that the Union movement was "an honest, manly and fair effort to unite all loyal men. . . ."⁷⁸

The opposition Democrats appreciated Morton's strategy and were quick to impeach his motives. They asserted that he had refused to appoint a Republican because that might interfere with his own future senatorial ambitions. They mocked the Republican candidates who had been "slighted" and "insulted" by the Governor's action. Moreover, jeered the *Sentinel,* Morton's first consideration had been "to make an appointment which would . . . be most damaging to the Democratic party." Wright, it added, could never have secured that position unless he had first "abjured his party . . . [and] surrendered the principles which he had advocated during his political career."⁷⁹

As the fall of 1861 passed it was evident that the truce between Republicans and Democrats was ended, and that the Republican-dominated Union party was not bridging

---

⁷⁷ U. S. *Senate Journal,* 37 Congress, 2 session, 175-76; Indianapolis *Daily Journal,* February 7, 1862. The *Journal* confessed that the evidence against Bright was not sufficient to try him for treason, but insisted that he was not a desirable man to have in the Senate.

⁷⁸ Indianapolis *Daily Journal,* February 25, 1862; Centreville *Indiana True Republican,* March 6, 1862; New Albany *Weekly Ledger,* March 26, 1862; Robert N. Hudson, Washington, to Richard W. Thompson, February 12, 1862, in Richard W. Thompson MSS., Indiana Division, Indiana State Library.

⁷⁹ Indianapolis *Daily State Sentinel,* February 25, March 5, 7, 1862; Richmond *Jeffersonian,* quoted in Centreville *Indiana True Republican,* March 13, 1862; Indianapolis *Daily Journal,* March 6, 1862.

the gap. By the beginning of 1862, the traditional political alignments, while shifting slightly, had reformed in a basically familiar pattern. The remarkable unity of purpose which followed the firing on Fort Sumter proved to be a mere interlude. Soon the rival politicians were again debating the old issues and abusing each other on the Indiana hustings. Neither the smoke of battle nor the subterfuge of no-partyism could conceal the fundamental disagreements among the Hoosiers. Actually it was the eloquent Hendricks and the implacable Voorhees, and not the "turncoat" Wright, who spoke for the masses of Indiana Democrats. Their criticisms of the ruling party during the first year of the war prefaced their text for the campaign of 1862.

CHAPTER 6
MOBILIZING A SOVEREIGN STATE

THE Federal government soon found that it would be no easy task to organize the popular enthusiasm which followed the attack upon Fort Sumter into a unified war effort. Aside from the ever-present problem of political expediency, civil and military leaders struggled through a perplexing labyrinth of administrative difficulties in raising the Union armies.[1] Not the least of these was the need to co-ordinate the activities of many proud and jealous states. Lincoln's first call for troops was upon the militia of the various states, and his subsequent calls depended upon the state governments to provide the volunteers. In this matter the power wielded by the governors of the various commonwealths at first far exceeded that of the President and commander-in-chief. While the volunteers entered Federal service, neither they nor state officials forgot their original source. The blue-clad regiments fought to vindicate national authority, but they battled beneath the vigilant eyes of their native states.

Indiana entered the war determined, from the chief executive to the humblest private, to achieve a distinguished position among the loyal supporters of the Union.

---

[1] The best general treatment of the problems presented in this chapter is Fred A. Shannon, *The Organization and Administration of the Union Army, 1861-1865* (2 vols. Cleveland, 1928).

To this end Governor Morton applied his executive genius and created with remarkable speed the semblance of an army out of the local recruits. He quickly filled the positions of state adjutant general, quartermaster, and commissary, and drove these departments to vigorous action under his direction.[2]

Satisfied with the seeming dexterity of their own military preparations, state officials looked impatiently for swift results from Washington. When the expected action was not forthcoming, they proceeded to chide at the inefficiency, the "red tapism," and lack of vision manifested there. Most local dignitaries cherished their own distinct opinions regarding national policy and military strategy, and they did not hesitate to acquaint the Federal administration with their views. When their admonitions were ignored, they generally attributed it to criminal negligence and fell back on their own resources and authority. The "vigilant, energetic, expedient [sic]" Morton, recorded Indiana's adjutant general, was not deterred by the "slow and cumbrous movements of the authorities at Washington."[3]

Secretary of War Simon Cameron gave ample cause for complaint, for that astute Pennsylvania politician proved to be an incompetent administrator. Nevertheless, the difficulties confronting the War Department at the outbreak of hostilities were almost insuperable. With much of its personnel of War of 1812 vintage, with a tradition of inefficiency cultivated in the soil of martial apathy, and with a complete lack of military prepared-

[2] Terrell, *Report*, 1:4-5, 444-46, 451-52; Wallace, *Autobiography*, 1:263-65.

[3] Terrell, *Report*, 1:18-19. For a critical view of Washington officialdom and praise for the state administrators, see William B. Weeden, *War Government, Federal and State in Massachusetts, New York, Pennsylvania and Indiana 1861-1865* (Boston and New York, 1906), 74, 146-47, 155-56. See also William B. Hesseltine, *Lincoln and the War Governors* (New York, 1948).

ness, the problem would have taxed a man of greater talents than Cameron.[4]

Nor did the ceaseless clamor of a score of exacting, though well-meaning state governors alleviate the situation. Nothing vexed Lincoln and Cameron more than the need to defer to these dignified officials and to pander to the local interests they represented. Throughout the war it took all of Lincoln's capacities as a statesman and a politician to maintain a degree of harmony between the states and the Federal government.[5]

2

The eager response to Lincoln's first appeal for troops at once threw state officers and the War Department into a quandary. The filling of Indiana's quota of six regiments and the subsequent dispatch of four more did not allay the tide of onrushing volunteers. Those who came too late were keenly disappointed and they indiscriminately abused local and national politicians for rejecting them. Morton urged these men to preserve their organization and to continue their drill in order to be ready for the future calls he anticipated.[6] Simultaneously he offered six additional regiments to Cameron and promised to have them in the field within six days. But to the dismay of both the Governor and men, the War Department replied that more troops were not needed and would not be accepted.[7]

The passage of the Six Regiments bill by the General Assembly absorbed part of the surplus volunteers, but the pressure was still great. In May Indiana was assigned

[4] Meneely, *War Department*, 13-23, 25, 140-41, 200.

[5] James F. Rhodes, *History of the United States from the Compromise of 1850* (7 vols. New York, 1896-1919), 5:235-37; Hesseltine, *Lincoln and the War Governors*, *passim*.

[6] Indianapolis *Daily State Sentinel*, April 22, 1861; Indianapolis *Daily Journal*, April 23, 1861.

[7] Correspondence between Morton and Cameron, April 17-26, 1861, in *Official Records*, 3 series, 1:75, 80, 93, 102-3, 115-16; Terrell, *Report*, 1:7-8.

four additional regiments when the President called for a limited number of men to serve for three years. This relieved the situation very little, since the regiments were taken from the troops mustered into the state service. The distracted Governor renewed with less patience his demands that the government accept more troops from Indiana. On May 13 he sent strong demands for aid to Secretary of the Interior Caleb Smith in Washington and told him of the local ill feeling that was rising "from the apprehension that Indiana has nobody in Washington to speak for her." On the same day six additional regiments of three-year men were offered to the Secretary of War, but were not accepted.[8] On May 19 the state adjutant general notified the remaining companies that there was no assurance of their ultimately being accepted and that they would have to assume the risk of maintaining their organization.[9] Whereupon many of them angrily disbanded and returned to their homes. State authorities received the blame for their chagrin and disappointment. One company organized an indignation meeting, bitterly denounced Governor Morton, and burned him in effigy.[10]

Secretary Cameron's apparent indecision was especially provoking, for he intimated once or twice that more regiments might be accepted but said no more about it. After Morton sharply rebuked him for this vacillation, the Secretary replied with an official notification that Indiana's whole quota was ten regiments. His advice to the state governors was to reduce, rather than enlarge the number of troops held for call into service, and in no event to increase it.[11]

---

[8] See Morton to Smith and to D. P. Holloway, and John S. Bobbs to Cameron, May 13, 1861, in *Telegraphic Correspondence,* 1:42, 52.

[9] Adjutant General's Office, General Orders No. 2, printed in Indianapolis *Daily Journal,* May 22, 1861.

[10] *Ibid.,* May 25, 1861; Indianapolis *Daily State Sentinel,* May 23, 1861.

[11] Morton to Cameron, May 10, 14, 1861, and Cameron to the governors, May 16, 1861, in *Official Records,* 3 series, 1:85, 198-99, 203.

The ensuing Federal policy of restricted recruiting annoyed Morton, who wanted to enlist at once the largest force possible and overwhelm the rebels by sheer numbers. The Governor was convinced that he and the people of the West were far in advance of the faltering steps of the general government. The administration in Washington, he believed, was still unaware of the size of the rebellion, fearful that it might do too much, and inclined to smother the spirit of the excited masses.[12]

Meanwhile, the War Department, laboring with its creaking, antiquated machinery, could scarcely supply and muster into Federal service the limited number of volunteers for which it had called. Indiana was only one of many states that flooded it with demands that it receive more regiments. For such technicalities, however, state officials had little patience and ascribed them all to the needless red tape which encumbered the army.

By early summer the confusion was partially abated, and, while no new calls were issued, the President and Secretary of War yielded more readily to additional tenders of troops. In June Lincoln agreed to accept ten more regiments from Indiana, and the next month he took the last two regiments of state troops for Federal service. But Morton was still contemptuous of the blundering Washington officials and continued to scheme for the further enlargement of the Union armies. Then came the disaster at Bull Run, General Frémont's urgent requests for reinforcements in Missouri, and the movement of Union forces into Kentucky, all of which changed temporarily the government's restricted recruiting policy. For a few months it received volunteers in unlimited numbers and asked that they be sent forward without delay.[13]

In Indiana the Governor immediately launched a vigorous campaign to raise new regiments, and with the

---

[12] Terrell, *Report*, 1:18-19, 24-25; Weeden, *War Government*, xiii, 86-87.
[13] Frémont to Morton, and Morton to Frémont, August 13, 1861, in *Telegraphic Correspondence*, 1:146, 147; Cameron to Morton, August 13,

barriers removed recruiting went on briskly.[14] Morton created a central camp for instruction and drill at Indianapolis and established local volunteer rendezvous in each Congressional district. He enlisted the services of influential citizens to forward the work with stirring war meetings and recruiting drives.[15] By September Morton was able to report sixteen new regiments virtually completed; by October the state had furnished 34,448 men, and twenty more regiments were in the process of organization.[16] At the end of the year Indiana proudly tabulated her achievement for 1861: 61,341 volunteers enlisted, although the state's quota had been only 38,832.[17]

By December, however, the administration had returned to its original policy of limited recruiting. When Governor Morton proposed the creation of another brigade to be called the "President's Legion," Lincoln gave him no encouragement and reported the existence of "some alarm lest we get more men than we can arm, provide and pay." Secretary Cameron confessed, in his report on December 1, that the number of enlistments could have been doubled "had not the department felt compelled to restrict" them. A few days later the War Department ordered the state governors to raise no more troops without a special requisition.[18]

15, 1861, and Morton to Cameron, August 14, 1861; Morton to Frémont, August 4, 1861; Frémont to Assistant Secretary of War Thomas Scott, August 4, 1861; Scott to Frémont, August 6, 1861, in *Official Records,* 1 series, 3:425-26, 428, 439; 3 series, 1:410, 413.

[14] See correspondence between Thomas A. Scott, Assistant Secretary of War, and Morton, August 30, 31, September 1, 2, 1861, in *ibid.,* 3 series, 1:466, 473-76.

[15] Terrell, *Report,* 1:16.

[16] Morton to Cameron, September 16, 1861, Holloway to Cameron, October 27, 1861, in *Official Records,* 2 series, 1:520, 601-2; Indianapolis *Daily Journal,* October 22, 1861.

[17] *Official Records,* 3 series, 1:384n; Terrell, *Report,* 1:16-17.

[18] Morton to Lincoln, November 6, 1861, and Lincoln to Morton, November 10, 1861, in Telegraphic Correspondence, 2:183-84; *Official Records,* 3 series, 1:700, 722-23; Indianapolis *Daily Journal,* December 17, 1861.

With that action Indiana's alacritous response to the call to arms was substantially checked. The ensuing winter was unusually severe, and reports of the resulting hardships among the troops in the field cooled the original ardor for military service. Consequently enlistments in Indiana declined until they nearly ceased.[19] Thereafter army recruiting became an increasingly difficult problem.

3

If the Federal and state governments were unprepared to receive the early rush of volunteers, they were even less prepared to equip them with the necessary arms and supplies. Governor Morton's prewar efforts to obtain a store of weapons were almost futile. In April Indiana had only a few hundred guns most of which were outdated flintlocks and altered-to-percussion muskets. The national arsenals were scantily stocked, and the War Department had neither the materials nor the technical proficiency to fill the demands of a large army.[20] These shortages, together with the deficiency in trained personnel, prevented the United States commissary and quartermaster departments from sending their own officers to Indianapolis until late in August.

Meanwhile, the problem of supplying the men in state recruiting camps was left to local officials. The volunteers who came forward, impatient to obtain the regalia which made them soldiers, chafed at the inevitable delays in providing and distributing arms, uniforms, and other equipment. Their insatiable needs could never be satisfied by the hard-pressed state officers.[21]

Plagued by thousands of irritated soldiers at home, Governor Morton in turn pursued without restraint officials in Washington. While he brandished his demands for the acceptance of more troops, he bombarded every division of the War Department with requests for the

[19] Terrell, *Report*, 1:17.
[20] *Ibid.*, 1:2-3; Meneely, *War Department*, 114.
[21] Terrell, *Report*, 1:445-46.

immediate delivery of arms and accouterments. With the same contempt for alleged inefficiency and needless red tape, he enlisted the aid of his staff, numerous special messengers, and several congressmen in forcing his requisitions upon the attention of the Secretary of War. When all these efforts yielded nothing but half-filled promises, the Governor accused Cameron of neglecting Indiana.[22] That adequate supplies did not exist and that every other state was equally clamorous, did not deter these impetuous local officials from seeking special consideration for their own requests.

At the same time Governor Morton, with Cameron's approval, joined the other state executives in efforts to contract for additional supplies of guns and accouterments in the open market.[23] The Governor sent banker Calvin Fletcher, Schuyler Colfax, Robert N. Hudson, and several special agents to Philadelphia, New York, New England, and Canada to negotiate these purchases.[24] On May 30 Robert Dale Owen, son of the founder of New Harmony, social reformer and former Democrat, received a commission to procure arms for Indiana in the East or from Europe, and thereafter he assumed responsibility for negotiating all such contracts. He entered the work

[22] The *Official Records,* 3 series, volume 1, and the Telegraphic Correspondence, volume 2, contain many exchanges between Morton and the War Department on the subject of supplies for the troops. See also Terrell, *Report,* 1:429-31.

[23] Cameron to Morton, April 26, 1861, Morton to Cameron, April 28, 1861, in *Official Records,* 3 series, 1:115-16, 126. The legislature appropriated $500,000 for the purchase of arms and accouterments. *Laws o Indiana,* 1861 (spec. sess.), 13.

[24] Among many communications regarding arms purchases in the Telegraphic Correspondence and Morton Letter Books, see particularly Morton to Calvin Fletcher, April 28, 1861, in Morton Letter Copybook, April 1861-September 1862, pp. 23-24; Morton to R. N. Hudson, New York, April 22, 1861, W. H. Walker, Philadelphia, to Morton, May 1, 1861, and Fletcher and Colfax to Morton, May 3, 1861, in Telegraphic Correspondence, 1:6, 21, 27. See also Terrell, *Report,* 1:6-7, 431-32; Diary of Calvin Fletcher, April 27, 1861, and following entries, May 29, 1861, in Indiana Historical Society Library.

with diligence and had considerable success in obtaining the desired equipment. Late in the summer of 1861 state purchasing of supplies still continued without opposition from the War Department.[25] In the fall state agents contracted for large quantities of overcoats when requisitions for them were not filled speedily enough in Washington.[26]

Similarly Governor Morton, "acting solely upon his own responsibility, and without the authority of law," sought to supply Indiana's troops with ammunition by the establishment of a state arsenal. Expecting the project to be a temporary one, Captain Herman Sturm, who had some experience in the fabrication of munitions, accepted its direction. When the shortage continued, the arsenal expanded its activities and new buildings were erected for its use. By the end of 1861 it was producing large quantities of cartridges at a price reputedly lower than the government paid to private contractors. After state funds had been exhausted Sturm operated the arsenal upon credit and loans from friends, and Morton began extended negotiations to commit the War Department to the assumption of its expenses.[27]

But trouble developed when Gen. James W. Ripley, head of the Federal ordnance department, favored the

---

[25] A copy of Owen's appointment is in the Morton Letter Copybook, April 1861-September 1862, p. 45. Before Owen completed his work in February, 1863, the state had contracted for more than 43,000 arms of all kind. Some were paid for by the national government, others by the state, which expected to be reimbursed eventually. Owen also purchased a large amount of clothing, blankets, and other equipment. A large body of correspondence regarding these purchases is in the Morton Letter Books and Telegraphic Correspondence. See also Terrell, *Report*, 1:433-34; Richard W. Leopold, *Robert Dale Owen. A Biography* (Harvard University Press, 1940), 346 ff.

[26] William H. Schlater, secretary to Morton, Washington, D. C., to Governor Morton, August 19, 20, 1861, Morton to [Schlater], August 20, 1861, and Morton to Holloway, October 26, 1861, in Telegraphic Correspondence, 1:160, 163, 2:172; Indianapolis *Daily Journal*, October 15, 29, 1861.

[27] Terrell, *Report*, 1:413-16.

liquidation of the state arsenal. Morton, Sturm, and Robert Dale Owen promptly journeyed to Washington and obtained Cameron's approval for its continued operation. Disputes with the ordnance department did not cease, however, and renewed appeals by Morton to the Secretary of War were a regular occurrence. Ripley, explained Indiana's adjutant general, belonged to the " 'fossiliferous period' of the old army" and was unable to comprehend Morton's "innovations upon ancient departmental usage." In 1862, after Congress sanctioned the establishment of Federal arsenals at Indianapolis and other western cities, the indignant ordnance chief was dismayed to learn that the state enterprise would still be maintained. Despite Ripley's constant opposition, the local arsenal was not discontinued until 1864.[28]

However honorable their intentions, and in spite of the early tacit approval of the War Department, the entrance of Indiana and other states into the business of securing military supplies hardly served the national interest. To the eminent satisfaction of merchants, manufacturers, and speculators, these enterprising state agents competed with each other, with Federal officers, and with private contractors in a mad race to find war materials.[29] Since the

[28] W. H. H. Terrell, adjutant general, to W. R. Holloway, December 8, 1862, in Morton Letter Press Books, 1(June 1862-January 1863):474; Morton to Stanton and Stanton to Morton, in *Official Records*, 3 series, 2:913; Terrell, *Report*, 1:415-16, 418, 424-25. See also report of Colonel Sturm to Governor Morton, February 12, 1863, printed in Indiana *House Journal*, 1863, pp. 552-56, giving an account of the arsenal to January 1. The military auditing committee and a special committee of the Democratic legislature of 1863 made a thorough investigation of the state arsenal and reported that "they were much gratified with the system and economy and also the neatness and dispatch with which the business was conducted." The report of the Military Auditing Committee is printed in Indiana *Senate Journal*, 1865, pp. 228-47. The arsenal made a total profit of $77,457.32 for the state. *Report of the Committee on Public Expenditures of the Expenses of the Executive Department of the State of Indiana* (Indianapolis, 1867), 6.

[29] Meneely, *War Department*, 115. When the state contracted for uniforms, the officers and men sometimes decided upon the kind and color

states expected the Federal government eventually to reimburse them, local officials disregarded soaring prices and the opportunities they presented to the crafty speculator. On one occasion Robert Dale Owen was offered $15,000 for one of Indiana's arms contracts which would probably have meant a neat profit to the state.[30]

As this sordid system became progressively worse, the general government made an effort to check it. In October, 1861, Quartermaster General Montgomery C. Meigs urged Governor Morton to desist from future contracting for overcoats, since his efforts only added to the extravagant and speculative price. The practice of competing with United States purchasers, he explained, did not increase the available supply, but it aided the speculators who were "breaking faith and contracts with Western Governors, persuading them to bid against each other and the United States, [and] selling to one State what they have contracted to deliver to another or to the United States. . . ."[31] The next month the Secretary of War condemned state purchases of arms as "highly detrimental to the public service" and asked Morton to withdraw his agents from the market.[32] But in spite of this advice the state officials long continued their efforts to fill the needs and desires of the local volunteers.

The unsavory practices of avaricious contractors crept into the early business of the state commissary and quartermaster departments in the provisioning and equipping of Indiana's troops. The activities of these departments

to be purchased. The results were often ludicrous. The Indianapolis Zouaves in Col. Lew Wallace's regiment uniformed themselves with gold-laced blue jackets, baggy scarlet trousers, orange leggings and shirts, white belts, and rimless scarlet caps with tassels. Holliday, *Indianapolis and the Civil War,* 551-52.

[30] W. R. Holloway, New York, to the state executive department, August 18, 1861, and W. H. S[chlater] to Morton, Washington, D. C., August 18, 1861, in Telegraphic Correspondence, 1:158, 159.

[31] Meigs to Morton, October 19, 1861, in Telegraphic Correspondence, 2:158.

[32] Cameron to Morton, November 25, 1861, in *ibid.,* 2:200.

reflected the general turmoil of the first months of the war and revealed a confusing mixture of inexperience, incompetence, and actual peculation.

Difficulties arose almost at once in the commissary department which was directed by Isaiah Mansur, a local meat packer and a personal friend of Governor Morton. Soldiers at Camp Morton complained strenuously about receiving adulterated coffee, bad meats, spoiled fruit, and other inferior rations. Local citizens grew indignant at the scandalous treatment of Indiana's volunteers.[33] The situation, however, was not as bad as the loud complaints of the raw recruits might have led the solicitous citizenry to believe.

The special session of the General Assembly joined in the criticism and demanded an explanation from Mansur. After receiving two vague and unsatisfactory reports, the legislature created a joint committee to make a thorough investigation of the commissary department. The resulting report revealed that the coffee had been "basely adulterated" and that inferior meat had come from Mansur's own pork house at higher than market prices. The commissary general had rejected outside offers to supply pork. His defense was that, since his position was a difficult one, he had as good a right as anyone to make the profits. The accounts of his department were in a chaotic condition, and nothing could be learned from them. On May 25 the lower house unanimously requested Mansur's removal for malfeasance and incompetency. A few days later he resigned and was succeeded by State Senator Asahel Stone.[34]

The quartermaster department under J. H. Vajen, an Indianapolis hardware dealer, fared little better. During

---

[33] Indianapolis *Daily Journal,* April 30, 1861; Foulke, *Oliver P. Morton,* 1:151; Terrell, *Report,* 1:451-54.

[34] *Brevier Legislative Reports,* 5(spec. sess. 1861):10, 17, 23, 30, 36, 41, 63, 72, 74, 112, 148-50, 175-79, 190-92, 199-201; Indianapolis *Daily State Sentinel,* May 27, June 8, 1861; Indianapolis *Daily Journal,* June 8, 1861; Winslow and Moore, *Camp Morton,* 247-49.

1861 there was much criticism of his methods of letting contracts for equipment, and the legislative auditing committee refused to accept a number of vouchers for clothing condemned as inferior.[35] When a Congressional committee examining government contracts at Cincinnati obtained evidence which called into question the administration of military affairs in Indiana, Morton urged it to come to Indianapolis and make a complete investigation.[36]

The committee arrived early in 1862 and questioned Vajen and a host of witnesses. Its subsequent report exonerated the Governor completely but exposed serious malpractices in Vajen's department. The quartermaster general attributed his mistakes to the early demand for swift results and charged that the Democrats had provided the witnesses simply to make party capital. He complained that they were trying to make him "the scapegoat of the sins of all connected with the Quartermaster General's Department!"[37] By the end of 1862, however, Morton was still unable to obtain a satisfactory report from Vajen to include in his message to the General Assembly.[38] Cameron's War Department, it appears, had no monopoly on loose administrative practices.

4

While Indiana's ardent state officers engaged in the business of raising and equipping troops, they also evolved definite ideas of how the war should be conducted. That national policy did not always conform with the plans of these local strategists, was not due to any failure on their part to acquaint Federal officials with their opinions.

[35] Holloway to Morton, January 25, 1862, in Telegraphic Correspondence, 2:241.
[36] Morton to Congressman William S. Holman, January 9, 20, 1862, and Holman to Morton, January 10, 1862, in *ibid.*, 2:231, 232, 237; Indianapolis *Daily Journal,* January 22, 1862.
[37] Indianapolis *Daily Journal,* December 17, 22, 1862; Indianapolis *Daily State Sentinel,* December 15, 16, 18, 20, 1862.
[38] Morton to Vajen, December 13, 1862, in Morton Letter Press Books, 1 (June 1862-January 1863) :501-2.

After a sweeping survey of the potential battle lines, Governor Morton, with his accustomed scorn for delay, developed comprehensive plans for immediate military action. From his post in the West he expounded his war views to Lincoln, Cameron, and the generals in the field and defended them with characteristic vigor.

The anomalous position of Indiana's Kentucky neighbors at once demanded the attention of state politicians. Governor Beriah Magoffin, whose southern sympathies were thinly disguised, had refused to respond to Lincoln's call for troops. In May the Kentucky legislature approved a policy of neutrality which was designed to exclude both Union and Confederate troops from the state. Lincoln cautiously acquiesced and permitted General George B. McClellan to agree to hold off the Union forces as long as the Kentucky militia could bar the Confederates.[39]

While the neutrality policy was not without sympathy in Indiana,[40] Lincoln's "timid" action toward Kentucky was anathema to the warlike Morton. The Governor was disturbed by reports of frenzied panic along the Indiana border. The river counties were terrified by the possibility that Kentucky might secede and thus bring the war to their doors, expose them to recurrent rebel raids, and threaten the destruction of lives and property.[41] To these border communities the Ohio River "front" was clearly the most vital battle line of the war, and their delegations descended upon Indianapolis with petitions for arms and

---

[39] Stampp, "Kentucky's Influence Upon Indiana in the Crisis of 1861," in *Indiana Magazine of History*, 39:268-76; Magoffin to Cameron, April 15, 1861, in *Official Records*, 3 series, 1:70; Indianapolis *Daily Journal*, May 2, 1861; Indianapolis *Daily State Sentinel*, April 20, May 21, 23, 1861; Smith, *The Borderland in the Civil War*, 173, 263 ff.

[40] Indianapolis *Daily State Sentinel*, May 6, 1861; Indianapolis *Daily Journal*, May 21, 1861.

[41] J. H. Barkam, Lawrenceburg, to Morton, April 18, 1861,AGO, Civil War Telegrams, Archives Division, Indiana State Library; Morton to Cameron, April 23, 24, 1861, in *Official Records*, 3 series, 1:102-3, 108; Morton to Caleb B. Smith, May 13, 1861, in Telegraphic Correspondence, 1:52; Indianapolis *Daily Journal*, May 10, 1861.

with much advice regarding military strategy. Displaying his own alarm, Morton wrote urgently to General McClellan at Cincinnati and explained the defenselessness of the river towns in the face of the allegedly rampant disloyalty in Kentucky.[42] Believing that the best defense was to keep the war as far as possible from the Ohio River, he would have occupied Kentucky at once, repudiated her neutrality, and ignored the advice of the Kentucky Unionists in whose loyalty he had little confidence. If the dissemination of such opinions embarrassed the President, Morton apparently gave it little thought. His chief concern was to protect the border of his state.

Throughout the spring and summer the Indiana executive and his aids continued to criticize Lincoln's border state policy and to intervene in Kentucky affairs.[43] His secret agents crossed the Ohio to ferret out the plans of the secessionists; he aided in the distribution of arms to Kentucky Unionists; he encouraged recruiting for the Union army at Camp Dick Robinson near Danville, Kentucky, and at Cincinnati, Jeffersonville, and other cities north of the river. On May 24 Morton and the governors of Ohio and Illinois prepared a memorial to Winfield Scott, General-in-chief of the Army, which urged the immediate occupation of various strategic points in Kentucky. The aged Scott's response to the advice of "these high functionaries" was extremely cold and critical. He observed that the Kentucky Unionists advised against such a policy and suggested that "probably the danger can be better estimated at home than by friends abroad." McClellan also opposed the governors' recommendations, and so they were ignored.[44] Morton then angrily re-

---

[42] Morton to McClellan, May 9, 1861, in Morton Letter Copybook, April 1861-September 1862, pp. 32-33. See also *Official Records*, 3 series, 1:93, 102-3, 125-26; Terrell, *Report*, 1:432-33.

[43] Terrell, *Report*, 1:213-15, 221-22, 223-24; Foulke, *Oliver P. Morton*, 1:140-41, 147-48; Smith, *Borderland in the Civil War*, 269, 278-80.

[44] The memorial and Scott's comment on it are in *Official Records*, 1 series, 52:pt. 1:146-47, 147-48.

buked the War Department for disregarding the imminent danger.

Kentucky's neutrality terminated abruptly in September, 1861, when the Confederates seized Columbus and Bowling Green. General Grant at once countered with the occupation of Paducah. The state legislature demanded the immediate withdrawal of the southern troops and prepared to employ the Kentucky militia to drive them out.

The success of Lincoln's strategy in forcing the Confederates to make the first move apparently escaped Governor Morton. Instead he saw in the southern invasion of Kentucky a complete vindication of his own position and a manifestation of the administration's stupidity in allowing the Confederacy to take the initiative. The Indianapolis *Journal* exploded with anger at the nation's humiliation in Kentucky. Had Morton's admonitions so uselessly given to the administration been heeded, it raged, the rebel invasion of Kentucky could have been averted.[45] Subsequently the President and the Governor exchanged icy letters of mutual criticism. "In this contest," Morton reminded Lincoln, "the Government is compelled to lean upon the States for its Armies, and in my opinion the hands of the men who labor without ceasing to sustain the Government should be held up and not deposed by indifference to their recommendations or demands."[46]

With the movement of Confederate forces into Kentucky, however small, to Indiana that sector became the main theater of the war. The border counties, more agitated than ever, redoubled their demands for adequate defense, and Morton excitedly endorsed their appeals. A thousand conflicting rumors poured in on the Governor

[45] Indianapolis *Daily Journal*, September 24, 26, 28, 1861.
[46] Lincoln to Morton, September 29, 1861, in Nicolay and Hay (eds.), *Complete Works of Abraham Lincoln*, 7:1-3; Morton to Lincoln, October 7, 1861, in Morton Letter Copybook, April 1861-September 1862, pp. 103-7.

from the interior of Kentucky, from Louisville, and from the river border. Morton passed them on to Federal authorities in daily reports of rebel movements to which he attached pertinent advice regarding Union strategy. Lincoln's facetious and patronizing replies to these admonishments were well calculated to drive the humorless Morton to fury.[47]

Indiana's solicitude about Kentucky affairs and the security of her border never abated. Every rumor of rebel movements brought a flurry of excited reports to the Governor from the river counties. Despite the general concern, however, military operations in that state were on a small scale until the brief Confederate invasion in the fall of 1862.

5

The clash of state and Federal interests in the Kentucky arena illustrated the difficulties involved in the formulation of a co-ordinated national war policy. The disputes over military movements and the conflicts between state authorities and the War Department never ceased. Underlying them all was the self-assertiveness of numerous local dignitaries. The multiform character of their activities was revealed in Governor Morton's endless exchanges of letters and his many personal conferences with the President, the Secretary of War, the generals in the field, and other state governors. Members of Morton's staff hovered about Washington to guard and advance the interests of their state; Robert Dale Owen remained there as a sort of liaison agent between the Governor and the administration. But the varying

---

[47] Morton to Cameron and to Seward, September 12, 1861, and to Lincoln, September 21, 25, 26, 1861, and Lincoln to Morton, September 21, 26, 1861, in Telegraphic Correspondence, 2:21, 23, 55, 56, 87, 88, 91. Said Morton petulantly, "From the spirit of your dispatches and from other information I am satisfied my dispatches in regard to Ky are not highly honored. I have said what I thought it was my duty to say. A few days will tell the story in Ky." See also Indianapolis *Daily Journal*, September 20, October 8, 1861.

perspectives attained at Indianapolis and Washington apparently could not be harmonized.

The resulting friction developed over many issues: Morton and other western governors dabbled in the secret service business;[48] they quarreled over promotions to brigadier and major generalships;[49] Morton protested when the War Department instructed him to stop transferring officers in the field to newly organized regiments;[50] he insisted that the Federal government should accept larger military companies than it had originally proposed; despite the objections of military leaders, he preferred to raise new regiments rather than keep old ones filled;[51] he protested against recruiting from the volunteer regiments for the regular army;[52] he fought with the War Department regularly over alleged abuses of military furloughs.[53] Conflicts such as these went on throughout the war.

Similarly state officials had decided opinions as to where the Indiana troops ought to be placed. At the start of the war the volunteers complained when they were not moved to the front with sufficient speed. Objecting to the special treatment which some regiments obtained through the

---

[48] William Dennison, governor of Ohio, to Morton, May 10, 1861, Colonel James M. Shackelford to Morton, and W. R. Holloway to Shackelford, October 8, 1862, in Telegraphic Correspondence, 1:39, 9:55, 61, 62. Dennison's telegram asked openly, "Will you join Ohio, Pennsylvania, Illinois, Wisconsin, Michigan in maintaining a secret service organization in the South under the sole direction of Genl McClellan who alone will know the parties expense about eight thousand (8000) dollars per month. . . ."
[49] Indianapolis *Daily Journal,* March 4, 22, 1862.
[50] Secretary of War, Order Respecting Volunteers and Militia, August 14, 1862, in *Official Records,* 3 series, 2:380-81; Morton to Stanton, August 14, 1862, and Stanton to Morton, August 15, 1862, in Telegraphic Correspondence, 15:102, 103; Indianapolis *Daily Journal,* August 16, October 6, 1862; Terrell, *Report,* 1:91-92.
[51] Terrell, *Report,* 1:57.
[52] *Official Records,* 3 series, 2:694.
[53] See for example Morton to General Henry W. Halleck, April 25, 1862, and Halleck to Morton, April 26, 1862, in Telegraphic Correspondence, 3:186.

influence of their congressmen, Morton urged the immediate forwarding of certain troops who were "in tip top condition," and "wild to go to Virginia."⁵⁴ In September, following the capture of Bowling Green, Kentucky, by the Confederates, Morton frantically requested Cameron to order a regiment to Evansville to defend the state border. Cameron coolly replied that the request was being referred, but that the President thought Washington "the most important point."⁵⁵

After the Union armies entered Kentucky, Governor Morton asked for the transfer of the Indiana regiments in western Virginia to the new sphere of military operations. Criticizing their alleged neglect in the East, the *Journal* suggested that the officers there be left "to paddle their own canoe." Now, it asserted, there was work for the state troops nearer home "where every one will lend a helping hand instead of attempting to steal the clothing from their backs."⁵⁶ To that end the Governor addressed a strong memorial to the President and journeyed to Washington to press his demand. Complications arose when Ohio made a similar effort to transfer her troops, but ultimately Morton secured the removal of several of his regiments to Kentucky.⁵⁷

The local strictures against the conduct of the war went on intermittently. Besides the attacks upon Lincoln's Kentucky policy, the *Journal* complained that the President

---

⁵⁴ Senator Lane and Representative Albert G. Porter had secured orders for Lew Wallace's regiment to go to the Cumberland. Morton to Caleb B. Smith, to General McClellan, and to General T. A. Morris, June 5, 1861, in Telegraphic Correspondence, 1:64, 66.

⁵⁵ Morton to Cameron and Cameron to Morton, September 13, 1861, in *ibid.*, 2:27, 28.

⁵⁶ Indianapolis *Daily Journal*, October 8, November 4, 1861.

⁵⁷ Morton to General J. J. Reynolds, October 9, November 8, 1861, W. R. Holloway to General R. H. Milroy, November 2, 1861, Morton to Lincoln, November 14, 15, 1861, Morton to Caleb B. Smith, November 14, 1861, Morton to David Kilgore, Washington D. C., November 15, 1861, and Kilgore to Morton, November 18, 1861, in Telegraphic Correspondence, 2:135, 177, 185, 187, 188, 189.

did not show sufficient interest in the army and that he permitted politicians to "use up his time with personal solicitations." Secretary of the Navy Gideon Welles, it asserted, was an incompetent "old dotard." As for Cameron, the bulk of his time was spent "settling the conflicting claims of his friends for army contracts and laying out anchors to pull around a Presidential nomination."[58] So persistent was this criticism that the *Sentinel* professed to believe that the Morton faction was antiadministration.[59]

Perpetual feuds between local authorities and officers of the War Department further retarded cordial co-operation between state and Federal governments. No sooner had Major Alexander Montgomery, the United States quartermaster for Indiana, arrived at Indianapolis in August, 1861, than he was embroiled with Governor Morton. The Major was a dignified and methodical officer whose devotion to regulations was equalled by his determination to endure no interference with his duties. His attitude annoyed the Governor whose contempt for red tape and propensity for giving orders were too strong to yield to a mere subordinate. Soon Morton lodged complaints with Secretary of State Seward (rather than Cameron) that Montgomery would not co-operate, that he was "very technical," and that his "tune does not suit me at all." The Governor protested that the state military administration had become a double-headed concern and demanded freedom to carry on operations as he had done before.[60]

The climax came when Morton and Montgomery involved themselves in a petty dispute over who deserved credit for the negotiation of certain contracts for military overcoats. Denying reports that the Governor had made

[58] Indianapolis *Daily Journal*, August 21, 23, 1861.
[59] Indianapolis *Daily State Sentinel*, November 9, 1861.
[60] Morton to Seward, September 1, 21, 1861, in Telegraphic Correspondence, 1:184, 2:65.

the contracts, the quartermaster denounced this effort to
" 'steal thunder' " for Morton and put " 'wind into the
sails' of 'his Excellency,' at the expense of the officers
of the General Government." Morton replied in a published card which refuted the Major's claims. Then the
War Department relieved Montgomery of his duties
and transferred him to Pittsburgh.[61] His young successor, Captain James A. Ekin, had a happier facility for
working with the Governor and won high praise for his
efficiency and "non-adherence to *red-tapeism*."[62]

Secretary Cameron's removal and the appointment
of Edwin M. Stanton as his successor in January, 1862,
won general approval in Indiana. This change, however,
did not end the state's conflicts with the War Department. Morton's grudge against the ordnance chief,
General Ripley, increased when he refused to send arms
directly to state authorities. The Governor's vigorous
protests caused the Secretary of War to make an exception to the general rule for Indiana. Morton also
criticized Col. John S. Simonson, the United States
mustering officer at Indianapolis, whom he accused of
being "superannuated, forgetful and slow, and not very
much superior to Gen. Ripley as a business man." Simonson, a long-time resident of Indiana, also left the state
to assume duties elsewhere.[63]

Despite the apparent respect for Stanton's ability, the
new secretary was no more able to avoid trouble with
disputatious local officials than were his subordinates.

---

[61] Indianapolis *Daily Journal,* October 11, 15, 29, November 4, 7, 1861; Indianapolis *Daily State Sentinel,* October 16, November 5, 6, 7, 19, 1861.

[62] Morton to Quartermaster General Montgomery C. Meigs, November 25, 1861, in Telegraphic Correspondence, 2:201; Morton to Stanton, March 5, 1862, in Morton Letter Copybook, April 1861-September 1862, p. 135; Indianapolis *Daily Journal,* November 9, 1861, February 22, 1862.

[63] Morton to Stanton, July 14, 1862, in Telegraphic Correspondence, 4:98; same to same, and Peter H. Watson, assistant secretary of war, to Morton, August 11, 1862, in *Official Records,* 2 series, 2:351-52.

On one occasion Governor Morton was offended and "painfully surprised" by the War Department's reluctance to grant certain requests and objected to their being "regarded in the light of favors, to be strictly scrutinized, and granted if at all, with hesitation."[64] A few weeks later Morton complained of the slowness in mustering men into the army. Stanton promised to remedy the situation, "but without hope of preventing dissatisfaction." Offended, the Governor replied that he regretted that his suggestions should be considered as "complaints and dissatisfaction." "I give you credit for doing what you can for the cause," he added testily, "and I claim the same for myself in my limited position. If the government understands the conditions of affairs in Indiana, of course information from me is not required."[65] With that, all correspondence between Morton and Stanton, except through intermediaries, ceased for some time. Such were the tribulations of politicians while the armies battled in the field.

6

Beneath the surface of Indiana's disputes with Federal authorities was an undercurrent of interstate jealousy and sectional prejudice. These feelings decidedly influenced her opinions on the conduct of the war.

Governor Morton carefully watched the other state executives to make sure that none ever obtained some unfair advantage from the War Department. Such a spirit of emulation might have had its advantages, but it was not an unmixed blessing. Mutual suspicion that special favors were being extended to one or another of the states brought a host of local emissaries to Washington to sue for a share in the concessions.

One of Morton's early protests resulted from his belief

---

[64] Peter H. Watson to Morton, July 25, 26, 1862, Morton to Watson, July 25, 26, 1862, in *Official Records,* 3 series, 2:251-54.

[65] Morton to Stanton, August 12, 13, 1862, Stanton to Morton, August 13, 1862, in *Official Records,* 3 series, 2:375, 376.

that the Federal government had accepted a disproportionately large number of Ohio regiments. "Why this great discrimination?" he asked Secretary of the Interior Smith. "Will you not see that justice is done Indiana?"[66] But Ohio's leaders complained that in the securing of guns and supplies Governor Morton had "out-generaled" Governor William Dennison, and that Cameron had been "partial to the appeals of Indiana politicians."[67] Similarly, late in 1861 Indiana objected because she had no major general and not a fair proportion of the brigadiers. And Morton persuaded Lincoln to accept six additional brigadier generals from his state.[68] Then Illinois protested that too many generals came from Indiana, and a debate ensued as to which state had been most neglected in that respect.[69] A persistent demand that Indiana's contracts for military supplies be filled exclusively in the state portrayed a kindred spirit.[70]

In viewing the military campaigns most Hoosier strategists were swayed by their desire to expedite the reopening of the Mississippi River. Thoroughly convinced that the war would be won in the West, they fretted at Easterners for their lack of perspective. As early as May, 1861, Morton and other western governors appealed to the President: "We hope that the West will

[66] Morton to Smith, May 24, 1861, in Telegraphic Correspondence, 1:54.

[67] Cincinnati *Commercial,* quoted in the Indianapolis *Daily Journal,* June 11, 1861. The Washington correspondent of the *Journal* boasted that Morton possessed influence with the administration "surpassed by few men in the General Government. . . . He is here now, working most assiduously for the interest of his State." *Ibid.,* July 23, 1861.

[68] Morton, Washington, D. C., to [W. R. Holloway], March 27, 1862, in Telegraphic Correspondence, 3:109; Indianapolis *Daily State Sentinel,* November 28, 1861; Indianapolis *Daily Journal,* March 27, April 2, 14, 1862.

[69] Chicago *Tribune,* quoted in Indianapolis *Daily Journal,* May 6, 1862.

[70] Morton to Quartermaster Ekin, August 26, 1862, in Morton Letter Press Books, 1(June 1862-January 1863):75-77; Indianapolis *Daily State Sentinel,* May 20, 1861; Indianapolis *Daily Journal,* August 30, 1862.

not long be held back but will be permitted to take its part in the contest and push the war to a prompt conclusion."⁷¹

In a short time Indiana newspapers began to criticize eastern states for their alleged failure to fill their quotas as quickly as the West. "Where is the patriotism of the East when compared with that of the West?" they cried.⁷² The Indianapolis *Journal* attacked the East's "stolid indifference . . . to the condition and conduct of the West" and wondered whether its press would ever regard "a Western victory of any value, or worth as much notice as an Eastern defeat."⁷³ As for the policy of "stripping the West to protect the East, and the capital," few Hoosiers could see its merit. The *Journal* proposed instead that western soldiers be sent to Sherman and Frémont for a drive down the Mississippi, "and Washington may go to the only place its swindling, selfish society is fit for."⁷⁴

In February, 1862, the capture of Forts Henry and Donelson in Tennessee by General Grant's western army marked the first decisive Union victory. Indiana glowed with pride in the belief that the West alone had revealed sufficient energy and zeal to prosecute the war successfully.⁷⁵

7

A striking example of sovereign state action was the system developed in Indiana for supplying the needs of her soldiers and caring for the sick and wounded. The initial effort for that purpose emanated from the desire of the people and the Governor, in his role of "soldiers'

---

[71] W[illiam] D[ennison], R[ichard] Y[ates], L[yman] T[rumbull], M[orton], and G[eorge] B. McC[lellan], to Lincoln, May 24, 1861, in Telegraphic Correspondence, 1:56.
[72] Indianapolis *Daily Journal*, September 2, 1861; New Albany *Weekly Ledger*, September 18, 1861.
[73] Indianapolis *Daily Journal*, November 1, 1861.
[74] *Ibid.*, October 15, 1861.
[75] Indianapolis *Daily State Sentinel*, February 18, 1862.

friend," to relieve the expected suffering of the state volunteers during the first winter of war. In October, 1861, Morton issued an appeal "to the Patriotic Women of Indiana" which solicited their aid in furnishing clothing and other supplies for the men in the field. The women responded enthusiastically, and many of them formed societies to advance the cause. Before long the state commissary general reported that he had an abundance of everything needed.[76]

Early in 1862, when the shortage of sanitary stores continued, the Governor created an elaborate permanent relief organization. Thereafter, with William Hannaman, a prominent Indianapolis businessman, as its director, the Indiana Sanitary Commission procured the needed supplies, and the General Military Agency of Indiana supervised their distribution. Subordinate to the central organization was a maze of auxiliary societies, solicitors, agents who followed the Indiana troops, and permanent agencies in more than a dozen cities where military hospitals were located. This state enterprise was close to the heart of Governor Morton, and he fostered it with meticulous care.

The itinerant sanitary agents engaged in a multiplicity of activities. Besides distributing clothing and sanitary stores, they wrote letters and did other favors for the men, saw to the burial of the dead, kept registers of the names of local soldiers in hospitals, reported upon their general health and comfort, talked with the officers and privates, and checked on all complaints. In short, they were the Governor's ambassadors-at-large to the army. The offices of the permanent agencies were supposed to provide a welcome haven for Indiana soldiers, and the directors were instructed to aid in securing furloughs for the sick and wounded, to visit the hospitals, to pro-

---

[76] Indianapolis *Daily Journal,* October 10, November 23, 1861; Terrell, *Report,* 1:315-16; Foulke, *Oliver P. Morton,* 1:159-60.

vide reading matter and other diversions, and to be "careful, affectionate, watchful guardians."[77]

The Indiana Sanitary Commission's first opportunity for vigorous work came during General Grant's campaigns against Forts Henry and Donelson and after the sanguinary battle at Shiloh. Thousands of Indiana troops were in these engagements, and the state commission poured in a steady stream of sanitary supplies. The Governor raised a corps of special surgeons and chartered several river steamers to bring the wounded home. During these operations Morton and other state officers went to the field to supervise the work.[78] These early activities formed the pattern for the later work of the state sanitary commission.

That such pursuits by a state organization should have been a prolific source of trouble to those charged with army administration was perhaps inevitable. However laudable the purpose, the local enterprise soon caused jealousy and dissatisfaction among the soldiers of other states. Generals in the field complained that the state agents interfered with army discipline, and the United States Surgeon General insisted that they caused confusion in the dispensing of medical care.[79] Indiana officials, however, attributed this opposition to the prejudices

[77] A detailed account of the organization and work of the Indiana Sanitary Commission is in Terrell, *Report*, 1:320 ff., 341-43, 349-50, 362-66, and appendix, 109. Correspondence relating to it is in the Telegraphic Correspondence, the Chicago-Morton Collection, and in the files of the Adjutant General's Office, Archives Division, Indiana State Library.

[78] See Telegraphic Correspondence, 2:32 ff.; Indianapolis *Daily Journal*, February 18, March 7, April 10, 11, 1862; Indianapolis *Daily State Sentinel*, February 18, April 11, 15, 16, 23, 1862; Terrell, *Report*, 1:322, 350-51.

[79] Major J. S. Wilson to Morton, Stanton to Morton, and Morton to General Halleck, April 17, 1862, in Telegraphic Correspondence, 3:161, 164, 165; Miles J. Fletcher, St. Louis, to Morton, May 6, 1862, C. F. Kimball, military agent, to Morton, August 15, 1863, Chicago-Morton Collection; Morton to General Grant, July 30, 1863, in Morton Executive Office file, Archives Division, Indiana State Library; Morton to Stanton,

of regular army officers who knew "nothing outside of the regulations."[80]

Relations between the Indiana Sanitary Commission and the United States Sanitary Commission were always hostile, and the former often complained that the latter tried to embarrass it. The state enterprise refused all proposals to unite with the national organization and asserted that it could "better look after the interests, welfare and comfort of . . . [Indiana's] men than anyone else.[81] But spokesmen for the national commission condemned the "indiscreet zeal which was willing to recognize State lines even in its ministrations of mercy on the battle-field." Here, they felt, was another manifestation of "that obnoxious heresy of State-sovereignty, against which the whole war was directed."[82]

Despite this criticism Governor Morton persisted in maintaining Indiana's own sanitary commission, and the Hoosier soldiers thus had additional evidence of his work in their behalf. "I trust I have sustained your reputation for patriotic interest in the military movement of our country," wrote one of Morton's earliest agents. This agent was especially gratified to hear his state "so frequently spoken of in praise," and the Governor's policy "so often applauded by the best citizens of other states."[83] The Governor, too, was gratified.

April 21, 1862, in *Official Records,* 3 series, 2:23-24; Stanton to General Sherman, October 4, 1864, and Sherman to Stanton October 20, 1864, in *ibid.,* 1 series, 39: pt. 3:63, 369.

[80] Terrell, *Report,* 1:323.

[81] Morton to Stanton, February 5, 1863, and Terrell to Peter H. Watson, assistant secretary of war, April 21, 1863, in Telegraphic Correspondence, 16:112, 178; Morton to W. Birch, superintendent U. S. Sanitary Commission, Louisville, December 14, 1863, in *ibid.,* 12:238; W. R. Holloway to D. P. Henderson, U. S. Sanitary Commission, February 16, 1863, in Morton Letter Press Book, 2(January-June, 1863):231-34; D. B. Scott to Morton, August 27, 1862, Archives Division.

[82] Charles J. Stillé, *History of the United States Sanitary Commission* . . . (Philadelphia, 1866), 150-53.

[83] David G. Rose to Morton, August 26, 1861, in Chicago-Morton Collection.

Amid these conflicts between local and national authorities and between the politicians and professional soldiers, the sovereign state of Indiana mobilized for the defense of the nation. Her people and her leaders were eager, enthusiastic for the cause and proud of the part they played. That the needs of the nation were so often confused with local interests provided striking evidence that, in Indiana at least, none waged the war to obliterate the states.

CHAPTER 7
REPUBLICANISM REPUDIATED

ALTHOUGH party politics gradually revived even during Indiana's early martial preparations, it did not regain its full prewar vigor until 1862. Then with the approach of state and Congressional elections, the conduct of the war and its many social ramifications came under the critical scrutiny of the Hoosier electorate.

The campaign of 1862 could scarcely have begun less propitiously for the Indiana Democracy. Still staggering under the load of factionalism inherited from earlier years, the party now bore the added burden of a war in whose inception it claimed no part and whose results it had reason to dread. But the Democracy of Indiana rallied, spurred on by the Indianapolis *Sentinel* and other party organs, and by the assembling of county conventions. After stating their unalterable attachment to the Union, these local political gatherings seldom failed to deplore "the intolerable spirit of extreme men which prevented an honorable compromise before the commencement of hostilities." But since war had come, they came out for its vigorous prosecution to the end. They defended their partisan activity on constitutional grounds, or as a Scott County Democratic meeting resolved, "that the people of this country are the only sovereign and source of political power, and we cannot consent that they should be denied the right, within the limits of the constitution and law, to fully canvass, approve or condemn the acts of those in authority, who, at the most, are but the servants of the people. The adoption of an opposite doctrine would be to destroy the very essence of free institutions."

Democratic criticism of Republican war policies had not taken definite form when the party's central committee issued a call for a state convention to assemble in Indianapolis on January 8. Nor had the one issue that was to be a deciding factor in the October election —emancipation—attained its coming significance. It had become the custom for the Democratic state convention to assemble on or near the anniversary of the Battle of New Orleans, and, said the *Sentinel,* the pursuance of the usages of the party was the maintenance of democratic principles. The convention call issued in October was an invitation to those who desired both "the Union as it was, and the supremacy of the Constitution," to meet to consider the condition of the country. The convention, it suggested, could take such action in regard to the nomination of candidates "as may be deemed advisable." Gradually more specific aims emerged. In November, the *Sentinel* stated that the Convention was to assemble to express its condemnation of corruption and extravagance, and to define the objects for which the war was being fought—re-establishment of the Union and maintenance of the Constitution—and to state its opposition to making it an "abolition" war.[1]

Many Democrats, especially those in southern Indiana who feared most a successful rebellion, voiced considerable opposition to the committee's call. This group doubted the wisdom of a party demonstration at that early date, "when the country was in such a distracted

[1] Indianapolis *Daily Journal,* October 18, 1861; Indianapolis *Daily State Sentinel,* October 9, November 18, 1861; report of Delaware County Democratic convention, in *ibid.,* January 1, 1862. The convention was called and dominated by Douglas Democrats.

condition, and when the platform . . ." might "have no reference to the state of things existing in October."² The New Albany *Ledger,* which still eyed the rebel batteries commanding the Mississippi River, expressed the views of these critics. The *Ledger* was "astonished" by the call and doubted that it would meet the approval of many Democrats. It scolded the party leaders in northern Indiana whom it accused of lacking enthusiasm for the war. It warned these leaders that they could fight the "black Republicans" alone if the southern part of the state was not to be consulted. Finally, it reproached the Democratic state committee for not falling in with Democrats elsewhere in supporting the President in his stand against abolitionists, and declared that the only test of Democracy according to the state committee was blind opposition to any presidential policy.³ To which the Democratic *Sentinel* replied that "it was high time that the party in power was held to strict accountability," that even Republicans were condemning the "inefficiency and imbecility of the Administration in its efforts to put down the rebellion."⁴

Despite the open hostility of the substantial minority represented by the *Ledger,* the Democratic state convention assembled on the appointed day. Republicans had already assured loyal Hoosiers that the gathering would be a "Bright affair" dominated by traitors appropriating the name Democrat "to gild . . . [their] disloyal designs."⁵ Indeed a coterie of peace men were present, and John G. Davis of Parke County gave vigorous

---

² Smith Jones, Bartholomew County, to Allen Hamilton, November 23, 1861, Allen Hamilton MSS.; Evansville *Weekly Gazette,* October 19, 1861. The New Albany *Weekly Ledger,* October 23, November 6, 1861, listed ten Democratic newspapers, besides itself, which opposed the call.

³ New Albany *Weekly Ledger,* October 16, 23, 30, November 6, 27, 1861.

⁴ Indianapolis *Daily State Sentinel,* October 18, 1861, January 1, 1862.

⁵ Indianapolis *Daily Journal,* December 3, 1861, January 7, 8, 1862; Jesse D. Bright to William H. English, January 5, 1862, English Collection.

expression to their opinions. In a lengthy discourse while the convention awaited the report of the platform committee, he deplored the cost of the war, doubted the wisdom of coercion, and longed for "one hour of General [Andrew] Jackson at Washington" to deal with the "plunderers of the people." Such remarks did not please the majority of delegates, and their repetition was avoided by a decision to refer all resolutions to the proper committee without debate. But the opposition from the other wing was not so easily suppressed, and many delegates from southern Indiana strenuously protested against the convention's decision to nominate candidates for state offices at this time for the election the following October.[6]

The resolutions which constituted the party platform were criticized by a few dissenters at both extremes, but they were generally approved by the Democratic masses. The platform again attributed responsibility for the war to the triumph of sectionalism, and affirmed that the Union could be restored only by the success of the conservative Democracy. Resolutions repeated the substance of the Crittenden resolution and opposed emancipation and the subjugation of the South. But the platform also promised to support "a war for the maintenance of the Constitution, and of the integrity of the Union *under the Constitution.*" Finally it refuted the Republican *"no-party dodge"* and expressed a doubt that the majority party's record for the past year had demonstrated anything but its incapacity to administer the government.

Thomas A. Hendricks, the president of the convention, delivered an eloquent keynote address in which he described vividly the present plight of the West. He cried out against the subversion of civil liberty and mourned over the "ruins of a violated Constitution." He

---

[6] A resolution to postpone nominations, offered by William H. English, of Scott County, was voted down 326 to 72.

deplored the tactics of the Republican party which had divided the nation by teaching the North that its interests were opposed to those of the South. Yet Democrats, he asserted, would loyally support the administration in its prosecution of the war, although they refused to permit the fabric of the Constitution to be soiled or torn in the process. Race prejudice and the fear of Negro competition with white labor crept into his attacks upon the abolitionist who, he vowed, preferred the destruction of the South to the restoration of the Union.

Turning to New England, Hendricks said he would speak for the first time as a sectional man. He was appalled by the dismal prospect of Westerners becoming "the 'hewers of wood and drawers of water' for the capitalists of New England and Pennsylvania." He scourged the eastern manufacturers who exploited the West with the protective tariff. The exorbitant freight rates charged by the railroads, he insisted, placed western farmers in a position of dependence upon the southern market and the cheap transportation of the rivers. Hence a "political party that would destroy that market is our greatest foe." The first interest of the Northwest lay in the restoration of the Union, "but if the failure and folly and wickedness of the party in power render a union impossible; then the mighty Northwest must take care of herself and her own interests. She must not allow the arts and finesse of New England to dispoil her of her richest commerce and trade, and to render her labor wholly subservient to an eastern, sectional, and selfish policy—Eastern lust of power, commerce, and gain."[7]

[7] Indianapolis *Daily Journal,* January 9, 10, 1862; Indianapolis *Daily State Sentinel,* January 8, 9, 10, 1862; New Albany *Weekly Ledger,* January 15, 1862. The *Ledger* of January 15 quoted from the Louisville *Democrat,* "that sterling Democratic Union paper," on the convention: "The Democratic convention at Indianapolis, we observe, is not likely to be satisfactory to the Democratic party; not that their resolutions contain any doctrine unsound, but that they do not contain much condemnation of Secession, and the tone of the speeches was more exception-

The words of Hendricks and the resolutions of the January 8 convention, both steeped in Democratic lore, were the views of the western Jacksonian Democracy. Because these agrarians saw little to commend in the basic national changes that seemed to be occurring during the war, their eyes were turned wistfully toward the past. The arguments of those who stood for "progress" had no appeal for men content with "the Union as it was."

2

Meanwhile, the champions of the Republican-dominated Union party movement were confidently developing their plans for the approaching campaign. All the signs seemed to promise them an easy victory. The winter and spring of 1862 witnessed military events which augured swift success for the Union armies. Much was expected of General McClellan who had organized and drilled the Army of the Potomac to a fine point. In the West the fall of Forts Henry and Donelson, the bloody battle at Shiloh, and the occupation of Memphis and Corinth were regarded as indications of the imminent collapse of the Confederacy. People in the river towns grew more optimistic, and business revived with the expectation that the Mississippi would soon be open again to western commerce.[8] The Indianapolis *Journal* had already assured Hoosiers that the North would never resort to the draft.[9] In April, 1862, despite the many protests among the loudest of which was Morton's, the War Department stopped recruiting. The assumption was that the Union armies were sufficiently large to complete the crushing of the rebellion.[10]

---

able than the resolutions. . . . In fact, this convention has left room for a conservative party to take the field and sweep the State."
  [8] Indianapolis *Daily Journal,* February 17, 18, April 10, May 1, June 14, 1862; Indianapolis *Daily State Sentinel,* February 18, 1862.
  [9] Indianapolis *Daily Journal,* August 20, 1861.
  [10] Terrell, *Report,* 1:25; Weeden, *War Government,* 114; Foulke, *Oliver P. Morton,* 1:179.

Amid this optimism the Union party began to take definite form in numerous local conventions which eschewed party organizations and platforms during the national crisis. While many Democrats hesitated and awaited subsequent developments,[11] Republican leaders instructed them regularly in the duties of the hour and paraded forth the leading "War Democrats" on every possible occasion. The *Journal* reported that Milton B. Hopkins, nominated by the eighth of January convention as state school superintendent, had declined the nomination, and in March it triumphantly proclaimed that the purely partisan eighth of January movement was dead.[12]

On April 30, Union party leaders issued a call for a state convention to assemble at Indianapolis on June 18. Their call proclaimed that with 60,000 Indianans defending their country in the Federal armies, it would be "unbecoming those who remain at home to array themselves in partisan warfare against each other." Hence they invited everyone, "without respect to past political associations," who favored a vigorous prosecution of the war for the preservation of the Union and the maintenance of the Constitution and were opposed to the disloyal convention of the eighth of January, to attend the convention. This appeal was circulated through the state in the form of petitions. Soon each county had sent in an impressive list of signatures, among which were those of many prominent Democrats.[13]

But the call for a state convention also provoked the first serious expressions of discontent with the Union

---

[11] Despite its hostility to the January 8 convention the New Albany *Ledger* never gave wholehearted support to the Republican Union party movement. In the fourth district Congressman William S. Holman was also undecided about his future course. "I should not willingly abandon my old political connection, though I do not like the 8th of January platform." Holman to Allen Hamilton, May 16, 1862, Allen Hamilton MSS.

[12] Indianapolis *Daily Journal*, March 4, April 30, 1862.

[13] *Ibid.*, April 30, 1862. Subsequent issues printed the lists of signatures.

movement. This criticism came from within the ranks of the Republican party itself. Julian and many other radicals looked upon the movement as a conservative surrender to the Democracy and as an evasion of the real issues of the war. They denounced it as "the 'Morton-Wright' plan of bringing together the fag-ends of all the office-seeking plunder-grabbing cliques of Indiana."[14] Besides the radicals, some of Governor Morton's old party foes in southern Indiana renewed their attacks upon him. To them the Union party movement was Morton's political machine, and so they openly opposed it. They urged Republicans to stand by their principles and nominate a purely Republican state ticket. Morton was clearly alarmed by the activities of these men, and his secretary addressed frantic letters to his friends, urging them to make sure that reliable men were sent to the convention.[15]

A challenge was thrown to the Union meeting by the active editor of the New Albany *Ledger*, who predicted success for its ticket if it took a firm stand against the country's two enemies, southern secessionists and northern abolitionists, and repudiated all ideas of freeing the slaves and confiscating rebel property, and resolved in favor of a vigorous prosecution of the war for the sole purpose of restoring the Union and maintaining the Constitution. What the *Ledger* apparently wanted was the eighth of January platform written in firmer, bolder language by a Union party. Mindful of its Democratic tradition, the *Ledger* assured the Union party that the Democrats joining with it were not forgetting either their name or their well-known principles, and that they would stand where they stood when they supported Douglas—"regarding abolitionism and secessionism equally as heresies."[16]

[14] Centreville *Indiana True Republican*, April 10, 17, 1862; Julian, *Political Recollections*, 223-24.
[15] William R. Holloway to Henry Taylor, to W. L. Lingle, to J. L. Mansfield, to N. W. Williams, and to J. Jenkenson, May 30, 1862, Morton Letter Press Books.
[16] New Albany *Weekly Ledger*, May 7, 14, 1862.

As soon as the Union state convention began, its conservative sponsors elected the officers and got control of its proceedings. The delegates chose Governor Morton to serve as president, and he opened the meeting with a keynote address which enlarged upon his usual plea for the abandonment of parties. "We come together now on the platform of saving the country," he began. "Parties may be formed hereafter, dividing us on this side or that. But till peace shall be secured, I trust that we shall give up everything as one man for the salvation of the nation." The Governor denounced the "wild and wicked dream" of ambitious men who allegedly plotted to form a Northwest Confederacy in alliance with the South. He announced dramatically that secret treasonable societies existed in the state and warned that the government might be compelled to use strong measures to suppress them. These were broad hints that opposition Democrats were closely identified with disloyalty.

Except for Morton most of the principal speakers were "War Democrats" whose participation in the convention was expected to make a favorable impression upon the Democratic masses. From Washington Senator Wright wrote a letter to the meeting which lauded the Union movement and urged that ultraism be suppressed in both the North and South. Henry Secrest, another prominent "War Democrat," spoke in reverent praise of Andrew Jackson and compared the eighth of January meeting with the Hartford Convention which had brought shame and ruin to the Federalist party. Inevitably, he affirmed, an opposition party in time of war soon found itself in a position of hostility to the war itself.

The promoters of the Union convention were especially pleased with a speech by State Senator Martin M. Ray which signified his adherence to their group. While he continued to be a Democrat, he professed to have no politics in relation to the war or to the government when it was in danger. "In this meeting we do

not abandon our old party creeds . . . we do not lose
our political identity, we do not adopt each other's supposed political heresies. We waive, for the time, political
differences, and suspend mere party warfare for the
public good . . . ."[17]

The convention divided the nominations for state offices
between the Republicans and "War Democrats." The
platform ignored every issue that might have caused disagreement. Except for resolutions praising the soldiers
and demanding governmental economy, it simply reiterated the Crittenden resolution as the basis for a continued
vigorous war policy. Thus the Indiana Union party, like
the Democrats, endorsed the original conception of a
war for the Union and not for the abolition of slavery.
The spirit of conservatism was firmly intrenched in both
of the state parties.[18] Radical doctrines still appealed
only to a minority of Hoosiers.

During the campaign Union party leaders continued
to emphasize their nonpartisan pretensions. On every
public occasion Governor Morton assumed his no-party
pose and spoke only as the champion of his country's
cause. Most of the state and Congressional candidates
canvassed the voters with a similar appeal. The "War
Democrats" always received the most flattering attention,
and Republican newspapers never tired of commending
the virtues of these unselfish patriots.

Nothing galled the regular Democrats more than the
Union movement's affectation of nonpartisanship and
its effort to monopolize the virtues of loyalty and patriotism. Angrily they berated the "base ingrates and
fawning parasites" who deserted the Democratic party
for "government pap."[19] In a letter to the Indianapolis

---

[17] Indianapolis *Daily Journal*, June 19, 20, 21, 23, 1862. Ray's speech
was printed and circulated as a campaign document.
[18] *Ibid.*, June 19, 1862; Indianapolis *Daily State Sentinel*, June 19,
1862.
[19] Indianapolis *Daily State Sentinel*, July 8, 24, August 1, October 2,
1862; Evansville *Weekly Gazette*, December 7 1861.

Sentinel, William H. English reminded his Democratic friends that their affiliation with the Union party would associate them with men "whose lives have been mainly devoted to unscrupulous and vindictive warfare against the Democratic party." In such an organization they would be "the mere tail-pieces to a political kite."[20] Exposing the hypocrisy of the "no-party dodge," the *Sentinel* begged to know when the Republicans had discarded a single party dogma for the good of the country. It asked for the evidence of Morton's nonpartisanship beyond the studied phrases of his campaign oratory.[21] It asserted that the only material difference between the Democratic and Union platforms was that the former "condemned alike the heresies of abolitionism and secessionism, while the 'Union' had no censure for abolition disunion and no condemnation for the proposed schemes for emancipation and confiscation by Republicans in Congress."[22] Yet the very bitterness of this Democratic criticism demonstrated the initial success of the Union party movement.

3

Though the Indiana Union party began auspiciously, the dismal events of the summer of 1862 promised a less happy conclusion for its first venture in local politics. Many of the Democrats who had long wavered between the two parties were becoming alarmed about some of the revolutionary changes in government policy. Behind the camouflage of war they perceived the steady abandonment of their ancient Democratic principles and the adoption of various parts of the old Whig creed. When that appeared to be the objective of the majority in Congress, few Democrats could be distracted any longer by the Union party plea. The war then ceased to be a

[20] Indianapolis *Daily State Sentinel,* June 28, 1862.
[21] *Ibid.,* August 27, October 10, 1862.
[22] *Ibid.,* June 19, 1862.

simple struggle for the integrity of the nation. Every new alarm further depleted the ranks of the "War Democrats" and brought them back to the regular party fold.

The dissenters had plenty of grievances. Some complained about the huge land grant incorporated in the Pacific railroad bill and insisted that it would injure the poor settlers by fostering land monopolies.[23] Hoosier farmers resented the rapid rise of consumer prices and the mounting burden of war taxes which, they feared, might make every man "a mere vassal to the Government."[24] From Washington, Representative Holman wrote in horror that Republicans had adopted the Hamiltonian heresy "that a public debt is a public blessing."[25] Similarly western Jacksonians viewed suspiciously the issuance of legal tender notes through which they anticipated "inflation, speculation and, possibly, financial ruin." They refused to accept the Republican plea of war necessity. That was "the despot's argument."[26]

Democrats were particularly bitter about the revival of the protective tariff. They branded western Republicans who accepted it as apostates to their section.[27] These "unfaithful servants" had "devoted their energies for months in fixing upon the country a tariff policy of taxation which enriches the manufacturing monopolists of the East and North by subjecting the great agricultural West to onerous and unequal burdens." How, asked a party campaign document, could "the imagination picture a scene more revolting than that of Con-

---

[23] Aurora *Commercial*, May 29, 1862.

[24] Indianapolis *Daily State Sentinel*, December 25, 1861, January 14, April 16, 1862. Voorhees promised his constituents in the Wabash Valley that he would "stand between the farmer and the tax gatherer." *Ibid.*, July 17, 1862; Indianapolis *Daily Journal*, July 16, 1862.

[25] Holman to Allen Hamilton, March 2, 1862, Allen Hamilton MSS.

[26] Indianapolis *Daily State Sentinel*, February 2, 1862.

[27] *Ibid.*, June 30, August 19, 1862; Corydon *Democrat*, quoted in *ibid.*, February 17, 1862. The protective tariff was the object of particularly bitter attacks by Voorhees. *Congressional Globe*, 37 Congress, 2 session, 1150.

gress discussing, for weeks and months, and finally *adopting this policy of increasing the semi-annual dividends of the Eastern manufacturers,* and, at the same moment, throwing additional burdens on the working classes of the people?"[28]

Defending the national policies of earlier and purer days, the Democrats deplored the revolution they saw in progress. The Republicans were prosecuting the war solely with the hope that a new order of things would be its end, declared the *Sentinel.* "A long war is their elysium," for without it "all their fancy schemes for taxing, banking and plundering would pass away . . . ." Republicans currently ridiculed the "butternut Democracy" it observed. "It used to be the 'barefoot' Democracy in Jackson's time—then it was the 'poke berry' Democracy, . . . but they all, as used, mean the same thing—a contempt for those who earn their bread by honest toil."[29]

Because of their fears of economic change Democratic agrarians speculated anxiously about the fate of their former southern allies. Their party was weakened by the loss of the South, and so they deplored the radical schemes for the subjugation of the seceded states and demanded generous terms for them. They had denounced confiscation of rebel property in their platform, and, echoing the sentiments of his constituents, Voorhees spoke out against a war of conquest.[30] Many Indiana Democrats would not abandon their conviction that western interests remained more akin to those of the South than of the East.

Equally alarming was the continued tendency of Fed-

---

[28] Democratic State Central Committee, "Appeal to the People of Indiana," in Indianapolis *Daily State Sentinel,* August 11, 12, 1862. The appeal was printed as a campaign document entitled *Facts for the People.*

[29] Indianapolis *Daily State Sentinel,* January 24, June 26, August 1, 1862.

[30] *Ibid.,* April 11, 19, 1862; *Congressional Globe,* 37 Congress, 2 session, 903.

eral officials to infringe upon personal liberties. The Democrats had denounced such practices in their January platform. The Union party might excuse such instances with the plea of war necessity, but the indignant opposition could see no validity in that argument. They indicted the ruling party for sanctioning arbitrary arrests and for seeking to destroy free speech and a free press. Many Hoosiers were deeply disturbed by the resort to military arrests in their own state where the courts were open and ordinary processes of law appeared entirely adequate. The *Sentinel* warned that such persecution "for opinion's sake" might well justify the formation of associations to defend constitutional liberty.[31] Impassioned denunciations of the " *'lettres de cachet'* by which men are imprisoned in our political bastiles" made effective themes for Democratic campaigners.[32]

In September Democrats saw what was to them the climax of political proscription when President Lincoln suspended the writ of habeas corpus for all persons charged with disloyal practices and subjected them to the arbitrary processes of martial law. Indiana then witnessed the arrest of a number of her citizens by military officers. To the opposition these at once became martyrs to the cause of constitutional liberty. Since some of these arrests, especially of several opposition candidates, looked suspiciously partisan, Democrats also charged that Republicans were resorting to intimidation to insure their own triumph.[33] So insistent were the protests that

---

[31] Indianapolis *Daily State Sentinel,* June 24, 1862; Indianapolis *Daily Journal,* June 12, 1862; Weeden, *War Government,* 236-37.

[32] Indianapolis *Daily State Sentinel,* June 20, 1862; Huntington *Democrat,* quoted in Indianapolis *Daily Journal,* July 12, 1862.

[33] Indianapolis *Daily Journal,* November 8, 27, 1862; Indianapolis *Daily State Sentinel,* September 8, October 13, November 19, 1862; Rushville *Jacksonian,* quoted in *ibid.,* November 7, 1862; New Albany *Weekly Ledger,* September 10, 1862. Among those arrested were Richard D. Slater, representative from Dearborn County; Jason B. Brown, Democratic candidate for the General Assembly from Jackson County; Harris Reynolds, of Fountain County; and Theodore Horton, Wells County.

the Indianapolis *Journal* at length felt the need to explain that the arrests were executed by United States officers and not by Governor Morton.[34] Nevertheless, Hoosier Democrats gained a distinct advantage over the Union party by making themselves the defenders of personal liberty.

4

Concurrent with these growing domestic apprehensions there occurred some startling military reverses which destroyed all hopes that the war would be won before the end of the year. The failure of General McClellan's campaign against Richmond and the stunning operations of "Stonewall" Jackson in the Shenandoah Valley dampened the war spirit of the West. While the Indianapolis *Journal* cast the responsibility for these failures upon McClellan, it could not ignore "the universal feeling of discouragement, not to say despondency," which it had produced among loyal men.[35] Continued military defeats, especially at the second battle of Manassas, prompted Colfax and other Republican candidates to furbish their appeal with the promise of a more vigorous war.[36] But the Hoosier people responded indifferently. They were appalled at the apparent waste of blood and treasure.

In June the President and War Department suddenly sent out urgent appeals to the governors for more volunteers. This was an added shock to the public since it followed so quickly the supposed permanent cessation of recruiting. Morton went to work at once to raise five additional regiments with all possible speed. To advance the enterprise he issued a proclamation which assured the

---

[34] Indianapolis *Daily Journal,* November 5, 1862. In November Lincoln suddenly ordered the release of all who had been subjected to military arrest.
[35] *Ibid.,* July 1, 2, 1862.
[36] Hollister, *Schuyler Colfax,* 194.

people that the new call, "which I trust is the last," was only "to complete the crushing out of the present rebellion."³⁷

But this was not the last call. By the end of June Lincoln saw the need for still more troops, and he searched desperately for a means of securing them that would not create a public panic. At last Secretary Seward aided the President by secretly persuading Morton and the other governors to sign a memorial which urged the government to recruit as many more volunteers as were needed to win the war. Early in July the appeal of the governors (known to the President and Stanton beforehand) and Lincoln's resulting call for 300,000 additional troops were published simultaneously in the local press.³⁸

During the following weeks the state administration worked vigorously to fill its quota of 31,250 volunteers. Morton issued a second proclamation which described the failure of the Richmond campaign as a "short and temporary retreat" and explained that new troops were needed to hold the territory recently taken from the rebels. He drafted the services of Lew Wallace and Schuyler Colfax, among others, to aid the recruiting drive. The local commandants sent out fervent appeals and sponsored stirring war meetings; men of wealth raised large sums of money for the support of soldiers' families; many localities paid additional bounty money to each new volunteer.³⁹ Still, none of these efforts could revive the early enthusiasm. Recruiting was no longer a

---

37 Indianapolis *Daily Journal*, June 25, 1862.

38 Governors Edwin D. Morgan and Andrew G. Curtin to Morton, June 30, 1862, in Telegraphic Correspondence, 15:5-6; Morton to Morgan and Curtin, July 1, 1862, in *ibid.*, 4:46; Lincoln to Seward, June 28, 1862; the Governors to the President, June 28, 1862; Seward to Stanton, June 30, 1862, in *Official Records*, 3 series, 2:179-80, 181-82. See also pages 186-88, 204.

39 Morton to Colfax, July 10, 1862, in Morton Letter Press Books, 1(June 1862-January 1863):48-49; Indianapolis *Daily Journal*, July 7, 14, 15, 26, 1862; Wallace, *Autobiography*, 2:589-91.

spontaneous outpouring of patriots eager to defend their country, but a laborious task.

The result of the languid progress of enlistments was a feeble effort to supplement volunteering with the application of a draft upon the state militias. On July 17 an act of Congress authorized the President to call out the militia of the various states for nine months and to apply a draft upon those organizations if necessary. On August 4, in conformity with this act, President Lincoln issued another call for 300,000 troops. In Indiana preparations were made at once for the necessary enrollment of the militia.[40] The reaction of the state was far from favorable. Few events did more to strengthen the opposition than this first crude attempt to administer a draft.

Military defeats and the lagging war spirit had another unfavorable effect upon public opinion in Indiana. Now there seemed to be little chance that the Mississippi River would soon be reopened. This was a serious matter for the people of southern Indiana who were already complaining strenuously about the high cost of railroad transportation. To them one of the most desirable consequences of a military victory over the South was the breaking of the railroads' monopolistic control of western commerce. Were the rebellion to succeed, they would lose the free navigation of the Mississippi and be at the mercy of the private corporations which controlled the artificial eastern outlets. The New Albany *Ledger* insisted that no real effort had yet been made to open the river and suggested that it was not "to the interest of Northern capitalists and corporations to do it."[41] Clearly the war had not dispelled western suspicion of eastern Yankees.

[40] Indianapolis *Daily Journal*, August 6, 1862.
[41] New Albany *Weekly Ledger*, October 2, 9, 23, 30, 1861, January 22, May 14, October 15, 1862; Terre Haute *Journal*, quoted in Indianapolis *Daily State Sentinel*, February 15, 1862; Smith, *Borderland in the Civil War*, 325-26.

5

Military failures and domestic discontent severely impaired the campaign of the Union party. Another problem grew out of the bitter conflict between radical and conservative Republicans over the government's policy toward slavery. The increasing influence of the radical wing threatened to weaken still more the Union party's appeal. Indiana Democrats, steeped in race prejudice and fearing a rush of free blacks into the Northwest, sounded the alarm as they watched the growth of abolitionism. They used every radical utterance and every measure touching upon slavery as evidence that the war for the Union was being transformed into an abolition crusade.

Whatever the exigencies of national politics and international relations, the majority of Hoosiers were still opposed to any tampering with the institution of slavery. The Indianapolis *Gazette*, a radical Republican paper, noted that it was common talk among many volunteers that when they had disposed of the secessionists they would deal out similar treatment to the abolitionists.[42] Local Union meetings everywhere re-endorsed the Crittenden resolution and declared their opposition to antislavery measures.[43] In the United States Senate, Henry S. Lane showed no sympathy for the abolitionists and Wright opposed every radical scheme.[44] In the House Republican Congressman William M. Dunn warned that the abolition of slavery would destroy the Union forever and vowed that he would "fight these Northern fanatics at every step."[45] The Indianapolis *Journal* took

---

[42] Indianapolis *Gazette,* February 6, 1862.
[43] Indianapolis *Daily Journal,* February 13, May 2, June 18, 1862.
[44] *Ibid.,* April 4, 1862; Indianapolis *Daily State Sentinel,* April 9, 1862.
[45] William M. Dunn to Allen Hamilton, January 17, 1862, Allen Hamilton MSS.; Indianapolis *Daily Journal,* January 14, 1862.

decided ground against any meddling with slavery and lauded the President for not yielding to the radicals.⁴⁶ Events, however, moved swiftly the other way. Lincoln's proposal for compensated emancipation in April, the abolition of slavery in the District of Columbia the same month, the exclusion of slavery from all the territories in June, and the passage of the second Confiscation Act in July, all signified the growth of radical power. Each new measure increased the fears of Indiana conservatives and gave added credence to the Democratic charge that the purpose of the war was being changed.⁴⁷

In July, during the days of national gloom and confusion, the abolitionists vigorously pressed their demands. While they redoubled their attacks upon the President, their friends in Indiana ignored the advice of conservative Union party leaders and called for general emancipation. Colfax courted radical favor with a pronouncement for abolition and confiscation.⁴⁸ From the field his protégé, Gen. Robert H. Milroy, promised to turn his Indiana regiments into "the best abolitionists in the U. S."⁴⁹ Other radicals allegedly found growing dissatisfaction in the army because of the belief that it had been "sold out to the old line party."⁵⁰ By this time Robert Dale Owen had completed his metamorphosis from a Democratic opponent of coercion to a Republican pamphleteer for

⁴⁶ Indianapolis *Daily Journal,* May 12, August 11, 25, 1862.

⁴⁷ Indianapolis *Daily State Sentinel,* March 8, April 7, 18, July 17, 18, August 29, 1862; New Albany *Weekly Ledger,* August 6, 1862; Evansville *Weekly Gazette,* February 8, 1862; Aurora *Commercial,* May 22, 1862.

⁴⁸ Hollister, *Schuyler Colfax,* 185.

⁴⁹ Note of Gen. Robert H. Milroy, Clarksburg, Virginia, to Colfax, appended to printed General Order No. 28, October 22, 1862, Colfax MSS.

⁵⁰ W. H. Colescott, Headquarters 51st Indiana Volunteers near Decatur, Alabama, to Col. B. J. Spooner, July 6, 1862, Benjamin Spooner MSS. (photostats in Indiana State Library; originals in possession of Mrs. Frank Hutchinson, Lawrenceburg, Indiana, 1934).

emancipation.[51] Julian battled the conservatives in his district and denounced the "persistent purpose of the administration to save the Union and save slavery with it."[52] Radicals had long been attacking Senator Wright and Caleb Smith for their opposition to emancipation.[53]

On September 22 (the eve of the Indiana election) Lincoln finally yielded to the radical pressure and issued his preliminary proclamation of emancipation. The immediate hostile reaction in Indiana promised to validate Secretary Smith's warning that the measure would certainly cause the Republicans to lose his state.[54] Some conservative Union papers printed the proclamation without comment; but the New Albany *Ledger* denounced it angrily and then gave its support to the regular Democrats.[55] The *Sentinel* at once proclaimed that the abolition of slavery had now become the chief issue of the political campaign. It called the President's proclamation a confession of national weakness, a mortal blow to southern Union sentiment, and the final proof that the war had become a crusade against slavery. Caustically it asked the "War Democrats" whether they intended to "sit down to the abolition feast." A deluge of "lazy, helpless and thriftless negroes" would soon sweep into Indiana.[56]

The diminishing ranks of "War Democrats" were further depleted by the emancipation proclamation. Among those who now returned to the Democratic fold

[51] Indianapolis *Daily Journal*, August 11, 1862; Leopold, *Robert Dale Owen*, 351-56.
[52] Centreville *Indiana True Republican*, September 4, 11, 1862; Julian, *Political Recollections*, 214.
[53] Indianapolis *Daily Journal*, April 16, 1862; Hollister, *Schuyler Colfax*, 200.
[54] Francis B. Carpenter, *The Inner Life of Abraham Lincoln: Six Months at the White House* (Boston, 1883), 87-88; Bailey, "Caleb Blood Smith," in *Indiana Magazine of History*, 29:233.
[55] New Albany *Weekly Ledger*, October 1, 1862.
[56] Indianapolis *Daily State Sentinel*, September 24, October 13, 1862.

was Martin M. Ray whose stirring appeal at the Union party convention the previous June had been so widely circulated.⁵⁷ The "War Democrats" still had abundant leaders, but most of their followers had left them by October.

The friends of Morton had no alternative but to give Lincoln's proclamation their belated approval. The *Journal* now saw in it a heavy blow to the rebellion and defended it as retaliation for the rebel violations of the Constitution.⁵⁸ Morton passed over all moral justifications and defined the President's act as a "stratagem of war."⁵⁹ But most Hoosiers were not inclined at that time to accept the measure upon any grounds, and the Governor's best efforts were of no avail.

6

At length the harassed leaders of the Union party resorted to some desperate tactics in their efforts to check the growing strength of the opposition. Republicans were afraid to touch controversial issues like the tariff; they could not erase the national record of corruption and military failure. And so they avoided these questions, as did their platform, and tried to create a diversion. From every battlefield they brought lurid tales of rebel barbarism, and in every speech they stirred up hatred against the South.

But most important was the deliberate attempt of Union party spokesmen to make their opponents appear to be as disloyal as the southern rebels. Their strictures against "rebel sympathizers" increased as the campaign progressed. A victory for the Democracy, they insisted, would be a blow at the Union cause, for all dissent in time of war must end in disloyal acts against the government. The Democratic cry for free speech was only "a

---

⁵⁷ Indianapolis *Daily Journal*, October 27, 1862.
⁵⁸ *Ibid.*, September 27, 1862.
⁵⁹ *Ibid.*, October 10, 1862.

sanctified cloak for treason."⁶⁰ They described the disloyalty of Democrats in a long indictment: they cheered for Jeff Davis; they gloated over Union losses; they plotted to discourage enlistments; they wept only for slavery and had no tears "for the blood of our sons . . . and the agony of mothers." Voorhees and Hendricks were traitors at heart, more dangerous than rebels in arms, and the Confederates read all their speeches with delight.⁶¹ Fortunately loyal soldiers knew about the activities of these men and were ready, when necessary, to suppress "the enemy at home!"⁶²

To fortify their shadowy charges of treason Union party politicians described vaguely the machinations of secret pro-Confederate Democratic societies. Stories of such allegedly disloyal organizations began with various accounts (subsequently an "exposure") of a Mutual Protection Society formed to oppose the war and resist the collection of taxes.⁶³ From that point the theme found numerous variations as receptive politicians seized upon every rumor as "evidence." Governor Morton exploited the subject repeatedly, as did Senator Wright in depicting the degeneracy of the latter-day Democracy.

The most publicized of the local "treasonable" societies was the Knights of the Golden Circle, which supposedly sprang from a parent stem in the Confederacy itself. Throughout the campaign there were wild reports that its estimated 10,000 members were plotting to overthrow the government and that it was engaging in military drills and midnight meetings in secluded spots. Though the evidence of such activities did not exist, Republicans tried their best to create popular alarm. The first objective of such a conspiracy, they insinuated, would be the circulation of treasonable Democratic documents to secure the

---

60 *Ibid.*, June 30, July 29, August 12, 1862.
61 *Ibid.*, April 15, 30, May 2, 7, 23, July 15, August 1, 15, September 10, 1862.
62 Kokomo *Tribune*, quoted in *ibid.*, April 30, 1862.
63 *Ibid.*, December 3, 30, 1861, January 1, March 30, 1862.

victory of that party at the polls. Then the Knights would encounter no further obstacle to the execution of their traitorous plans.⁶⁴ As if to stress the imminent danger, a report went out from Indianapolis that the state militia was to be placed upon a war footing in preparation for any emergency.⁶⁵

The Union party press uncovered numerous incidents to illustrate the charge that the state was honeycombed with treason. In May there was a railroad accident in Sullivan County which caused the death of the state superintendent of public instruction, Miles J. Fletcher, son of Calvin Fletcher. Since Morton was also on the train, Republican papers at once asserted that the accident was the result of a plot to kill the Governor.⁶⁶ Indiana traitors were accused of co-operating with Kentucky guerrilla bands which operated along the border.⁶⁷ In July when one of these bands raided Newburgh, Indiana, there were reports that the guerrillas had been aided by disloyal citizens of that town. A local mob killed two of the

⁶⁴ Mayo Fesler, "Secret Political Societies in the North During the Civil War," in *Indiana Magazine of History*, 14(1918):203-4; Ollinger Crenshaw, "The Knights of the Golden Circle: The Career of George Bickley," in *American Historical Review*, 47(1941-42):23-50; Indianapolis *Daily Journal*, June 25, July 12, September 4, 1862; Brownstown *Jackson Union*, quoted in *ibid.*, July 14, 1862; Indianapolis *Daily State Sentinel*, September 11, 1862; New Castle *Courier*, quoted in Aurora *Commercial*, July 17, 1862.

⁶⁵ Cincinnati *Gazette*, quoted in Indianapolis *Daily State Sentinel*, June 23, 1862. See also Morton to Stanton, June 25, 1862, in Morton Letter Press Books, 1(June 1862-January 1863):9-17, printed in *Official Records*, 3 series, 2:176-77.

⁶⁶ Indianapolis *Daily Journal*, May 12, 13, 16, 1862; Indianapolis *Daily State Sentinel*, May 17, 22, 1862; Terrell, *Report*, 1:284. A group of Republicans from Sullivan County, in a letter to the *Journal*, May 21, denied and resented the imputations of treason against their county. Later, while testifying before a Sullivan County jury, Berry R. Sulgrove, the *Journal* editor, admitted the injustice of his charges since he knew none of the facts of the incident. Indianapolis *Daily Journal*, January 22, 1863. Governor Morton gave the details of the accident in a letter to Calvin Fletcher [May 11, 1862], Calvin Fletcher Papers, Indiana Historical Society Library.

⁶⁷ Indianapolis *Daily Journal*, July 2, 11, 1862.

suspected accomplices, and seven others were arrested.[68] All of these events supposedly illustrated the secret sentiments of the Democratic party.

The climax of the treason campaign came in August when the grand jury of the United States district court submitted a report on disloyalty in Indiana. With the aid of the Governor[69] this jury had examined numerous witnesses and returned many indictments for treason and conspiracy. Its report included a sensational exposé of the disloyal activities of the Knights of the Golden Circle and an elaborate description of the society's organization, ritual, and treasonable purposes. Actually these jurors had done little more than accept all the current rumors and thereby revealed their own gullibility. Moreover, the members of the jury were not free from the suspicion of partisanship, and their report was immediately distributed as a Union party campaign document. Its assertion that loyal soldiers were to be "treacherously betrayed in the bloody hour of battle" formed a lurid phrase for campaign oratory.[70]

Whatever the allegations of excited Republicans, the Indiana Democracy of 1862 was eminently loyal. While

[68] *Ibid.*, July 19, 21, 26, 1862; Indianapolis *Daily State Sentinel,* July 19, 28, 1862; Evansville *Weekly Gazette,* July 19, 29, 1862; Terrell, *Report,* 1:143-46; New Albany *Weekly Ledger,* July 23, 1862. See also the series of telegrams received and sent on the Newburgh affair in Telegraphic Correspondence, July 18-21, 1862, vol. 4:118 ff., and Adah Jackson, "Glimpses of Civil War Newburgh. . .," in *Indiana Magazine of History,* 41(1945):178-79. During the raid the guerrillas captured the military hospital and paroled the inmates. As was the case with every such incident, the state, especially the border, became very excited. "Indiana Invaded" was the large headline used by the *Journal.* But the invaders were small in number and left within a few hours.

[69] Morton to James Speed, July 9, 1862, in Telegraphic Correspondence, 4:72; W. H. H. Terrell to James H. Cravens, Osgood, July 10, 1862, and Morton to Osgood postmaster, July 16, 1862, in Morton Letter Press Books, 1(June 1862-January 1863):55, 56; Morton to E. B. Allen, July 14, 1862, E. B. Allen MSS., Indiana Division, Indiana State Library.

[70] Indianapolis *Daily Journal,* August 4, 1862; Indianapolis *Daily State Sentinel,* August 5, 7, 1862; Terrell, *Report,* 1:appendix, 295-96.

it criticized methods, it campaigned as a war party and demanded the suppression of the rebellion by force of arms. Voorhees, despite the insinuations of his opponents, was not then a peace man, and he boasted of the support that Democrats had given to measures providing the necessary men and money.[71] Hendricks repeatedly stated that it was the duty of all to support the war and that he favored its vigorous prosecution.[72] None exceeded Congressmen Holman and Cravens in their zealous support of the Union cause. Almost every local Democratic meeting endorsed an energetic war policy and vowed that nothing must obstruct that end.[73] The party press indignantly denied that the Democratic masses opposed the war and insisted that all Indiana remained united upon that question.[74]

7

Military events in Kentucky late in the summer of 1862 brought the Indiana Union party to the nadir of its fortunes. By the middle of August the Confederates had betrayed their plans for a large-scale invasion of Kentucky. Gen. Kirby Smith began the operations with a movement north from Knoxville, and Gen. Braxton Bragg moved in the same direction from Chattanooga a few days later. The approach of the Confederates once again brought terror and confusion to the Indiana border and to the threatened cities of Louisville and Cincinnati. Untrained regiments with temporary officers were rushed from Indiana to Kentucky in an effort to check the rebel

---

[71] *Congressional Globe,* 37 Congress, 2 session, 903; Indianapolis *Daily Journal,* September 6, 1862; Indianapolis *Daily State Sentinel,* July 18, 1862.

[72] Holcombe and Skinner, *Thomas A. Hendricks,* 238-39, 246-48; Indianapolis *Daily State Sentinel,* July 7, 18, 19, 1862.

[73] Indianapolis *Daily State Sentinel,* June 12, 26, 30, July 14, 16, 19, 25, August 20, 23, September 19, 1862.

[74] *Ibid.,* June 19, July 21, August 2, October 11, 1862; New Albany *Weekly Ledger,* May 14, 1862; Evansville *Weekly Gazette,* May 10, 1862.

march.⁷⁵ Eastern military failures had been dispiriting, but the invasion of Kentucky reduced the people of Indiana to despair. The ensuing six-weeks campaign was full of discouraging and humiliating events for Hoosiers. While Bragg and Gen. Don Carlos Buell raced northward, Kirby Smith's army fell upon some raw Indiana troops at Richmond, Kentucky, on August 30, and cut them to pieces. Indiana was horrified, and many citizens censured the Governor for sending green recruits to such a dangerous position.⁷⁶

As the Confederates moved closer to the Ohio River the panic-stricken border people rushed defense preparations. Both Cincinnati and Louisville expected to be the object of the rebel attack, and each demanded the full attention of the distracted military leaders. Gen. Lew Wallace was placed in command of the Cincinnati defenses. Governor Morton was active in both cities and once more sent many confusing reports along with much advice to the War Department.⁷⁷ On September 5 he declared martial law in the border counties and ordered every business establishment closed by three o'clock to permit able-bodied men to drill for the Legion.⁷⁸

---

⁷⁵ Gen. J. F. Boyle to Morton, August 31, 1862, in Telegraphic Correspondence, 15:215, 217; Indianapolis *Daily Journal*, August 18, 21, 1862; Wallace, *Autobiography*, 2:591-93.

⁷⁶ A. H. Burton, Mitchell, to Morton, September 4, 1862, Chicago-Morton Collection; Holloway to Morton, September 4, 5, 1862, and Morton to Gen. H. G. Wright, September 6, 1862, in Telegraphic Correspondence, 8:38, 42, 44, 15:250; Morton to Stanton, September 26, 27, 1862, in *Official Records*, 2 series, 4:562, 3 series, 2:590; Indianapolis *Daily Journal*, September 1, 5, 9, 1862; Indianapolis *Daily State Sentinel*, September 1, 2, 8, 1862; New Albany *Weekly Ledger*, September 3, 1862; Terrell, *Report*, 1:157-59, appendix, 296-97.

⁷⁷ Morton's Telegraphic Correspondence reflects the general panic and confusion, and records the work of Indiana officials during the crisis. See also Indianapolis *Daily Journal*, September 6, 9, 23, 1862; Indianapolis *Daily State Sentinel*, September 2, 5, 6, 12, 13, 1862; New Albany *Weekly Ledger*, September 10, 24, 1862; Terrell, *Report*, 1:157-59; Wallace, *Autobiography*, 2:612n, 624, 628n.

⁷⁸ Indianapolis *Journal*, September 6, 1862; Terrell, *Report*, 1:157.

In the midst of these military activities Indiana politicians and commanders in the field engaged in a sordid conflict which had an unfavorable effect upon both army morale and public opinion. For many months Morton and other western governors had been critical of General Buell who commanded the Army of the Ohio. Now they blamed his alleged "mismanagement and imbecility" for the rebel invasion of Kentucky.[79] When the Confederates captured Munfordville, Kentucky, and made prisoners of almost 5,000 Indiana troops, Morton and other politicians were furious with Buell. The Indianapolis *Journal* expressed regret that any state troops had been placed under his command and demanded his immediate removal. In fact, it wrote hysterically, "He richly deserves to be shot, and we hope he will be cashiered."[80]

Simultaneously Morton became embroiled with Gen. William Nelson, whom Buell had placed in command of the forces opposing Kirby Smith. Nelson's dislike for civilian interference led to trouble when Morton sent state agents into Kentucky to arrange bounty matters with the Indiana regiments at Richmond.[81] Further difficulties arose when Nelson relieved General Wallace from his command and when he blamed Indiana's Gen. Mahlon D. Manson for the Union defeat at Richmond. By then the *Journal* was calling Nelson's conduct "brutal and barbarous" and questioning his ability as an officer.[82] Late in September Morton and Nelson met in Louisville.

---

[79] Morton to Stanton, September 26, 27, 1862, in *Official Records,* 2 series, 4:562, 3 series, 2:590. The Indianapolis *Daily Journal* had long been sniping at Buell for his inactivity. It asserted that his men had no confidence in him and hinted that he might end his "career of ineffective patriotism with a display of very effective treason." January 11, 15, July 16, 18, August 16, 20, 1862.

[80] Indianapolis *Daily Journal,* September 19, 22, October 1, 1862.

[81] Morton to Gen. William Nelson, August, 1862, Holloway to Nelson, August 29, 1862, Nelson to Morton, August 28, 1862, in Telegraphic Correspondence, 15:194, 196, 197.

[82] Indianapolis *Daily Journal,* September 9, 1862.

Their relations were strained to the breaking point. At that juncture Nelson also had a bitter quarrel with Gen. Jefferson C. Davis of Indiana. He accused both Morton and Davis of plotting against him. On September 29 General Davis, after having been dismissed and insulted, shot and killed Nelson at the Galt House, Louisville. Morton witnessed the shooting, and since his rift with Nelson was widely known, there was a general disposition to implicate him in the dismal affair.[83] The Governor's political fortunes probably reached their lowest point at that time.

On October 8, the plans of Bragg and the Confederates to set up a secessionist government in Kentucky were terminated by the bloody battle at Perryville. Neither side could claim a clear victory, but the Confederates began an immediate withdrawal into Tennessee. Though the threat to the Indiana border was thus removed, the rebel campaign in Kentucky was not forgotten on election day. Nothing more completely disproved the Union party's prediction that the fall of the Confederacy was imminent.

Meanwhile Indiana continued her preparations for the execution of the unpopular draft. Morton found abundant excuses for delay, and state officials did some close figuring in an effort to prove that Indiana's quota had actually been filled by volunteers. Nevertheless, on October 6, a few days before the election, the state was obliged to apply a draft to raise 3,003 additional men.[84] The

---

[83] General Davis surrendered himself to military authorities and was placed under arrest. Subsequently, however, he was released. *Ibid.,* September 26, 30, October 1, 1862; Indianapolis *Daily State Sentinel,* September 30, October 7, 1862; New Albany *Weekly Ledger,* October 1, 15, 1862; Foulke, *Oliver P. Morton,* 1:193-95.

[84] Correspondence regarding the operation of the draft is in Morton's Telegraphic Correspondence, vol. 9. See also *Official Records,* 3 series, 2:338, 471, 485, 491, 495. Later corrections in the number of volunteers furnished by Indiana showed that the state had actually exceeded its quota and that the draft, therefore, was not necessary. Terrell, *Report,* 1:40-41, 43-44.

scene was a sorry one. Democrats, fearing partisanship, complained that the executers of the draft were all members of the Governor's party.[85] A system of passes had to be instituted to prevent draft dodgers from leaving the state. Forceful resistance occurred in a number of places, especially in Blackford County where an armed mob destroyed the enrollment lists and seized the draft box.[86] Democratic leaders counseled against such acts and urged the people to appeal instead to the ballot box. But Republicans pointed to this violence as the fruits of the teachings of Hendricks and Voorhees.[87] They would have been more accurate if they had attributed it to the fact that the draft was resented by most Hoosiers.

8

On October 14, in an atmosphere of gloom, the people of Indiana cast their votes in the state election. In spite of the frantic warnings of Union party politicians that their defeat would insure the success of the rebellion,[88] the Democrats won a clear victory. Their candidates for state offices triumphed by more than 9,000 majority; seven Democrats were elected in the eleven Congressional districts; the new legislature would have a substantial Democratic majority in both houses.[89]

Union party spokesmen were ready with hasty explanations: Union men had filled the armies, and state laws prevented them from voting in the field. The chairman

[85] Indianapolis *Daily State Sentinel,* August 6, 30, 1862.
[86] T. M. Brown, Muncie, to [J. P. Siddall, General Commissioner of the Draft], October 7, 1862, Telegraphic Correspondence, 9:46; Terrell, *Report,* 1:43, 282-83, 287.
[87] Indianapolis *Daily Journal* and *Daily State Sentinel,* October 9, 1862.
[88] Indianapolis *Daily Journal,* October 3, 11, 14, 1862.
[89] The four Republican congressmen elected were Julian in the fifth district, Ebenezer Dumont in the sixth, Godlove S. Orth in the eighth, and, by a slim margin, Colfax in the ninth district. Indianapolis *Daily State Sentinel,* October 20, 1862; Indianapolis *Daily Journal,* November 3, 1862.

of the Union state committee also charged that Democrats had been guilty of monstrous frauds.[90] But aside from any such irregularities, there were abundant causes for the Union party defeat in the welter of domestic discontent and military failures. The Indianapolis *Journal* explained the Democratic victory as a reaction against the "terrible inefficiency" with which the war had been conducted.[91]

On October 27 the Democratic state central committee issued an address "To the Freemen of Indiana" which refuted the accusations of treason lodged against the victorious party. The address reviewed the reasons for its criticism of the Republicans, rehearsed the issues of the past campaign, and re-endorsed the Crittenden resolution. "*Armed rebellion must be suppressed by force,*" it concluded, "and the insane and infuriated faction of Abolitionists *must retire before the ballots of a free people*. The first civic battle has been fought, and the first victory won in the contest. . . . The sun of Constitutional liberty beams upon this goodly land!"[92]

The triumph of the Hoosier Democracy in 1862 was not a repudiation of the war for the Union. It was a repudiation of Republicanism!

[90] Indianapolis *Daily Journal*, October 16, November 17, 1862.
[91] *Ibid.*, October 16, 1862.
[92] Indianapolis *Daily State Sentinel*, October 27, 1862.

CHAPTER 8

THE COLLAPSE OF CONSTITUTIONAL GOVERNMENT

PARTY politics in Indiana was traditionally an intensely serious business. But even that state had no precedent for the rancorous partisan conflict which unfolded in the months following the election of 1862. The issues in the conflict, aside from that of mere party advantage, were essentially those which had long divided Hoosiers, but the passions generated by war precluded calm and judicious discussion. In this political battle a vindicated, indignant, almost revengeful Democracy was pitted against a humiliated and bitterly disappointed Republican-dominated Union party. Both factions had an abundance of able leaders, but there were few men on either side who demonstrated any real capacity for statesmanship.

The Democratic victory caused Governor Morton and his friends to look to the future with feelings of panic and despair. Emotionally unbalanced by the war and overcome by their own lurid tales of treason, they seemed to expect revolution in their midst at any moment. When a Democratic paper exultantly proposed that Morton yield to the popular will and resign, Republicans regarded this as the beginning of a vast program of disloyalty.[1] They were equally upset by a Democratic

[1] Indianapolis *Daily Journal*, November 1, 10, 1862.

(158)

victory jubilee held at Cambridge City where Clement L. Vallandigham, the extreme peace Democrat from Ohio, George H. Pendleton, a moderate Democratic leader from the same state, and Hendricks addressed a boisterous crowd. Vallandigham recalled an earlier visit to Indiana when Morton's marshal and police had allegedly violated the state's hospitality. He asked these satraps of the Governor whether they had heard the election news and knew that their days were numbered. Then, according to Union party reports, the crowd cheered for Jeff Davis and whispered about their plans to aid the Confederacy. Individual Democrats made a brazen display of their Butternut pins.[2] Surely the peace of Indiana was seriously imperiled!

The alarmed Governor, amid Union party cries for vigorous action, tried desperately to check the trend toward political reaction and public discouragement. The first object of his attack was the hapless General Buell, for the election returns strengthened Morton's determination to secure a new commander for the Army of the Ohio. The Governor was never afraid to meddle in military affairs; nor did he have scruples about scheming with subordinate officers to achieve his ends. Soon the Indiana troops were fully acquainted with his attitude toward their commander.[3]

Buell's failure to pursue the Confederates after the battle of Perryville roused Morton to a fury and gave him excuse to send an angry complaint to the President.[4]

---

[2] *Ibid.*, November 21, 1862.

[3] See, for example, W. R. Holloway to Samuel E. Munford, Surgeon of the 7th Regiment, Bardstown, Kentucky, October 23, 1862, in Morton Letter Press Books, 1 (June 1862-January 1863) :224-25.

[4] "Nothing but success, speedy and decided," Lincoln was warned, "will save our cause from utter destruction in the North-west. Distrust and despair are seizing upon the hearts of the people." Morton, W. M. Dunn, A. Lange, and W. A. Peelle to Lincoln, October 21, 1862, in *Official Records*, 1 series, 16:pt. 2:634. See also W. R. Holloway to John G. Nicolay, October 24, 1862, in Morton Letter Press Books, 1 (June 1862-January 1863) :233-39.

Simultaneously he urged Governor Richard Yates of Illinois to join him in a trip to Washington to press for a change in command.⁵ On October 24, just before their departure, the news arrived that Buell had been removed and replaced by General William S. Rosecrans. That action made the journey to Washington unnecessary, but the two governors telegraphed Lincoln that the order came "not a moment too soon."⁶ Besides falling victim to civilian meddling and western discontent, Buell was something of a scapegoat for disappointed Union party politicians.⁷

Morton turned next to the problem of opening the Mississippi River. He was convinced that the failure to achieve that objective was a major cause for the recent Democratic victory. Indeed western anger at the continued closure of the river outlet grew more intense in the last weeks of 1862. Amid the grumbling came hints of what might happen if the mouth of the Mississippi remained permanently in the hands of a foreign nation.⁸ On October 27, the Governor poured out his fears to

---

⁵ Morton to Yates, October 20, 21, 1862, Yates to Morton, October 21, 1862, in Telegraphic Correspondence, 9:125, 126, 127, 128.

⁶ Morton and Yates to Lincoln, October 25, 1862, in *Official Records,* 1 series, 16:pt. 2:642. The Democrats, including some "War Democrats," denounced Buell's removal as the work of "a clique of intermeddling governors and strategic editors." New Albany *Weekly Ledger,* October 29, 1862.

⁷ In November a military commission, headed by Indiana's Lew Wallace, investigated Buell's Kentucky campaign. Although Judge Advocate Donn Piatt informed the commission that it was "organized to convict," Buell defended his course with great success. The western governors, who had been instrumental in securing his removal, refused to testify against him. To show the political influence at work to demoralize his army, Buell cited the editorial in the Indianapolis *Daily Journal* which had suggested that he ought to be shot; he observed that that newspaper usually reflected the views of Governor Morton. *Official Records,* 1 series, 16:pt. 1:8-12, 642; Wallace, *Autobiography,* 2:643-44; Alexander K. McClure, *Abraham Lincoln and Men of War Times* (Philadelphia, 1892), 356-60.

⁸ Indianapolis *Daily State Sentinel,* November 4, 1862; Evansville *Weekly Gazette,* December 13, 1862.

President Lincoln in a letter which vowed that the future of the Northwest was "trembling in the balance." After reviewing the causes of western complaint and relating the alleged Democratic program for a Northwest Confederacy, he predicted that a victorious South would bring civil war to his section. The only solution, Morton concluded, was an immediate effort to complete the conquest of the Mississippi. Thus Westerners would be assured that, whatever the outcome of the war, the free navigation of their great river would be secure.[9]

Capitalizing upon this sentiment, John A. McClernand, a political general from Illinois, obtained authority from Secretary Stanton to raise a new western army to capture Vicksburg. On October 23, McClernand conferred with Morton and won his enthusiastic support for the project.[10] The Governor immediately began a drive to recruit the needed men, and several Indiana colonels showed great eagerness to join the proposed expedition. By December 12, McClernand reported to Lincoln that 40,000 troops had already been raised in the West and asked permission to go forward at once.[11] Instead, however, much of his army was diverted to other commands, and he was sent with the rest to join General Grant.[12] Whereupon the Indianapolis *Journal* launched another bitter attack upon the administration and suggested that the Mississippi River would probably be blockaded at Cairo before it was opened at Vicksburg.[13]

To no small extent the fears of Republicans and the menacing appearance of the Democrats were due to the

---

[9] Terrell, *Report*, 1:21-22; Foulke, *Oliver P. Morton*, 1:208-11.

[10] McClernand to Stanton, November 10, 1862, in *Official Records*, 1 series, 17:pt. 2:332-34.

[11] *Ibid.*, 1 series, 17: pt 2:401.

[12] W. H. H. Terrell to Col. Cyrus L. Dunham, 50th Regiment, Indiana Volunteers, Columbus, Kentucky, December 15, 1862, in Morton Letter Press Books, 1(June 1862-January 1863): 505-6.

[13] Indianapolis *Daily Journal*, December 30, 1862.

continued military misfortunes which brought a universal feeling of depression and discontent. The failure to reduce Vicksburg, the disastrous Union defeat at Fredericksburg in December, and the bloody, but indecisive, battle at Murfreesboro, Tennessee, in the first days of the new year, all combined to make the administration's war policy appear to be a failure. On January 1, 1863, the President's final proclamation of emancipation brought no joy to the disheartened Hoosiers. State authorities feared that there would be violent demonstrations, but the conservatives were content with verbal expressions of angry criticism.[14]

It was in such an atmosphere that the early small group of peace advocates won for the first time in Indiana a more substantial following. By the beginning of 1863 numerous Democratic meetings and many party spokesmen suggested plans for an armistice, the holding of a national convention, and a settlement by negotiation and compromise. On January 8, 1863, an address of the Democratic state central committee spoke vaguely of the "great duty of pacification or honorable adjustment" and expressed regret that "every avenue to compromise has been closed in the face of the people."[15] Though Republicans sought to misconstrue their purpose into a disloyal desire to accept disunion or even to join the Confederacy, the peace men nearly always insisted that their program was premised upon a recognition of the nation's integrity. Most Democrats never repudiated the war, but even those who did, generally favored only peace *and* Union.[16] The cry for peace was the product of an accumulation of mili-

---

[14] Henry B. Carrington to Stanton, December 31, 1862, copy in bound volume labeled Carrington Papers, Archives Division; Indianapolis *Daily State Sentinel,* January 1, 8, 1863.
[15] Indianapolis *Daily State Sentinel,* January 8, 1863.
[16] For the war views of these Democratic meetings, see *ibid.,* December 25, 1862, January 9, 20, 28, 30, February 3, 5, 7, 10, 14, 23, 27, March 3, 4, 1863.

The Collapse of Constitutional Government 163

tary failures, and the influence of its sponsors always fluctuated with the fortunes of Union arms.

While this pervasive spirit of gloom and discouragement set men at home to talking of peace, it also permeated Indiana's troops in the field. A number of officers resigned their commissions in protest against the Emancipation Proclamation.[17] Recruiting was stagnant, and desertions increased at an alarming rate. Volunteer soldiers, having little understanding of the seriousness of their offense, simply tired of the service and went home.[18] Nothing testified more clearly to the waning of martial enthusiasm than this decline in the morale of the Federal armies. "The term of service of nearly one third of the army [is] about expired, and no prospect of re-filling the loss," wailed Gen. Lew Wallace. "Desertions occurring daily, and encouraged at home. . . . I am not disheartened —merely getting so."[19]

Unwilling to attribute desertions to the irresponsibility or discontent of individual soldiers, Morton insisted, publicly at least, that they were caused by the machinations of organized conspirators. He was ever on the verge of exposing a great secret society formed to aid deserters and discourage enlistments. According to current reports such an organization had even spread to the army itself.[20] The alleged discovery of many ungrammatical letters to soldiers urging them to desert supposedly established the truth of these charges. Here was

[17] Terrell, *Report*, 1:79.
[18] Carrington to Major J. P. Garishee, chief of staff and assistant adjutant general, Nashville, Tennessee, December 8, 1862, in volume labeled Carrington Papers, Archives Division; Gen. W. S. Rosecrans to Morton, February 21, 1863, in Telegraphic Correspondence, 16:125; Terrell, *Report*, 1:276-77; Berry R. Sulgrove, *History of Indianapolis and Marion County* (Philadelphia, 1884), 318-19.
[19] Wallace, Louisville, to Col. John Coburn, January 20, 1863, John Coburn MSS., Indiana Division, Indiana State Library.
[20] Indianapolis *Daily Journal*, January 17, 1863; Indianapolis *Gazette*, January 27, 1863; Carrington to Stanton, December 22, 1862, and January 24, 1863, in *Official Records*, 2 series, 5:108, 3 series, 3:19.

another means by which "the scourge of this war" would "be rolled back . . . upon the fair fields of our own glorious Northwest."[21]

Sporadic attempts to prevent the arrest and return of deserters to the field appeared equally sinister. Late in January, 1863, the most serious incident of that nature occurred in Morgan County where a band of men fired upon a military detail as it tried to apprehend deserters. A squad of cavalry had to be sent in to restore order. There were further exchanges of shots but no fatalities on either side. Three deserters and several citizens were finally arrested. The Republican press made much of the affair and suggested that it might well have carried the state into "the awful chasm of civil war."[22]

Other events added to the excitement and caused Democrats to feel as greatly alarmed as did the members of Governor Morton's party. Patriotic Indiana soldiers threatened Hendricks and Voorhees with violent treatment and reported that the army was ready to use force against domestic traitors. In January bands of soldiers destroyed Democratic newspapers at Rockport and Terre Haute.[23] Democrats also heard rumors that public arms were being distributed to the political organizations of

[21] W. R. Holloway to John Hanna, U. S. deputy attorney, February 24, 1863, in Morton Letter Press Books, 2(January-June, 1863), 295; Indianapolis *Daily Journal,* January 20, February 10, 23, 24, 1863; Indianapolis *Gazette,* February 11, 1863; Terrell, *Report,* 1:277, appendix, 356-57.

[22] Indianapolis *Daily Journal,* February 2, 3, March 4, 1863; Indianapolis *Daily State Sentinel,* February 3, 4, 1863; Indianapolis *Gazette,* February 2, 1863; Carrington to U. S. Adjutant General Thomas, February 2, 1863, typed copy in bound volume labeled Carrington Papers, Archives Division; Carrington to Lincoln, February 2, 1863, in *Official Records,* 2 series, 5:235.

[23] Col. W. H. Blake, headquarters of the 9th Indiana Volunteers near Glasgow, Kentucky, to Colfax, November 7, 1862, Colfax MSS.; Major James T. Embree, Camp near Nashville, to Mary Embree, December 17, 1862, Lucius C. Embree MSS., Indiana Division, Indiana State Library; Morton to Stanton, January 15, 1863, in Morton Letter Press Books, 1(June 1862-January 1863):671-72; Indianapolis *Daily State Sentinel,* February 3, 1863.

The Collapse of Constitutional Government 165

their opponents.[24] They read Republican accounts of unprecedented sales of weapons to private individuals and of incipient revolts by secret societies. And they heard their opponents make inflammatory appeals to loyal men to "be awake, look to your arms! Be prepared for *any* emergency."[25]

Union party leaders aggravated a tense situation with a volley of rash charges against their Democratic foes. They played upon war passions by insinuating that Democrats favored an abject surrender to the Confederacy. "It is no longer a secret, confined to the 'dark-lantern' halls of the Knights of the Golden Circle, and the conclaves of midnight assassins," the Indianapolis *Gazette* solemnly announced, "but is openly advocated, talked of and hinted at in public meetings, on the streets, and in the tory organs of the public press."[26] The *Journal* printed an elaborate description of how this Democratic conspiracy was to be executed. It concluded: "If we are not to be forced out of the Union by the temporary power of a party which already makes no secret of its designs, we must be ready to act.... Be prompt, vigilant and bold, and you will defeat their schemes."[27] This much-repeated text fell like a firebrand among a people already disturbed by the psychological dislocations of war.

Democrats responded with no greater restraint. They demanded the proof of their alleged disloyalty and vowed that Morton was "demented" upon the subject of treason and conspiracy. His real aim, they insisted, was to create a panic in order to have an excuse for declaring martial law and destroying the last vestige of personal liberty. They accused Republicans of forming their own secret societies and of securing arms to launch a war against

[24] Indianapolis *Daily State Sentinel,* February 18, 23, 1863; Indianapolis *Daily Journal,* February 21, 1863.
[25] Indianapolis *Gazette,* January 13, February 3, 1863; Terrell, *Report,* 1:278-93.
[26] Indianapolis *Gazette,* December 31, 1862, January 15, 1863.
[27] Indianapolis *Daily Journal,* January 19, 1863.

the Democracy. Though they did not deny that secret Democratic associations existed, they asserted that these organizations were merely for self-defense and for protection against arbitrary arrests and encroachments upon the purity of the ballot box.[28] H. H. Dodd, a member of the faction of extreme peace men, told Republicans that they would learn the purpose of these associations if they tried again to "place arms in the hands of their sons and send them to the polls in company with hired ruffians to intimidate and overawe peaceable citizens in the exercise of a constitutional right."[29]

Similarly, Democrats defined the "Northwest conspiracy" as Republican "clap trap" whose object was "to advance, in some way, dishonest partisan purposes."[30] But their press and public speakers still continued indignantly and somewhat demagogically to abuse New England. The *Sentinel* maintained that the war was being waged to give supremacy to that section and to advance its material interests. New England, it declared, had profited by the war and was growing rich, while other sections felt "its blighting influences." Consequently, it continued, "it is not the 'radical Democracy' ... who will ... separate the Northwestern States from New England. If it is ever done, it will result from the conviction of the people of the Northwest that a continued affiliation is detrimental to all her interests."[31]

With fanatical partisans, both Republican and Democratic, prating thus hysterically, it was not strange that domestic peace often hung by a thread.

2

On January 8, 1863, amid these military failures and outbursts of malignant partisanship, the state legislature

[28] New Albany *Weekly Ledger,* January 28, 1863; Indianapolis *Daily State Sentinel,* January 20, 21, 23, 1863.
[29] Indianapolis *Daily State Sentinel,* January 28, 1863.
[30] *Ibid.,* January 16, 20, February 2, 9, 1863.
[31] *Ibid.,* January 20, 1863.

The Collapse of Constitutional Government 167

began its biennial session. Despite the assurances of the Democratic majority that the Union cause would be sustained, Republicans had long been warning Hoosiers to expect the worst. The air was thick with evil rumors: the majority would sell out the Democrats to Jesse Bright and return him to the Senate; southern rebels waited expectantly while Democratic legislators conspired to seize the state arsenal, free the rebel prisoners at Camp Morton, and inaugurate a revolution; at the least they would repudiate and depose the Governor and take Indiana out of the war.[32] In alarm Morton telegraphed Stanton that the legislature intended to recognize the Confederacy and urge the Northwest to dissolve all constitutional relations with the New England states.[33]

Both houses organized quickly and elected the Democratic candidates for legislative offices. The opening day of the session was the anniversary of the Battle of New Orleans and the Republicans were ready with patriotic resolutions lauding the memory of Andrew Jackson for his devotion to the Union and praising General Rosecrans' army for its heroic conduct at Murfreesboro. The Democrats accepted and passed them.[34] At the end of the first day's proceedings the *Sentinel* noted sarcastically that peace still reigned in Indiana. "No women and children were slaughtered. The city was not destroyed. . . . Indiana was not voted out of the Union into the Southern Confederacy."[35]

Although treason failed to make its expected appearance, frayed tempers and political crimination were soon very much in evidence. The first partisan wrangle grew out of the need to elect a United States Senator for the remainder of Bright's unexpired term and one for the new

[32] Indianapolis *Daily Journal*, October 17, 25, 28, 1862, January 9, 1863; Terrell, *Report*, 1:296-97.
[33] Morton to Stanton, January 3, 1863, in *Official Records*, 1 series, 20:pt. 2:297.
[34] *Brevier Legislative Reports*, 6(1863):10, 12.
[35] Indianapolis *Daily State Sentinel*, January 9, 1863.

term which would begin in March. Trouble began when Republicans, even before introducing the above-mentioned patriotic resolutions, proposed a resolution that no man be elected to office by the legislature who did not favor a vigorous prosecution of the war and was not "unalterably opposed to the severance of any State or States from this Union." Some Democrats resented its implications, and others wanted to qualify it by adding the Crittenden resolution. Hence it was referred to the Committee on Federal Relations. Whereupon Republican senators defeated a proposal for a joint session to accomplish these elections by resorting to the old expedient of breaking a quorum.[36] The Republican bolt continued during the following two days. Democrats upbraided them bitterly for their factious course and vowed that legislation for that session was ended unless they were ready to yield.[37]

The dubious conduct of these Republican bolters failed to win the united approval of their party friends. Several of their senatorial compatriots and part of the Republican press denounced their action.[38] Ultimately the disorganizers abandoned their abortive attempt to block Democratic action and returned to their seats. On January 14, the joint session met and elected David Turpie, a moderate Democrat who supported the war, for the senatorial short term, and Hendricks for the long.[39]

During this turmoil another petty political conflict was taking shape. On the first day of the session Governor Morton agreed to deliver his message the following afternoon. At the appointed time the house invited the senate into joint session to hear the message, but the latter body replied that since some of its members had broken a quorum it was unable to accept the invitation. The house

[36] *Brevier Legislative Reports,* 6(1863):13.
[37] *Ibid.,* 6:13-14, 18; Indianapolis *Daily State Sentinel,* January 9, 12, 1863.
[38] *Brevier Legislative Reports,* 6(1863):15-18; Centreville *Indiana True Republican,* January 15, 1863.
[39] *Brevier Legislative Reports,* 6(1863):39, 46-47.

The Collapse of Constitutional Government 169

immediately notified the Governor of this fact and that it was uncertain as to when his message could be heard. At that juncture Morton sent his secretary with copies of his message in printed form to each house separately. The speaker of the house promptly ruled that the Governor's action was unconstitutional, and the majority voted to send the message back to him until it could be delivered properly.[40]

After the Republican bolters returned, the Governor made no further move to deliver his message. But both houses continued to maintain that the document had not been delivered officially and therefore could not be considered. On January 14, Bayless W. Hanna of Vigo County proposed that, since Governor Morton had neglected his duty, the house adopt "the exalted and patriotic sentiments" contained in the message of Horatio Seymour, Democratic governor of New York. The proposal was not voted upon, but the next day the house adopted a resolution thanking Seymour "for the able and patriotic defence of the Constitution, the laws and liberties of the American citizen" embraced in his message.[41]

Subsequently the legislature sent committees to the Governor to ask him when he expected to transmit his message. Morton replied with a long defense of his course and declined to act further on the matter. His message was thus never read in either house, although it was later referred to the proper committees and recommended to be printed.[42]

These trivial political tiffs were but a prelude to the more serious controversies which embroiled the legislators during the ensuing weeks. On the Democratic side there was a small but noisy faction of ultra men whose opposition to the war was mingled with a rabid desire for

---
[40] *Ibid.*, 6:21-22, 30-32, 41; Indianapolis *Daily Journal*, January 10, 12, 1863; Indianapolis *Daily State Sentinel*, January 10, 1863.
[41] *Brevier Legislative Reports*, 6(1863):37, 46, 49.
[42] *Ibid.*, 6:64, 67, 79, 85, 114; Indianapolis *Daily Journal*, January 21, 1863.

revenge against Morton and his Republican cohorts. They engaged in endless flights of grandiloquent oratory and introduced numerous proposals for peace through an armistice and some form of national compromise. "War alone," they asserted, "is no remedy for the evil of disunion," especially when waged "in the spirit of sectional hatred, for an unconstitutional purpose, or in a manner not sanctioned by the laws of civilized warfare." Indiana, suggested one delegate, should "never voluntarily contribute another man or another dollar, to be used for such wicked, inhuman and unholy purposes."[43]

Resolutions of that type were supplemented by rash speeches against the conduct of the war, particularly against the draft which had been "mercilessly enforced" in Indiana.[44] Government speculators, "that hoard of national 'horse leeches' . . . who have fattened and gloated upon the miseries of their country," received an abundant share of their abuse. Lincoln and Morton, asserted these critics, had lost all sympathy for the white soldier in their love for the Negro. They wailed bitterly at the decline of personal liberty and at the sight of men "ruthlessly kidnapped . . . cast into dungeons . . . to remain, sicken and die." They warned ominously of a terrible vengeance by an enraged people and asserted that Democrats would not "cowardly and basely submit" to military rule.[45]

But Republicans proved themselves to be at least as adept as their opponents in this sort of political demagoguery. Throughout the session the legislative halls rang with unsubstantiated charges of treason and conspiracy and with ceaseless impeachments of Democratic loyalty. Republican legislators pretended to be fighting desperately

[43] *Brevier Legislative Reports,* 6(1863):45, 49, 53, 56-57, 91-92, 94, 95, 100, 169, 174, 181, 227; Indianapolis *Daily Journal,* January 26, 1863; Indianapolis *Daily State Sentinel,* January 29, February 2, 3, 7, 1863.
[44] *Brevier Legislative Reports,* 6(1863): 54, 75, 95, 127, 178.
[45] *Ibid.,* 6(1863):57, 74-75, 77-78, 96, 114-15, 133-34, 193, 215, 216, 217.

to keep Indiana out of the Confederacy and reported that Democrats were already communicating with rebel emissaries at Indianapolis.[46] The Republican press joined vigorously in this sordid campaign of calumny. The Indianapolis *Journal* saw a conspiracy in every Democratic move, a rebel plot in every criticism of war policy. No charge appeared to be too rash to impose upon the gullibility of its readers.[47] One Republican delegate finally confessed that his party was as guilty as its opponents of unreasoning partisanship.[48]

Though the coterie of peace men made wild speeches and the Republicans denounced the whole majority party as disloyal, most Democratic legislators were more judicious in their critical review of the policies of the state and Federal governments. Without opposing the war itself, they challenged the expediency or constitutionality of many of the measures related to its prosecution. They vigorously denounced the sanctioning of arbitrary arrests and other infringements upon personal liberty, the abandonment of the Crittenden resolution, the Emancipation Proclamation which they believed would prolong the war, the arming of Negroes, and the exaltation of the powers of the central government.[49]

In addition to their criticism of war policy, Democrats engaged in an enlightening discussion of western grievances which reflected clearly their deep hostility to current economic changes. They protested against high freight rates. A few demanded state railroad regulation and thus foreshadowed a new field of political controversy which culminated in the postwar revolt of western farmers. They also revived the debate between river and railroad

[46] *Ibid.*, 6:15-16, 123-25, 159-60, 187.
[47] Indianapolis *Daily Journal*, January 13, 17, 30, 31, March 13, 1863; Indianapolis *Gazette*, January 30, March 4, 1863; Foulke, *Oliver P. Morton*, 1:240.
[48] *Brevier Legislative Reports*, 6(1863):38.
[49] *Ibid.*, 6:12, 28-29, 35, 41-43, 88, 111-12, 132-33, 140, 149, 181, 197, 227-28.

interests. At the same time Democrats ran through all of their time-tested arguments against Republican financial methods and against the protective tariff.[50] On these issues the prewar alignment of political and economic groups had shifted very little, for the old conflict between Whig and Democratic policies still survived.

3

The ebullitions of the peace faction, the more telling blows of the moderate Democratic majority, and the continued decline of the war spirit worried Hoosier Republicans. Hence during the session of the General Assembly party leaders staged a series of Union meetings. They pictured these gatherings as a spontaneous outburst of popular indignation caused by the traitorous conduct of Democratic legislators. Republican orators cursed their treason, and Governor Morton often rehearsed the livid details of Democratic disloyalty and of the plots for a Northwest Confederacy. The Governor informed his listeners pointedly that a divided North was the last hope of the rebellion. Domestic unity would swiftly end the war.

Each of these meetings endorsed a series of almost identical resolutions. They pledged support to a vigorous prosecution of the war, denounced all proposals for peace or an armistice until the rebels had laid down their arms, repudiated the idea of separation from New England, and lauded the patriotic conduct of Governor Morton. To make a distinction between the government and the administration, they affirmed, "is treasonable, and tends to the destruction of all government."[51]

Meanwhile, reports that the "disloyal" legislature intended to restrict Governor Morton's military powers caused his friends in the army to rally to his support. The

[50] *Brevier Legislative Reports*, 6(1863):78-79, 93-94, 125, 147-48, 153-54, 161, 164-65.
[51] Indianapolis *Daily Journal*, January 15, 20, 27, 29, February 5, 9, 13, 24, 25, 26, 28, March 2, 1863.

The Collapse of Constitutional Government 173

treason stories had a way of reaching Indiana soldiers, and soon the Republican press was filled with letters from them inquiring about the "fire in the rear." Some like General Milroy threatened to return to Indiana "to exterminate treason at the North."[52] Throughout the state furloughed officers were on the stump to speak in behalf of the "soldiers' friend."

The most significant political action taken by Hoosier soldiers in the field was their attempt to instruct the state legislature in its duties through the medium of memorials and resolutions. This movement had the support not only of Indiana troops but also of those from other states with Democratic legislatures. Indeed, the documents sent to various states from widely dispersed regiments were remarkably similar in their wording. Though the Republican press depicted the enterprise as the work of masses of irate volunteers, actually the real impulse seemed to come from small groups of army officers, working in behalf of their chief.

Governor Morton had advance knowledge of this movement among Indiana regiments, and he gave it his approval. To Colonel John T. Wilder, who proposed to begin the work in the Army of the Cumberland, the Governor's military secretary wrote a long letter of encouragement.[53] He described the Democratic legislators as "rampant, furious—crazy, almost, in their opposition to the war and to the State and National Governments." He complained that they "have already showed it to be their purpose to vilify, abuse, embarrass & annoy him [Governor Morton] in every possible way and shape." Therefore, that the soldiers "who know and appreciate his services should raise their voices in his favor in such an hour as this, is in my judgment peculiarly appropri-

---

[52] *Ibid.*, January 20, February 3, 9, 1863; Gen. W. P. Benton to Morton, January 12, 1863, in Telegraphic Correspondence, 10:69.

[53] W. H. H. Terrell to Colonel Wilder, January 24, 1863, J. T Wilder MSS., Indiana Division, Indiana State Library.

ate." Certainly the Governor would "never forget this mark of approbation."

By the end of January resolutions approved in one way or another by groups of Indiana soldiers began to pour in. The troops at Murfreesboro in the Department of the Cumberland sent a lengthy memorial and some resolutions which demanded that the legislature give its unqualified support to the war and cease its partisan wrangling.[54] The regiments at Corinth warned the "traitors" in the legislature to "beware of the terrible retribution that is falling upon your coadjutors at the South, and as [your] crime is tenfold blacker, [we] will swiftly smite you with tenfold more horror should you persist in your damnable deeds of treason." They tendered their thanks to the Governor for his work in their behalf. If he thought it were necessary for them to "return and crush out treason at home," they would "promptly obey a proper order to do so"; for they despised "a sneaking traitor in the rear more than open rebels in front."[55]

Throughout the month of February other soldiers' resolutions, together with an address from General Rosecrans, reached the Indiana legislators. Republicans rejoiced that the army had not "forgotten its citizenship." They declared that when the volunteers returned at the end of the war "the power to punish rebellion will only be changed in its implements, from bullets to ballots."[56] Governor Morton, the "soldiers' friend," was already receiving rich political rewards for his efforts.

In the legislature this action by Hoosier soldiers produced a heated debate. Democrats denounced the army

---

[54] Indianapolis *Daily Journal,* January 26, February 7, 12, 1863; Terrell, *Report,* 1:appendix, 352-54.

[55] Indianapolis *Daily Journal,* February 13, 1863; Terrell, *Report,* 1:appendix, 355-56.

[56] Indianapolis *Daily Journal,* January 26, February 7, 1863; Indianapolis *Gazette,* February 6, 1863.

The Collapse of Constitutional Government 175

officers who were interfering in state politics and attacked Republicans for misrepresenting them to the volunteers. They looked with special alarm upon the threats of military intervention in civil government. Asserting that the whole movement had been a scheme of Morton and his political tools, they refused to be intimidated and warned that any military demonstration would inaugurate revolution at home.[57] Democratic senators replied to the soldiers with a long address, defending their course and assuring them that they had been misled. The senators promised that they would favor no peace which was humiliating to the nation. After listing their efforts to aid the soldiers, they flayed "the political culporteurs sent among . . . [the soldiers] to slander and villify the majority of the legislature."[58] The Democratic press was equally perturbed by the attempt "to drag the soldiers into the politics of the country."[59]

Though various Republican legislators, Union meetings, and soldiers' resolutions accused the Democrats of treason, there was little factual basis for their charges. Most members of the majority party in the General Assembly continued to support the war. They received innumerable resolutions for peace through an immediate armistice and referred them to the proper committee, but it was significant that not one of them so much as reached the floor of either chamber for debate. The final report of the senate committee on Federal relations was a document the loyalty of which was above reproach. While the report eloquently expressed the grievances of the western Democracy, it ignored the proposals for peace and vigorously denounced secession and southern traitors. "The

[57] *Brevier Legislative Reports,* 6(1863) :88-90, 141-45, 154, 159, 169-72, 186, 187, 207, 208, 210, 211, 228-29.
[58] Indiana *Senate Journal,* 1863, pp. 667-81; Indianapolis *Daily State Sentinel,* March 7, 1863.
[59] Indianapolis *Daily State Sentinel,* January 27, February 6, 10, 13, March 5, 1863; New Albany *Weekly Ledger,* January 28, February 18, March 11, 1863; Evansville *Weekly Gazette,* March 7, 1863.

ously denounced secession and southern traitors. "The Union of the States," it stated, "is a necessity; and under no consideration or circumstance will we ever consent to surrender it. We must be one people, under one government and one flag."[60]

It obviously served the ends of Republican politicians to say otherwise, but it was rank partisanship and not treason that discredited the Indiana legislature of 1863. For that Republicans and Democrats were equally responsible.

4

At length the dictates of party politics led to the complete disruption of the General Assembly and to the breakdown of constitutional government in Indiana. All this occurred because the Democratic majority sponsored several partisan measures which were particularly obnoxious to Republicans. Among them was a bill to reapportion the state for legislative and Congressional elections. Its provisions were probably as favorable to the Democrats as the one proposed in 1861 had been to the Republicans. Another bill favored by the majority would have reorganized the state board of benevolent institutions so that it could be packed with Democrats. The dominant party also wanted to create an executive council composed of the secretary of state, the state auditor, treasurer, and attorney general, to act as a curb on the Governor's power.[61]

But the most distasteful project to Republicans was the one through which the Democrats planned to modify the state militia system. Their aim was to reduce the Governor's power over the Indiana Legion by dividing its control between him and the Democratic officers of state. Though the minority swore that such a measure

[60] Indiana *Senate Journal*, 1863, pp. 695-700.
[61] *Brevier Legislative Reports*, 6(1863):119-21; Indianapolis *Daily Journal*, February 10, 1863; Indianapolis *Daily State Sentinel*, March 3, 1863.

should never pass, the Democrats framed a comprehensive military bill which Bayless W. Hanna introduced in the lower chamber on February 17. Among numerous changes in the existing law, this bill provided for the election of company and regimental officers by the men themselves. Brigadier and major generals were to be commissioned by the governor upon the recommendation of a military board comprising the other state officers. Thus Morton would have lost some of his military patronage in the state militia. Democrats could hardly conceal the partisan purpose of this measure, but it nevertheless conformed in every respect to the letter of the state constitution.[62]

As soon as the militia bill came before the legislature Republicans began to attack it violently. They called it an unconstitutional interference with the Governor's prerogatives, and they hauled out their customary charges of treason. They declared the bill a "usurpation and revolution," a device by which "the Copperheads mean to collect every weapon . . . with which they can make a sure blow at the Union, and when they feel fully armed to strike it down." Through control of the militia Democrats would be in a position to inaugurate their secession schemes, for the state would have lost its "only protection against a rebel conspiracy."[63]

That the minority would break a quorum to prevent the enactment of the military bill was generally expected. But the first Republican bolt occurred on February 25 in order to block the passage of the reapportionment bill and other measures which had not met their approval.[64] The next day, after the military bill was engrossed and ready for a vote, all but four of the house minority

[62] Indianapolis *Daily State Sentinel*, January 29, February 3, 18, 1863; *Brevier Legislative Reports*, 6(1863):99, 155; Pliny Hoagland to Allen Hamilton, February 20, 1863, Allen Hamilton MSS.; Terrell, *Report*, 1:262; Foulke, *Oliver P. Morton*, 1:237n.
[63] Indianapolis *Daily Journal*, January 30, February 6, 7, 19, 1863.
[64] *Ibid.*, February 28, 1863.

again left their seats. With the Governor's approval they went in a body to Madison on the Ohio River where they could escape to Kentucky if the majority sought to force their return.[65] Then the bolters notified the Democrats that they would remain away as long as the military bill was before the house. When all efforts at compromise failed, legislative business was at a standstill.

On March 8, the regular session of the General Assembly came to an end as prescribed by the constitution. The members had passed no significant legislation, and they had made no appropriations for the following biennium. In retrospect the bald partisanship of the Democrats and the shabby attempt of Republicans to shield their disorganizing tactics behind the threadbare cloak of patriotism made a sordid picture. The pious comments of Democratic leaders upon the evils of bolting came with an ill grace from a party which had pursued the same course two years before. Yet the practice of breaking a quorum finds no justification in political ethics at any time. On this occasion it was clear that Republicans had bolted to prevent the passage of other measures besides the military bill.

Actually there is room for a reasonable doubt that the military bill could ever have passed.[66] Certainly the minority fled from the lower chamber with undue haste. The bill still had to pass through the senate, and the Governor still had the veto power. Moreover, the bolters refused to return even for the last two days of the session when there was not sufficient time to pass any measure which did not meet Republican approval.[67]

[65] *Brevier Legislative Reports*, 6(1863):175-76; Foulke, *Oliver P. Morton*, 1:237-39.

[66] Martin M. Ray insisted that the bill would have failed to pass even the house. *Brevier Legislative Reports*, 6(1863):233.

[67] To pass any measure during the last two days would have required the suspension of rules. Such action needed a two-thirds vote in either house, and Republicans were numerically strong enough to prevent it for any bill they opposed. Indianapolis *Daily State Sentinel*, March 6, 9, 1863.

Finally, Republicans, for political reasons, attached far greater significance to the military bill than it ever deserved. The whole wretched affair found most of its meaning in terms of a quest for political capital and a struggle for control of state military patronage.

But whatever the merits of the case, the Republicans apparently outmaneuvered their Democratic foes.[68] They assured the distracted Hoosiers that they had rescued the state from a "vile conspiracy" against the constitution and government.[69] Governor Morton at once incorporated the affair into his indictment of the Democracy for treason, and he never tired of rehearsing the story of how quick action had saved Indiana for the Union. The Governor waged many a future campaign upon no greater issue.

5

The farce which was played in Indiana's legislative halls in the winter of 1863 was followed by a more serious attempt at extralegal state government and finance. Since the General Assembly had failed to pass appropriation bills, Democrats expected that Morton would soon be forced to call a special session. But they underestimated his resourcefulness. Republicans frequently asserted that another meeting of the legislature would be a waste of the people's money, and vowed that the "rebels" should have no further opportunity "to consummate their schemes of revolution."[70] On June 9, the Governor conferred with the Republican legislators, and they readily endorsed his decision.[71] In consequence the Indiana General Assembly did not convene again until the regular session in January, 1865.

Posing as the last refuge for loyal Hoosiers, Governor

---

[68] F. W. Matthis to William H. English, March 6, 1863, English Collection.
[69] Indianapolis *Daily Journal*, March 11, 1863.
[70] *Ibid.*, March 6, June 13, 16, July 16, December 14, 1863.
[71] Indianapolis *Daily State Sentinel*, June 10, 1863; Foulke, *Oliver P. Morton*, 1:259.

Morton then set out to administer the state alone. His first problem was to secure money to support his government for the next two years. The Federal War Department immediately gave him limited aid by assuming some of the state's outstanding military debts.[72] But from that point on the Governor ignored the constitution and laws and resorted to devious methods to raise funds.

In March Morton went to Washington to collect $90,000 due the state for ammunition furnished by the Indiana arsenal. The *Journal* announced in triumph that the money would be used to support the benevolent institutions and carry on the other functions of the government.[73] Democrats insisted that the money must be paid immediately into the state treasury unless the Governor wished to expose himself to the penalties of the embezzlement law.[74] Morton assumed the risk, refused to surrender the funds, and continued to operate the arsenal as a kind of private enterprise.

At the same time the Governor directed his secretaries to send appeals to Republican county officials for additional funds to help him avoid a special legislative session. Sixteen counties responded with loans amounting to $90,000 for which they received Morton's personal receipt and a promise of a reasonable rate of interest. By the terms of these agreements the money was to be used to help support state institutions and to aid sick and wounded Indiana soldiers.[75] Morton also obtained loans, totaling $45,000, from private sources.[76]

[72] Morton to Gen. J. T. Boyle, March 20, 1863, in Telegraphic Correspondence, 16:150; Foulke, *Oliver P. Morton,* 1:255-56.

[73] Indianapolis *Daily Journal,* April 3, 4, 1863.

[74] Indianapolis *Daily State Sentinel,* April 3, 6, August 12, 13, 15, 1863.

[75] Many letters dealing with these negotiations are in the Morton Letter Press Books and Telegraphic Correspondence. See also Financial Secretary Terrell's report of the state bureau of finance in Indiana *Documentary Journal,* 1865, pt. 1:no. 1.

[76] Twenty thousand dollars were received from citizens of Wayne County; $15,000 from the Terre Haute and Richmond Railroad; and $10,000 from the W. R. McKeen Bank of Terre Haute. *Ibid.,* 1865, pt. 1:no. 1:10.

The Collapse of Constitutional Government 181

Finally, the Governor again approached the national administration for further financial aid. Neither Secretary Chase nor President Lincoln could find authority to grant his request, but they referred him to the War Department. Stanton, who completely approved of Morton's plans, had at his disposal a $2,000,000 fund for use in states threatened with rebellion. The Secretary of War decided that Indiana came within that category, and he gave Morton $250,000 to support the Legion and for other military purposes.[77] With these combined funds, and with careful financial management, the Governor carried on the state government almost to the end of the war.

Morton could not deposit this money in the state treasury because he would have no means of forcing the Democratic treasurer to pay it out again. Therefore he simply ignored the state auditor and treasurer and created his own financial department. In April he organized a bureau of finance and placed it under the direction of W. H. H. Terrell who had previously been his military secretary. The funds were kept in a safe which the Governor had purchased and placed in his office.[78] Terrell was responsible to Morton alone; the regular state officers virtually ceased to function. In that extraordinary fashion Indiana finances were administered until 1865.

The last fiscal problem which confronted Governor Morton was the payment of the interest upon the public debt. The money for the interest, which would fall due on July 1, 1863, and every sixth month thereafter, was in the state treasury, but the legislature had made no specific appropriation for its payment. Attorney General Oscar B. Hord informed Auditor Joseph Ristine that in

---

[77] J. J. Brown to Morton, April 27, 1863, and Morton to Brown, April 29, 1863, in Telegraphic Correspondence, 10:233-34; Foulke, *Oliver P. Morton*, 1:260-61, 267-68; Indiana *House Journal*, 1865, pp. 36-37; Indiana *Documentary Journal*, 1865, pt. 2:no. 3.

[78] Indianapolis *Daily State Sentinel*, June 10, 1863. See also report of bureau of finance in Indiana *Documentary Journal*, 1865, pt. 1:no. 1.

his opinion no funds could be drawn from the treasury for any purpose without a specific appropriation. Hord cited statutory and constitutional law to substantiate his position. Therefore, he concluded, if the state defaulted, the responsibility would rest solely upon the Republican party.[79]

Morton replied to this opinion in a long letter to James Winslow of the New York banking firm of Winslow, Lanier & Company. The letter was printed and circulated in pamphlet form. In it the Governor developed an elaborate argument to prove that no legislative appropriation was needed for the payment of the interest on the state debt. Republicans and Democrats debated the issue for many weeks, but after much legal hairsplitting they merely established the fact that the law was not clear upon the point involved.[80]

To fortify their position Hord and Ristine arranged a test case which they ultimately carried to the state supreme court. On June 5 the court ruled that the auditor and treasurer had no authority to pay the interest without a specific legislative appropriation. Since Democratic judges controlled the court, the Governor's friends attacked the decision as partisan and accused the judges of conspiring with the "repudiators." When State Treasurer Matthew L. Brett subsequently refused to pay the interest, the Republicans declared that his action was only justified by "contemptible quibbles, and the hocus-pocus of a sham lawsuit."[81]

After the Democratic state officers refused to cooperate with him, Morton turned to Winslow, Lanier & Company for help. The interest of this New York

---

[79] Indianapolis *Daily State Sentinel,* April 8, 1863.

[80] Indiana *Documentary Journal,* 1865, pt. 2:no. 16; Indianapolis *Daily State Sentinel,* May 5, 9, 11, 1863; Indianapolis *Daily Journal,* May 4, 1863.

[81] Indiana Supreme Court *Reports,* 20:345-83; Indianapolis *Daily Journal,* May 12, June 12, 13, 1863; Indianapolis *Daily State Sentinel,* May 14, 16, 19, June 6, 8, 1863; Foulke, *Oliver P. Morton,* 1:257-59.

banking house in Indiana finances caused it to be deeply concerned about the success of the Governor's schemes. In June Lanier agreed to place $160,000 to Indiana's credit and authorized the agent of state to draw upon that sum to pay the interest due on July 1. He also agreed to make similar provisions for all subsequent interest payments through January 1, 1865. Lanier, "trusting entirely in the good faith of the State," asked Morton for no specific understanding regarding interest or compensation for the advances made.[82]

But this extraordinary arrangement did not entirely solve the problem. To pay the interest it was necessary to obtain a list of the bona fide bondholders from John C. Walker, the Democratic state agent, because many of Stover's fraudulent bonds remained in circulation. When Lanier asked him for the list, Walker refused to surrender it. In a public letter the state agent asserted that he would not become a party to the Governor's illegal acts. He denied that Morton's arrangement with Lanier actually paid the interest; instead it simply transferred part of the state debt from the bondholders to Lanier's bank. The Governor's objective, he insisted, was not to save the state's credit but to advance "his partisan politics and his selfish ambition." Lanier then suggested that Walker would not be held personally responsible for these financial transactions, but Walker still would not give up the list. The proper remedy, he said, was to call a special legislative session.[83] In consequence July 1 passed without the interest being paid.

[82] Foulke, *Oliver P. Morton,* 1:262; Indianapolis *Daily Journal,* June 29, 1863. During these negotiations Auditor Ristine refused all requests for his co-operation. He insisted that a special session of the legislature was the proper remedy and produced numerous letters from Democratic legislators promising that appropriations would be made immediately. Morton, however, was not interested. Telegraphic Correspondence, 11:77; Indianapolis *Daily State Sentinel,* December 16, 1863.

[83] The correspondence between Walker and Lanier was printed in Indianapolis *Daily State Sentinel,* July 1, 1863; Indianapolis *Daily Journal,* July 2, 6, 1863; Indiana *Documentary Journal,* 1865, pt. 2:560-67.

Near the end of the year Auditor Ristine, convinced that Morton could not be forced to call the legislature into session, finally agreed to let the Governor's secretary take from his books the names of the holders of state bonds. In December the victorious Governor issued a proclamation to the people of Indiana in which he announced that Winslow, Lanier & Company would begin at once to pay the July interest. From then until 1865 these bankers advanced approximately $600,000 to the state for that purpose.[84] Meanwhile, the Democratic press asserted that these transactions were fraudulent, that the payments were a "gratuity," and that Morton's financial allies would never be reimbursed if it could be prevented.[85]

6

Governor Morton's triumph over the Indiana Democracy was complete. None knew better than the Democrats themselves how effective his strategy had been, and they deeply resented his ruthless methods. They accused him of having Napoleonic ambitions to create a personal dictatorship. He had, they said, destroyed Indiana's representative government. He was laboring under the hallucination that he was the State. Because the Governor could not tolerate criticism, he fell back on such warnings as "Remember, when you strike at me, you strike at *the* Government." Through his pretended patriotism he was "forever trying to shelter himself under the wings of the Government."[86] "The people of Indian-

---

[84] W. H. H. Terrell to Morton, November 25, 26, 1863, and Morton to Terrell, November 25, 1863, in Telegraphic Correspondence, 5:56-57; Indianapolis *Daily Journal*, December 11, 1863, January 13, February 23, April 2, 1864; Cottman, "James F. D. Lanier," in *Indiana Magazine of History*, 22:201; Foulke, *Oliver P. Morton*, 1:268-69; Indiana *House Journal*, 1865, p. 40.

[85] Indianapolis *Daily State Sentinel*, December 12, 1863; Covington *Friend*, quoted in *ibid.*, December 31, 1863.

[86] *Ibid.*, March 12, April 16, June 9, 10, 17, 18, 22, August 1, 12, 13, 1863; New Albany *Weekly Ledger*, May 18, 27, November 18, 1863.

The Collapse of Constitutional Government 185

apolis were blessed with a refreshing shower of rain yesterday," mocked the *Sentinel*. "They should be thankful, therefore, to the 'gigantic efforts' of O. P. M."[87]

But from this fierce partisanship one ominous fact protruded: in Indiana the bitter hatreds and swift social changes generated by the Civil War had caused a temporary collapse of constitutional government. Like the Tudors of old, with the similar excuse of a national emergency, Governor Morton had established himself as a virtual dictator. His only restraint was the influence of public opinion, and that influence was distorted by war hysteria. Standing as a bright beacon for loyal men, Morton could justify his course—and he often felt the need to do it—in terms of a patriotic desire to save the nation from its enemies.[88] It was an ominous precedent.

Those were revolutionary times, and Morton obviously enjoyed his part in building a new nation. Only the conservative Democracy shrieked in protest, for its worst fears now seemed to have been realized.

[87] Indianapolis *Daily State Sentinel*, August 4, 1863.
[88] For a constitutional justification of Morton's acts, through a singularly broad interpretation of executive powers, see Indianapolis *Daily Journal*, June 30, 1863.

CHAPTER 9
THE BACKWASH OF WAR

AMID the confusion and discord caused by the clash of armies and angry politicians the Hoosiers became increasingly aware that the Civil War was reshaping the national character. Distracted by the excitement of battles, and living too close to unfolding events for a clear perspective, few men could grasp the full meaning of these momentous changes. Yet it seemed apparent enough to almost everyone that henceforth the Americans would be "a different people" and that the country was entering upon "a new stage of being."[1] "Verily," exulted Julian, "the day of Conservatism is over, and the reign of Radicalism has been fairly ushered in."[2]

The local sponsors of "Progress" welcomed these revolutionary results of military strife and pronounced them good. They pictured the war as a "refining ordeal" which would develop "the virtues of the American people" and strengthen the national heritage of liberty and democratic government. The United States would "from the crucible of war and the sacrifice of blood, present a more perfect civilization . . . than the world has ever seen."[3]

---

[1] Evansville *Weekly Gazette,* October 12, 1861; Indianapolis *Gazette,* February 6, 1864; Kenneth M. Stampp, "The Impact of the Civil War upon Hoosier Society," in *Indiana Magazine of History,* 38(1942):1-16.

[2] Centreville *Indiana True Republican,* June 11, 1863.

[3] Indianapolis *Daily Journal,* February 9, June 28, 1864.

But this optimistic description of a regenerate people distorted the Indiana scene during these four years of civil strife. Actually Hoosier society was a perplexing mixture of heroic, self-sacrificing patriotism and unblushing avarice, of warm idealism and calloused cynicism. There was much to commend in the devotion of the common people to the soldiers' welfare and in the efforts stimulated by Governor Morton to aid the destitute families of the volunteers. Such endeavors manifested a social consciousness and co-operative spirit rarely seen in that individualistic age.

Unfortunately there was another and less attractive side to Indiana's wartime society. The suffering and privation, the broken families, the growing lists of native sons killed in action, the mutilated men, and the coffins lining the walls of the Indianapolis depot—all these formed parts of the war experience. Soon people became hardened and habituated to such incidences of war. Moreover, the appeal to arms seemed to encourage the growth of vice at least as much as it did virtue, for the war brought with it a decided slackening of moral standards.[4] Gambling and heavy drinking were common; prostitutes plied their trade unmolested; crime increased. Newspapers abounded in accounts of street brawls, of the depredations of lawless bands of men, of murders and thefts.

For the Hoosier volunteers the hardships of army life and close association with death appeared to be anything but a "refining ordeal." Soldiers made rash threats of forcible intervention in local politics, and some of them committed acts of violence against those whose conduct or opinions failed to meet their approval. Private citizens registered countless complaints against soldiers who disregarded other men's rights and property, and to no small extent the volunteers shared responsibility for many

---

[4] Holliday, *Indianapolis and the Civil* War, 574, 585-86.

of the disturbances that occurred in Indiana.⁵ Discipline in the Union army was often lax. In May, 1863, the commander of the district of Indiana issued a general order which called attention to the numerous reports of soldiers on duty in the state exceeding their authority and acting in an "arrogant overbearing manner." Such reprehensible conduct, he warned, must cease for the public good.⁶ Difficulties of this nature were perhaps inevitable when a civilian army was temporarily released from normal legal restraints.

Equally distressing was the unhappy spectacle of war profiteering. It appeared during the first year of war when state bonds were marketed.⁷ Indiana also had its quota of "shoddy contractors" who were willing to make huge profits by swindling state and national governments in filling war orders.⁸ Some of the critics defined the conflict as a "contractors war" and cried out against the patriots who had "enriched themselves out of the . . . very miseries of the country."⁹

While heavy taxes and the inevitable wartime inflation brought distress to men on fixed salaries and to soldiers' families, others grew rich and lived accordingly. For some the war was a period of prosperity and material abundance. But dissatisfied Hoosiers called it an era of "criminal extravagance . . . without parallel," and asserted that the resources of the country were being

---

⁵ W. H. H. Terrell, military secretary to Governor Morton, to Col. Isaac P. Gray, November 6, 1862, in Morton Letter Press Books, 1(June 1862-January 1863):286-87; Indianapolis *Daily Journal,* August 6, 1863; Indianapolis *Daily State Sentinel,* August 6, 11, 1863; New Albany *Weekly Ledger,* July 1, 1863; Terrell, *Report,* 1:398.

⁶ Indianapolis *Daily Journal,* May 2, 1863.

⁷ *Ibid.,* July 9, 1861.

⁸ General Carrington to U. S. Adjutant General Thomas, October 26, 1862, typed copy in bound volume labeled Carrington Papers, Archives Division; Indianapolis *Daily Journal,* August 23, 1861; Indianapolis *Daily State Sentinel,* November 21, 23, 1861.

⁹ Indianapolis *Daily State Sentinel,* September 4, 1863, March 6, 1865.

"wasted in riotous living."[10] These were inauspicious beginnings for the nation's "new stage of being."

2

Meanwhile, vast economic changes were sweeping across Indiana and the nation. Democratic concepts of political economy, so long predominant, were giving way to the new principles of Republicanism. Sadly the old Jacksonians watched the destruction of their system and the advance of industrial capitalism.

In southern Indiana the prostrate river interests still refused to abandon their fear of railroad transportation and attributed all their adversities to grasping eastern capitalists.[11] Yet ultimately they were forced to adjust themselves to the fact that the war was ruining their southern market and changing the paths of commerce. The demands of Europe and of the East had diverted much of their trade, and consolidating railroads were fast growing up to the needs of the country.[12] The Indianapolis *Journal* mocked those who clung to the tradition of western dependence upon the South and noted that the eastern and southern markets could not be compared "with the arithmetic of five years ago."[13]

Not only the high tariff, but changes in Federal banking and currency policies further enraged the Jacksonian Democrats. Secession had almost ruined some of Indiana's free banks which had invested heavily in southern state bonds, and even the state bank was soon forced to suspend specie payments.[14] These blows to local banking and the government's issuance of large quantities of "greenbacks" raised a protest against the growth of a

---

[10] *Ibid.*, May 4, 1864.

[11] Indianapolis *Daily Journal*, September 9, 1861, February 17, 1862, June 3, 1863; New Albany *Weekly Ledger*, February 11, April 15, August 26, September 16, 1863; Evansville *Weekly Gazette*, December 19, 1863.

[12] New Albany *Weekly Ledger*, September 2, 1863; Smith, *The Borderland in the Civil War*, 324-26.

[13] Indianapolis *Daily Journal*, November 3, 1862.

[14] *Ibid.*, July 8, 9, 1861, March 10, 1862.

"political money power" whose financial policies were based upon a "foundation of sand." Democrats pessimistically predicted that economic ruin and the collapse of government credit were imminent.[15]

Early in 1863 western Jacksonians were shocked when Congress created a new system of national banking. In their eyes this act was a symbol of the complete abandonment of Democratic doctrines. But Republican businessmen and some wealthy Democrats welcomed it. Beginning with the First National Bank of Indianapolis, directed by William H. English (a Democratic politician), a network of these institutions quickly covered the state. By 1864 Indiana possessed thirty-one national banks which had all but won the field from the state banks.[16] Old-line Democrats predicted disastrous consequences from the revival of this Whig heresy. The inevitable result, they said, would be the growth of a northern financial aristocracy which simply wished to replace what they termed the "slavocracy." "Mr. Chase," added the *Sentinel,* "says the aristocrats of the South lord it over black men, but what will the people gain if there is substituted in its place an aristocracy that will domineer over white men?"[17]

Despite Democratic pessimism and the inevitable changes and dislocations of these years, the war brought an unprecedented degree of prosperity to Indiana. Increasing eastern and foreign markets meant high prices for the products of her farms; agriculture flourished and expanded as never before. Local railroads, like all commercial enterprises, did a thriving business and made

[15] Indianapolis *Daily State Sentinel,* February 10, September 22, 25, November 23, 1863.

[16] Indianapolis *Daily Journal,* June 6, 1863, January 4, June 29, 1864, March 8, 1865. Hugh McCulloch, former president of the Indiana State Bank, became comptroller of the currency under the national banking system. Most branches of the state bank obtained national bank charters after the war.

[17] Indianapolis *Daily State Sentinel,* October 27, 1863.

handsome profits.[18] The invigorating influence of the war was especially noticeable at Indianapolis where old industries grew rapidly, new establishments sprang up in mushroom fashion, and the population doubled.[19] In the midst of all this activity the *Journal* glowed at "the universal prosperity of all classes" and noted contentedly that "the nation wages war and prospers!"[20]

The war also seemed destined to modify the structure of American government. Conservative Indiana Democrats clung stubbornly to the principles of state rights, and local party gatherings frequently re-endorsed the Virginia and Kentucky Resolutions. They expressed alarm at the current trend toward a centralization of power and deplored the abject surrender of northern governors to Federal tyranny. State governors, they said, acted "as though they themselves and their fellow-citizens *belonged* to the Administration." They also feared that the growing power of military authorities responsible only to the central government would lead to the final obliteration of state lines and to the reduction of states to mere administrative districts. And so the Democracy accused Republicans of attempting a revolution in government and of returning to the "sentiments entertained by Hamilton and Adams."[21]

3

By 1863 the Civil War had assumed the proportions of a protracted and gigantic struggle which promised to modify most of America's institutions. Then many Hoosiers began to look upon the Crittenden resolution of 1861 as an inadequate justification for their cause.

---

[18] Terrell, *Report,* 1:396.
[19] Indianapolis *Daily State Sentinel,* May 25, 1862, August 24, September 16, 1864; Indianapolis *Daily Journal,* July 12, 1862, April 28, 1863, November 9, 1864; Centreville *Indiana True Republican,* December 25, 1862; Holliday, *Indianapolis and the Civil War,* 560, 569, 583-84, 588.
[20] Indianapolis *Daily Journal,* February 9, 1864.
[21] Indianapolis *Daily State Sentinel,* October 29, 1861, April 22, July 18, September 8, 19, November 6, 1863.

Hence the state's war leaders proceeded to formulate a broader moral appeal. Gradually their propaganda organizations unfolded and described a series of issues and objectives which identified the Union cause with every human virtue. Thereafter, Indiana's sons fought and died for something far more sublime than the mere preservation of the Union. The Indianapolis *Journal* assured them that they were engaged in a crusade for freedom "against one of the most cruel and profligate despotisms in the history of time—against a blasphemous attempt to rear an empire on the corner stone of human slavery. We are fighting for national existence, for good government, for law and order, for liberty and civilization."[22]

Fortified with these lofty principles, loyal speakers and the loyal press worked zealously to bring this message to the Indiana people. The Union party supplemented their efforts by circulating thousands of pamphlets which discussed the causes and aims of the war as well as the record of the "disloyal Democracy." Additional floods of propaganda pamphlets poured into Indiana from the East, especially from the New York and New England Loyal Publications Societies and from the Union League. In the spring of 1863 A. H. Conner established a loyal-documents room in Indianapolis from which these pamphlets could be distributed throughout the state.[23] The New England Loyal Publications Society also sent out large quantities of printed material to the Indiana press, and

---

[22] Indianapolis *Daily Journal,* April 30, 1863.

[23] W. H. H. Terrell to G. W. Nichols, June 5, 1863, and Terrell to Charles Eliot Norton, June 27, 1863, in New England Loyal Publications Society MSS., Boston Public Library. The author is indebted to Professor Frank Freidel of Vassar College for the use of photostatic copies of items in the collection. Morton to W. Wallace, May 2, 1863, Henry K. English MSS., Indiana Division, Indiana State Library; W. R. Holloway to —, May 8, 1863, in Morton Letter Press Books; W. R. Holloway to Terrell, May 16, 1863, in Telegraphic Correspondence, 11:6; Indianapolis *Daily Journal,* May 12, 1863.

by 1863 at least seventy-six Union newspapers were publishing its items more or less regularly.[24]

Republican secret societies provided still another means of disseminating Union propaganda. The Union clubs which appeared in Indiana in 1862 were the first local organizations of that nature. National headquarters were at Louisville, but Indiana had a central state organization with the power to grant charters to subordinate clubs. Each club possessed all the usual paraphernalia common to secret societies: codes, passwords, mysterious signs, elaborate rituals, and a cryptographical alphabet for secret messages. These Union clubs were formed upon a military basis and spoke much of arming against disloyal Hoosiers, but their greatest work appeared to be the distribution of loyal documents.[25]

By 1863 the Indiana Union Clubs had been replaced by new secret organizations, especially the Strong Bands, National Leagues, and Loyal Leagues. These societies were also supposed to provide defense against "northern rebels," but like their predecessors they served primarily as propaganda agencies.[26] This was equally true of the Indiana Union Leagues whose proceedings were often secret and who sought occasionally to secure public arms to suppress domestic "traitors."[27] All of these groups provided broad channels for the circulation of the Union party's political and war propaganda.

[24] J. B. Harrison to Charles Eliot Norton, June 27, August 10, 1863, and printed circular dated February 1, 1864, in New England Loyal Publications Society MSS.

[25] Correspondence between the officers of the Union clubs, as well as charters, circulars, codes, and other material, is in the Henry K. English MSS.

[26] Indianapolis *Daily Journal,* April 21, 1863, June 20, 1865; Indianapolis *Gazette,* March 6, 1863; Fesler, "Secret Political Societies," in *Indiana Magazine of History,* 14:239-40.

[27] A. C. Harris to Morton, May 6, 1863, Archives Division, Indiana State Library; Indianapolis *Gazette,* March 28, 1863.

4

Despite the contemporary justification of the conflict in terms of great moral issues, the Civil War had a strange and appalling effect upon the minds of Hoosiers. The bitter dispute between the champions and opponents of social and economic change, the inevitable physical and mental distress experienced by a nation at war, and the powerful influence of Union propaganda transformed many people into blind fanatics. They seemed to have lost their capacity to think rationally, for the virus of war hysteria poisoned the minds of leaders and people alike.

War hysteria was manifested not only in the Hoosiers' hatred of the South but also in their morbid suspicion of those at home whose opinions did not coincide with their own. Loyal citizens lived in panicky fear of their own neighbors and lumped all dissenters in the single category of traitors. The Republicans assured people that peace could come only "through the red gates of war," and that unless a man gave unqualified support to the war and was "openly, heartily, and intensely loyal," he would be "suspected of secession proclivities."[28] Upon that premise Union party advocates continued to denounce the Democracy as disloyal.

The columns of Republican papers were filled with accounts of the military drills and traitorous plots of secret Democratic societies. These allegedly illustrated that the state was, "as Governor Morton strikingly expressed it, 'perfectly cavernous' with disloyal organizations."[29] Union editors printed every rumor and wild report they received in letters from frenzied patriots. The authors of these letters described the conspiracies

---

[28] Indianapolis *Daily Journal,* January 17, March 16, 1863, February 27, 1864.

[29] *Ibid.,* February 2, 21, March 12, 21, 23, April 1, 3, 14, June 13, August 20, 1863. The same kind of material filled the columns of the Indianapolis *Gazette.*

being hatched by their neighbors, the secret aid being given to the rebels, and the shameful persecution of Union men. They expressed horror that some men boldly wore "Copperhead" emblems and were so depraved as to "glory in being butternuts." Often they demanded that all such traitors be arrested and tried for treason, or that they be "cleaned out" through the action of vigilance committees.[30] The Governor also received frantic letters from every quarter of the state which related the activities of Democrats who cursed Union men and cheered for Jeff Davis and reported the drills and meetings of treasonable societies in adjoining townships or counties.[31] The general war hysteria was equally well portrayed in the correspondence of Republican secret societies whose members regarded themselves as the last bulwark against domestic revolution.[32]

It was not strange that such an atmosphere of partisanship, suspicion, and fear produced numerous instances of personal violence. Outbreaks of that nature first became serious in the spring of 1863 and continued sporadically thereafter. As usual the Republican press pictured these affairs as the products of a widespread treasonable conspiracy. Actually they were the fruits of the general hysteria, of lawless bands associated with neither party, of refractory soldiers, and of local and personal feuds.[33]

Many affrays grew out of soldiers' attacks upon Democratic newspapers, their brawls with private citizens,

[30] See especially Indianapolis *Daily Journal,* September 2, 25, 1861, March 18, 1863.

[31] Many such letters are in the files pertaining to Governor Morton's administration in the Archives Division, Indiana State Library. Several are printed in Harvey Wish (ed.), "Civil War Letters and Dispatches," in *Indiana Magazine of History,* 33(1937):62-74.

[32] See, for example, Corresponding Secretary Indiana Union Club to J. K. English, June 23 [1862?], Henry K. English MSS.

[33] Terrell, *Report,* 1:278 ff.; Fesler, "Secret Political Societies," in *Indiana Magazine of History,* 14:208-10.

and their efforts to vote illegally in the spring elections.[34] Republican reports that Representative Voorhees had denounced the soldiers as "Lincoln Dogs" (which he vigorously denied) brought him into an encounter with a band of volunteers.[35] Conflicts among private citizens were most common in the hilly and wooded counties south of Indianapolis, though they also occurred in the northern counties. From the southern region emanated endless accounts of riots at political meetings, of depredations by mobs of armed men, of organized efforts to protect deserters, and of private quarrels which ended in shooting. These incidents often caused state or military authorities to send out troops who would seize quantities of arms, make arrests, and at times only aggravate the situation by their own indecorous conduct.[36] Few Hoosiers, it appeared, were finding the war to be a refining ordeal.

5

During the general excitement in the spring of 1863 Democrats were further alarmed by the conduct of officers in the military Department of the Ohio to which

[34] Indianapolis *Daily State Sentinel,* March 17, April 7, 9, 1863, March 7, 1864; Indianapolis *Daily Journal,* March 18, 31, April 7, 1863; Centreville *Indiana True Republican,* March 19, 1863.

[35] Indianapolis *Daily Journal,* August 14, September 13, 16, 1863; Indianapolis *Daily State Sentinel,* September 15, 1863; New Albany *Weekly Ledger,* September 25, 1863.

[36] Indianapolis *Daily State Sentinel,* March 30, April 6, 20, 23, 27, June 25, September 14, October 16, 1863; Indianapolis *Daily Journal,* March 12, 31, April 20, 22, August 4, 13, 14, September 7, 8, 24, 1863. The following dispatch to the Executive Department, dated May 5, 1863, gives an account of an outbreak at Fort Wayne: "The riot here was an organized attempt to break up our union meeting. Threats had been made that it should not be held. During the day several attempts were made but promptly put down by Union men. In the evening, squads of Butternuts, armed with clubs, stones, &c, made attacks in different parts of the city, badly wounding many Union men. A force of seventy five (75) to one hundred (100) attacked the excursion train leaving on the Chicago road, stoned the train, hurting several persons badly. No lives were lost. Our city officials were entirely indifferent. The election passing off quietly today." Telegraphic Correspondence, 10:247.

Indiana was attached. The tactless and highhanded action of various generals who had authority in the state intensified the local political conflict.

In March, 1863, General Horatio G. Wright, commander of the Department of the Ohio, organized Indiana into a subordinate military district and placed it under the command of General Henry B. Carrington of the U. S. Volunteers.[37] Carrington assumed his new position with a somewhat officious proclamation instructing the people in their duties as loyal citizens, but he tried thereafter to conduct himself judiciously. Nevertheless, the *Sentinel* saw in the General's presence "a new feature in the history of our State," for never before had "Indiana been placed under military rule." His power "overrides the sovereignty and independence of the State."[38]

A few days later General Ambrose E. Burnside superseded General Wright in the Department of the Ohio. Burnside immediately displayed a propensity for arbitrary rule and a singular disregard for the finer points of democratic government. As soon as he reached Cincinnati he caused a furor by issuing General Order Number 38, which proclaimed that he, as commanding general, would not tolerate "the habit of declaring sympathy for the enemy" or permit "expressed or implied" treasonable conduct.[39] Democrats raised an angry protest against the unheard of principle of "implied treason," especially when its interpretation rested solely in the hands of a military officer. The subsequent arrest of Clement L. Vallandigham of Ohio and the suppression of the Chicago *Times* gave Indiana Democrats new opportunities to mourn the death of constitutional liberty.

Even Morton objected to Burnside's frequent resort

---

[37] *Official Records,* 1 series, 23:pt. 2:168.
[38] Indianapolis *Daily State Sentinel,* March 27, 1863.
[39] *Official Records,* 1 series, 23:pt. 2:147, 237.

to arbitrary arrests.⁴⁰ But Burnside advised Carrington that in his opinion the military power "used prudently and quietly" would silence the disaffection in the West.⁴¹ The General had little faith in the loyalty of Indiana, and it was only Morton's protest that prevented the establishment of martial law in his state. ⁴² The Governor's political sense stood him in good stead on that occasion.

On April 22, despite the opposition of Morton, General Milo S. Hascall, a native Hoosier, was appointed to replace Carrington as commander of the District of Indiana.⁴³ Hascall had less faith in Indiana's loyalty than Burnside, and arrived with the belief that the state was in virtual rebellion.⁴⁴ Feeling the need for immediate vigorous action, he issued General Order Number 9, which stated that newspapers or speakers who encouraged resistance to the laws of Congress or endeavored "to bring the war policy of the Government into disrepute" would be treated as violators of Burnside's earlier edict.⁴⁵

The Republican press blessed Hascall's action as "most admirable," but the Democrats vigorously defended their right to discuss administration policies and denounced the order as incendiary. Congressman Joseph K. Edger-

---

⁴⁰ W. R. Holloway to Stanton, October 1, 1863, in Morton Letter Press Books, 3(September 1863-December 1866):28-29; Indianapolis *Daily State Sentinel,* May 25, 1863.

⁴¹ Burnside to Carrington, April 21, 1863, typed copy in bound volume labeled Carrington Papers, Archives Division, Indiana State Library.

⁴²Morton to Burnside, July 11, 1863, in Telegraphic Correspondence, 16:254; *Official Records,* 1 series, 23:pt. 1:398, 728.

⁴³ *Official Records,* 1 series, 23:pt. 2:193-94, 216-17, 326; Indianapolis *Daily Journal,* April 23, 1863. See also typed copy of documents relating to this in bound volume labeled Carrington Papers, Archives Division.

⁴⁴ Hascall's account of his service as commander of the District of Indiana is included in a brief manuscript autobiography in the Archives Division, Indiana State Library. See also his report to Adjutant General Terrell in Terrell's *Report,* 1:appendix, 276-77.

⁴⁵ Indianapolis *Daily State Sentinel,* April 27, 1863; *Official Records,* 2 series, 5:485.

ton, of Fort Wayne, wrote a public letter to the commander deploring the fact that free speech and a free press were to be suppressed in Indiana.[46] Several Democratic newspapers courted martyrdom by openly declaring their intention to violate the order and by attacking its author. In each case Hascall informed them promptly that they must retract their statements or cease publication.[47] The Plymouth *Democrat* was one of the newspapers which refused to recant, and its editor was arrested and sent to Cincinnati.[48] The Columbia City *News* came out dressed in mourning when it printed Hascall's letter. "We have nothing to retract," it replied. "We await the order of General Hascall with pleasure. The wicked alone flee from the wrath of an offended Diety."[49]

On May 20, the Indiana Democracy assembled in a great mass convention at Indianapolis and thus brought on the state's most dramatic experience with wartime violence and military meddling. The recent acts of Burnside and Hascall and the memory of past difficulties at Democratic gatherings in Indianapolis caused many of the party faithful to attend the meeting prepared for trouble.

Alarmed by rumors that the Knights of the Golden Circle planned to convert the convention into a revolutionary uprising, General Hascall mobilized the available infantry, cavalry, and artillery and placed the city upon a war footing. Cannon were drawn up to command one of the main arteries; infantry and cavalry patrolled the

---

[46] Indianapolis *Daily Journal*, May 6, 1863; Indianapolis *Daily State Sentinel*, May 13, 15, 1863.

[47] The Plymouth *Democrat*, Columbia City *News*, South Bend *Forum*, and Warsaw *Union* defied the order. *Official Records*, 2 series, 5:723-26; Indianapolis *Daily State Sentinel*, May 16, 18, 26, 1863.

[48] The proprietors of the paper were forced to obtain a "loyal" editor and post $5,000 bond which would be forfeited if the order were again violated. Indianapolis *Daily Journal*, May 7, 1863.

[49] Columbia City *News*, quoted in Indianapolis *Daily State Sentinel*, May 18, 1863.

Governor's Circle and principal streets; additional troops guarded the arsenal and other state property.⁵⁰ Hascall might have expected that the Democrats would make the most of such a remarkable military demonstration designed to overawe a political assemblage.

Voorhees, after being elected president of the meeting, began the proceedings with a defiant address. With all the eloquence at his command he denounced the growth of military power and defended free speech and the right of the people to meet and discuss public affairs. He directed pointed remarks at Hascall's General Order No. 9, even though, he said, "I may at this very moment be talking myself into a prison by uttering these ancient sentiments of liberty." Vallandigham, he affirmed, had "fallen a little sooner, perhaps, than the rest of us, a victim to base usurpation" which had "taken the place of popular rights and of the Constitution."⁵¹ Voorhees' address set the tone for the speeches that followed.

Although party leaders urged those who attended the convention to conduct themselves in a quiet and orderly manner, trouble began early in the afternoon. The first disturbance occurred when a body of armed soldiers rushed one of the speakers' platforms and stopped the speech of Samuel R. Hamill of Sullivan County. During the remainder of the day soldiers and citizens engaged in numerous battles, especially after the participants had got themselves well fortified with whisky. The bolder spirits then began to grow loud in their denunciations of Lincoln and Morton, and loyal patriots came to their defense with equal ardor. Many Democrats were arrested. Some were arraigned in the mayor's court for carrying concealed weapons, and others were taken

---

⁵⁰ Carrington to Morton, May 20, 1863, Carrington Papers; Hascall, MS. Autobiography; Indianapolis *Daily Journal,* May 19, 1863; Indianapolis *Daily State Sentinel,* May 16, 1863; Foulke, *Oliver P. Morton,* 1:273-74.

⁵¹ Indianapolis *Daily State Sentinel,* May 21, 22, 1863.

to military headquarters for expressing "disloyal" sentiments.[52]

Late in the afternoon Senator Hendricks addressed the convention. While he was speaking a group of soldiers advanced toward the platform with fixed bayonets and declared their intention to make a summary disposal of the Indiana senator. At the same time squads of cavalry clattered up the streets toward the meeting. Bloodshed appeared inevitable, until army officers hurried forward to order the soldiers away. But Hendricks concluded his speech and the convention adopted its resolutions in a near riot. After adjournment, soldiers and numerous Republicans who had been scattered through the audience seized the platform and staged a "loyal" demonstration of their own.[53]

That evening as the excursion trains departed from the city, a number of irate Democrats cursed their political opponents and fired their pistols into the air. Again the soldiers were on hand to deal with the situation. Placing a cannon on the tracks of the Indiana Central, they boarded the train and seized a large quantity of arms. Similarly they stopped the Cincinnati and Peru trains along Pogue's Run and confiscated all the pistols that were not thrown into the stream. In great glee the Republicans dubbed the incident the "Battle of Pogue's Run."[54]

Responsibility for the riotous events of that day was shared by inept military officials, undisciplined soldiers, and the hotspurs of both political parties. While Republicans pretended to have staved off a revolution and sneered at the cowardice of their opponents, Democrats

[52] *Ibid.*, May 27, 1863; Indianapolis *Daily Journal*, May 21, 1863. Those arrested were quickly released.

[53] Indianapolis *Daily State Sentinel*, May 21, 23, 1863; Indianapolis *Daily Journal*, May 21, 22, 1863.

[54] Hascall, MS. Autobiography; Indianapolis *Daily Journal* and *Daily State Sentinel*, May 21, 1863; Foulke, *Oliver P. Morton*, 1:274-77; Esarey, *History of Indiana*, 2:781-83.

asserted that their forbearance alone had prevented more serious consequences. "Indiana today is as completely under military rule as France, Russia or Austria," wailed the *Sentinel*. "A large portion of the people are willingly bowing their necks to receive the yoke of despotism."[55]

Although the Republican press defended Hascall's officious conduct, Morton soon had enough of him and privately petitioned for his removal. Secretary Stanton readily confessed to Burnside that the Indiana commander's indiscreet political meddling had aggravated the situation in that state.[56] In consequence, Indiana and Michigan were combined into a single military district under Gen. Orlando B. Willcox. As Democrats rejoiced, Hascall revoked his General Order Number 9 and relinquished his command.[57]

While General Willcox displayed, perhaps too openly for his position, an aptitude for political speechmaking, he proved to be more discreet in his official conduct than his predecessor. One of his first acts was to issue a proclamation which urged both Republicans and Democrats to abandon their secret orders. Though few criticized him for that suggestion, neither faction was willing to comply.[58] Local disorders and military arrests continued in the following months, and, as usual, they were attributed to the revolutionary designs of Democratic secret societies. The activities of these groups and the arrest and trials of some of the leaders will be taken up in following chapters.

6

Meanwhile, the system of national conscription adopted by Congress in March, 1863, was bringing additional

[55] Indianapolis *Daily State Sentinel*, May 21, 1863.
[56] *Official Records*, 1 series, 23:pt. 2:369; 2 series, 5:724.
[57] *Ibid.*, 2 series, 5:741; Indianapolis *Daily Journal* and *Daily State Sentinel*, June 8, 1863.
[58] Indianapolis *Daily State Sentinel*, June 15, July 1, 1863; Indianapolis *Daily Journal*, July 1, 1863; New Albany *Weekly Ledger*, July 8, 1863; Terrell, *Report*, 1:appendix, 278-79.

tribulations to Indiana. That conscription was odious to Hoosiers, especially when administered by national officials, did not long remain in doubt. Indiana Democrats promptly questioned the constitutionality of the measure. The Fort Wayne *Sentinel* called it "a death blow to all State Rights," which left the people "no better than serfs under a military despotism."[59] Republicans in turn blamed the draft upon Democrats whom they accused of discouraging enlistments and protecting deserters. At least the act would frustrate the Democratic strategy of leaving the fighting to the friends of the government while its enemies remained at home to do the voting.[60]

The conscription bill aroused particularly bitter criticism because it permitted a drafted man to escape military service by providing a substitute or by paying $300 in commutation money. Democrats generally denounced these clauses as an "unjust and oppressive discrimination against the poor." Because of them men of wealth would "laugh at the draft."[61] Some supporters of the Union party also complained that it did not look well "for a *democratic* government, which knows of no distinction among its citizens, while fighting for the perpetuity of *democratic* institutions to indulge in *class legislation*."[62] Morton, too, objected to these provisions, at least in private. Democratic secret societies, he feared, would be able to purchase exemptions for antiwar men.[63]

By the end of May enrollment boards had been created in each local district. The next month, amid great excite-

---

[59] Fort Wayne *Sentinel*, quoted in Indianapolis *Gazette*, March 11, 1863.

[60] See speech of Governor Morton in Indianapolis *Daily Journal*, April 16, 1863. See also *ibid.*, June 30, October 31, 1863; Indianapolis *Gazette*, March 11, April 2, 1863.

[61] Indianapolis *Daily State Sentinel*, March 5, July 17, 20, 1863; Evansville *Weekly Gazette*, March 7, 1863.

[62] Aurora *Commercial*, March 5, 1863.

[63] Colfax to Morton, January 7, 1864, Archives Division; Morton to Provost Marshal General Fry, February 1, 1864, in Morton Letter Press Books, 3(September 1863-December 1866):83-88; Terrell, *Report*, 1:49-53.

ment, enrolling officers began to compile their lists. Resistance to the enrollment occurred in several counties, generally in isolated regions. A number of officers were fired upon, a couple were killed, and some of their records were seized and burned. These acts of violence, like their predecessors, were largely the products of political feuds, of ill-founded suspicions of unfairness in the administration of the draft, of hostility to probing government officials, and of personal enmities and local prejudices against the men appointed as enrolling officers. Republican politicians could offer no evidence to substantiate their reckless charges that this resistance resulted from the organized activities of disloyal secret societies: nor was it as widespread or as serious as these partisans made it appear.[64]

General Burnside again proposed a declaration of martial law, but chary Indiana officials advised against such action.[65] Instead, Morton issued a proclamation warning the people of the penalties for resistance to Federal law and denouncing newspapers and organizations which allegedly incited men to violence.[66] At the same time Voorhees, Hendricks, and other Democratic leaders urged submission to the draft until it had been repealed or nullified by the courts. The only other legal remedy, they added, was an appeal to the ballot box.[67]

All these difficulties provided the material from which Republicans constructed the legend that in 1863 Indiana had reached the brink of revolution. This was Governor

[64] For accounts of resistance to the enrollment, see the files of the Indianapolis *Daily Journal* and *Daily State Sentinel* for June, 1863; *Official Records,* 3 series, 3:339-40, 370-71, 375, 391, 392-94, 396-98; Charles E. Canup, "Conscription and Draft in Indiana during the Civil War," in *Indiana Magazine of History,* 10(June, 1914):81.

[65] *Official Records,* 3 series, 3:371, 392.

[66] Indianapolis *Daily Journal,* June 12, 1863.

[67] *Ibid.,* June 27, 1863; Indianapolis *Daily State Sentinel,* June 18, 19, 26, 1863; New Albany *Weekly Ledger,* June 17, July 8, 1863; *Official Records,* 3 series, 3:339-40.

Morton's ammunition for his attacks upon the loyalty of the Hoosier Democracy. Yet the record of those critical days shows that there were many causes, other than sympathy for rebels, which explained the growing rage of the Governor's political foes.

7

For a few exciting days in the summer of 1863 the war swept northward to the hills of southern Indiana. The Hoosiers' brief experience with actual warfare on their own soil resulted from the activities of daring Confederate raiders. These military operations were of minor importance, but they gave the lie most effectively to the Republican assertion that a large element in Indiana society was disloyal.

In June Capt. Thomas Hines took his Confederate cavalry company on a horse-stealing expedition across the Ohio River a few miles above Cannelton. After eluding their pursuers for two days, they were finally trapped by the local Legion and home guards. Though Hines and a few followers escaped into Kentucky, the rest were either killed, drowned, or captured.[68] After that episode Governor Morton renewed his efforts to secure arms for state defense and to rebuild the Indiana Legion. He persuaded the War Department to assign General Carrington to him for special duty in advancing this work.[69]

Early in July a more serious invasion occurred when Gen. John Hunt Morgan received permission from the hard-pressed Bragg to make a diversion by leading some two thousand cavalrymen on another raid through Kentucky. In disobedience to his orders Morgan moved northward to the Ohio River, where, on July 7, he

[68] Indianapolis *Daily Journal,* June 20, 22, 23, 1863; Terrell, *Report,* 1:161-64, appendix, 278.
[69] Terrell, *Report,* 1:109-10; Morton to [W. R. Holloway], June 20, 1863, in Telegraphic Correspondence, 1:75; Indianapolis *Daily Journal,* July 1, 8, 1863; *Official Records,* 1 series, 52:pt. 1:382, 3 series, 3:391.

occupied Brandenburg on the south bank. The following day, with the aid of two captured steamers, he crossed his troops to the Indiana side and started for Corydon some fifteen miles to the north. Local members of the Legion put up what opposition they could but were forced to fall back to a line six miles south of Corydon. Here they remained until the following morning when Morgan attacked and forced some three hundred fifty of the poorly armed and trained Legionnaires to surrender. The invaders then pushed on to Corydon where they plundered the stores and seized a much-needed supply of fresh horses. After that Morgan was ready to move again, but his opponents could only guess his ultimate destination.[70]

The general hysteria and feverish activity that followed in Indiana was reminiscent of the days after the fall of Fort Sumter; the panic and chaos resembled the Kentucky campaign of 1862. At once Governor Morton received a volley of wild and conflicting reports about Morgan's movements and exaggerated estimates of the size of his force. Some told him that the raiders numbered as many as six thousand men.[71] Though the Governor was ill at the time of the invasion, he worked hard with his subordinates to organize the state's defenses. But panic rather than sound judgment seemed to rule his conduct.

Indiana was poorly defended when Morgan arrived. Most of her troops had previously been sent to Kentucky, and the Legion was inadequately armed and organized.

---

[70] Indianapolis *Daily Journal* and *Daily State Sentinel,* July 9, 1863; Margrette Boyer, "Morgan's Raid in Indiana," in *Indiana Magazine of History,* 8(1912):150, 153-59. Other accounts of the raid are in the bound volume of Carrington manuscripts; Terrell, *Report,* 1:166 ff., appendix, 279-80; Foulke, *Oliver P. Morton,* 1:278-85; Esarey, *History of Indiana,* 2:771-76; Cecil Holland, *Morgan and His Raiders* . . . (New York, 1942), 226-49.

[71] A large correspondence regarding the raid and the general excitement is in the Telegraphic Correspondence, vols. 11, 16. See also Indianapolis *Daily Journal,* July 9, 11, 1863; Terrell, *Report,* 1:169.

Consequently, Morton demanded that General Burnside immediately return the state regiments in Kentucky.[72] At the same time he called out the state militia south of the National Road and urged the people elsewhere to form military companies ready for future orders. On the night of July 10 he closed all business houses in Indianapolis to enable the men to perfect their militia organizations. General Willcox was given control of all troops raised for state defense; General Carrington was assigned the job of organizing and commanding the Legion; General Hascall was placed in charge of the defenses of Indianapolis; and General Lew Wallace was anxiously called from his home for special duty.[73]

Meanwhile, Morgan's raiders were following an uneven northeastward course through southern Indiana. They reached Salem, then swung eastward toward Scottsburg, Vernon, and Versailles. They plundered the towns in their path, seized all the available horses, burned bridges, and tore up railroad lines. Terrified citizens fled before them, carrying away as much personal property as they could move. Bankers hastily gathered up their funds and sent them north. Companies of the Legion impeded Morgan's progress as much as possible, while General Edward H. Hobson and the Federal cavalry continued a desperate pursuit.[74]

On July 10 Morton sent appeals to prominent men in northern Indiana to bring all available forces to Indianapolis at once and to send runners through the counties to spread the alarm. The response was astonishing. The

---

[72] Morton to Burnside, July 9, 1863, in Telegraphic Correspondence, 16:210; *Official Records,* 1 series, 23:pt. 1:716, 717, 723; Terrell, *Report,* 1:173-76; Boyer, "Morgan's Raid," in *Indiana Magazine of History,* 8:152.

[73] Hascall, MS. Autobiography; account of the raid in bound volume labeled Carrington Papers; Indianapolis *Daily Journal,* July 9, 10, 11, 1863; *Official Records,* 1 series, 52:pt. 1:398, 399; Wallace, *Autobiography,* 2:657; Terrell, *Report,* 1:179.

[74] Indianapolis *Daily Journal* and *Daily State Sentinel,* July 10, 11, 12, 13, 14, 1863; Terrell, *Report,* 1:181; Boyer, "Morgan's Raid," in *Indiana Magazine of History,* 8:155-59.

Legion in southern Indiana took form almost overnight; city companies drilled constantly at Indianapolis; volunteers came by the thousands from other parts of the state. Within two days Indianapolis had 20,000 disorderly but willing defenders who occupied every lot and vacant building in the city. Throughout the state 45,000 more recruits were ready to be called.[75]

During this crisis the much discussed "northern wing" of the Confederate army failed to make an appearance. The presence of Morgan's men afforded an excellent opportunity for the long-expected uprising, but the Confederates met only a hostile and united people. Once again the masses forgot for the moment their party differences and joined hands against the common danger. General Morgan alienated friends for the South as his men indiscriminately looted the property of Republicans and "Copperheads" alike. The Democrats cried as lustily as their opponents for the expulsion of the hungry, horse-stealing invaders, and the *Sentinel* glowed with tributes to the loyalty of the "butternut" Democracy. Indiana was still decidely in the Union![76]

But Governor Morton was not so easily convinced of the essential unity of his state. This fact helped to produce the most ludicrous phases of the rebel raid. Though Indianapolis teemed with armed defenders, the Governor continued to dread the possibility that the city might be captured by the raiders. In private he raged against domestic traitors and explained how, with their aid, Morgan could seize the arsenal, free the rebel prisoners, and thus gain control of the entire state.[77] In consequence Morton seemed to be more interested in keeping Morgan out of Indianapolis and in expelling him from the state

---

[75] Terrell, *Report*, 1:176-79; Holliday, *Indianapolis and the Civil War*, 582-83; Boyer, "Morgan's Raid," in *Indiana Magazine of History*, 8:153.

[76] Indianapolis *Daily State Sentinel*, July 10, 13, 14, 21, 1863; Indianapolis *Daily Journal*, July 15, 1863; Boyer, "Morgan's Raid," in *Indiana Magazine of History*, 8:149.

[77] See account in bound volume labeled Carrington Papers.

than in securing his capture.[78] Quite possibly the Governor's illness had clouded his judgment.

By July 12, Morgan's men were near exhaustion. With Indiana mobilized for defense and with General Hobson closing in, his raid had almost become a rout. The next day the Confederates, seeking a way to escape into Kentucky, entered Ohio near Harrison. Morton then tendered the services of Indiana troops to Governor David Tod, and on the afternoon of July 13, preparations were made to send three regiments under General Carrington to Hamilton, Ohio. Delays occurred in organizing the expedition, during which Carrington visited friends and became intoxicated. Whereupon General Willcox placed him under arrest and turned his command over to General Hascall.[79] The Indiana regiments arrived too late to be of service and went to Cincinnati where they remained until Morgan's final capture, which was accomplished on July 26, near Salineville, close to Ohio's eastern border.[80] Indiana then quickly demobilized, although Morton continued his efforts to strengthen the Legion for future emergencies.

The Hoosier party battle revived immediately upon Morgan's departure. The Confederate raid had provided a new field of controversy. Now Republicans gave Governor Morton full and almost exclusive credit for saving the state. Insinuating that the Knights of the Golden Circle had aided Morgan, the *Journal* cited the invasion as further justification for Republican resistance to the schemes of the Democratic legislature.[81] The Democrats in turn suggested that Republican accounts of domestic

---

[78] Indianapolis *Daily Journal*, July 13, 1863; Wallace, *Autobiography*, 2:657-59.

[79] Hascall, MS. Autobiography; Carrington's account in bound volume labeled Carrington Papers; Indianapolis *Daily Journal*, July 14, 1863.

[80] Julian, *Political Recollections*, 233; Boyer, "Morgan's Raid," in *Indiana Magazine of History*, 8:161-63.

[81] Indianapolis *Daily Journal*, July 15, 22, 25, 1863; Fesler, "Secret Political Societies," in *Indiana Magazine of History*, 14:213-14.

traitors had lured the Confederates into the state, and they criticized the failure of local authorities to achieve Morgan's capture. The hints of treason, asserted the *Sentinel,* were designed "to hide imbecility of those who assume to possess 'all the loyalty,' and who proved themselves . . . incapable of preventing Morgan's invasion of the state. . . ."[82] Hoosier politics had returned to its familiar pattern.

8

Despite the tense political situation and the endless rumors of rebellion, the masses of regular Indiana Democrats still maintained their position as a loyal and constitutional opposition. Many of them voiced sympathy for Vallandigham after his banishment to the Confederacy and his subsequent escape to Canada, but it was General Burnside who made a martyr of the Ohio "Copperhead" by subjecting him to military rule. Though some Hoosier Democrats continued to speak of peace through compromise, with few exceptions they still insisted that it must be based upon a reunited nation.

Even in 1863 most Democrats continued to support the war and believe that only its vigorous prosecution could restore the Union.[83] Governor Morton's confession that southern Indiana was the most loyal part of the state was substantiated by the enthusiastic crowds which cheered Democratic Colonel Dunham as he toured the river counties speaking for a united support of the Union armies.[84] The devotion of Congressmen Holman and Cravens to the Union's cause remained unsurpassed.[85]

---

[82] Indianapolis *Daily State Sentinel,* July 20, 23, 24, 1863; New Albany *Weekly Ledger,* July 29, 1863.

[83] New Albany *Weekly Ledger,* July 17, September 2, 9, 14, 1863, Indianapolis *Daily State Sentinel,* May 4, June 9, 15, 20, August 12, September 10, 11, October 7, 1863.

[84] Morton to General Rosecrans, February 28, 1863, in Morton Letter Press Books, 2(January-June, 1863):305-6; Indianapolis *Daily Journal,* April 10, 1863; Indianapolis *Daily State Sentinel,* April 14, 1863; New Albany *Weekly Ledger,* April 8, 1863.

[85] Holman to Allen Hamilton, October 9, 1863, Allen Hamilton MSS.

The New Albany *Ledger* would not relinquish its war views, although it criticized the treatment of Vallandigham.[86] The Indianapolis *Sentinel* too, despite its blind partisanship and occasional digressions upon compromise, spoke often for the suppression of the rebellion by force of arms.[87]

Daniel W. Voorhees, whom the Republicans abused most violently, was the representative man of the Indiana "Copperheads." By 1863 he had begun to speak boldly of peace and to make angry attacks upon the policies of the Lincoln administration. Yet the Republicans were unable to find evidence of the disloyalty which they so often tried to pin upon him. It was the effectiveness of his oratory and the devotedness of his followers which caused his enemies to pursue him with such fury.

There was an earthy quality in Voorhees, "the tall sycamore of the Wabash." On the stump his hot temper, passionate partisanship, and stirring eloquence made an irresistible appeal to the western Democracy. His bitter cries against protective tariffs and national banks, his intense race prejudice, his suspicion of the eastern Yankee, his devotion to personal liberty, his defense of the Constitution and state rights faithfully reflected the views of his constituents. Like other Jacksonian agrarians he resented the political and economic revolution then in progress. Voorhees idealized a way of life which he thought was being destroyed by the current rulers of his country. His bold protests against these dangerous trends made him the idol of the Democracy of the Wabash Valley.[88]

---

[86] New Albany *Weekly Ledger*, April 8, July 29, September 9, 1863.

[87] Indianapolis *Daily State Sentinel*, June 1, 27, August 22, October 20, 1863.

[88] Leonard S. Kenworthy, *The Tall Sycamore of the Wabash. Daniel Wolsey Voorhees* (Boston, 1936), *passim;* Jordan, "Daniel Wolsey Voorhees," in *Mississippi Valley Historical Review*, 6(1919-20):532 ff.; Frank S. Bogardus, "Daniel W. Voorhees," in *Indiana Magazine of History*, 27(1931):91 ff.

In Indiana, then, the everlasting cry of treason had meaning only in terms of war hysteria and political strategy. The Republican appeal in the local spring elections to "vote squarely against the traitors" went far toward explaining the phenomena.[89] Again in October, during the state elections in Pennsylvania and Ohio and the county elections in Indiana, the Republican press reported that the rebels' last hope was a Democratic victory. "To elect the Copperhead ticket ... is to send down to Lee and Bragg the shout of arriving reinforcements," they cried. "A Union victory at the polls will be a more crushing blow to the Southern Confederacy than defeat at Chattanooga or on the Rapidan."[90]

The results of these elections brought much satisfaction to all Republicans. Andrew G. Curtin was re-elected governor of Pennsylvania; Vallandigham was overwhelmingly defeated in his campaign for the governorship of Ohio; Indiana Republicans made gains in the counties. The New Albany *Ledger* frankly attributed responsibility for this outcome to the burden thrown upon the Democracy by spokesmen like Vallandigham and the Cincinnati *Enquirer*.[91] But the *Sentinel* concluded that Republicans would "rejoice more over the subjugation of the Democratic party than in subduing the Rebel States."[92] Its real fear was that both might occur together.

9

Hoosiers were obviously much concerned about domestic issues, but their attention was still chiefly focused upon military events and the conduct of the war. Though they recoiled from the sting of Union defeats and sickened at the enormous lists of casualties, the campaigns of 1863 ultimately showed a marked improvement in the fortunes

---

[89] Indianapolis *Daily Journal*, March 20, April 6, 1863; New Albany *Weekly Ledger*, April 15, 1863.
[90] Indianapolis *Daily Journal*, October 9, 13, 1863.
[91] New Albany *Weekly Ledger*, October 21, 1863.
[92] Indianapolis *Daily State Sentinel*, July 21, 1863.

of Union arms and presaged the final collapse of the Confederacy. In the East a series of Union reverses, beginning with the battle of Chancellorsville, at last ended in a victory at Gettysburg. In the West the great rejoicing over the final fall of Vicksburg in July and the opening of the Mississippi subsided before the bloody defeat at Chickamauga in September. Yet, by the end of the year the Confederates had been cleared out of Tennessee and Bragg had been defeated and driven from the Chattanooga region. The way had been prepared for the advances of Grant and Sherman in 1864.

Meanwhile, in Indiana the business of building armies continued, and the people watched a steady stream of new recruits leave the state to fill the gaps in the Union lines. In spite of all the hardships and discouragement, the difficulties of enrollment, and the talk of conspiracies to resist the draft, until the fall of 1864, except for the militia draft of 1862, the state filled its quotas without resorting to conscription.

Indiana's generous response to the President's calls was due in part to her devotion to the Union cause and in part to her fear of the draft which increased recruiting efforts.[93] A portion of the credit also belonged to Morton, Carrington, and other energetic leaders who applied every means at their disposal to stimulate enlistments. With the hope that each call would be the last and that the conflict would soon be won, they sponsored war meetings throughout the state to keep up the patriotic spirit and to raise funds for the support of soldiers' families. The Governor spoke at many of these gatherings and often observed that the avenues to future positions and honor passed through the gates of military service. Hired speakers toured the state to advance the work of raising volunteers.[94]

---

[93] Terrell, *Report*, 1:54.
[94] The files of the Indianapolis *Daily Journal* and *Daily State Sentinel* for October and November, 1863, contain almost daily reports of these meetings.

Governor Morton was always fertile with ideas to encourage recruiting, and many of them won the War Department's approval. In the late summer of 1863 he anticipated another presidential call for troops and obtained permission to raise eleven new regiments to apply to future state quotas.[95] At his suggestion speakers and recruiting officers were paid a premium of six dollars for each volunteer they obtained.[96] In the fall Morton arranged to have one noncommissioned officer from each company in the field sent home for recruiting purposes until his unit was filled.[97] Finally, the Governor proposed a plan for the re-enlistment of the three-year men as their terms expired. By its provisions any regiment in which three-fourths of the men would re-enlist was to have a thirty-day furlough for rest and recruiting before its full term had expired. After the War Department accepted the plan, Morton's agents went to the field and had considerable success in securing re-enlistments.[98]

Unfortunately there were other and less happy results from Indiana's efforts to meet its obligations under Lincoln's various calls for troops. The horror of the draft often made the state more eager to fill its quotas nominally by any expedient than actually to supply the army with the needed men. As a result brokers did a thriving business in the sale of "credits" to counties and townships

[95] Provost Marshal General Fry to Morton, September 14, 1863, in *Official Records,* 3 series, 3:795; Indianapolis *Daily Journal,* September 15, October 20, 1863.

[96] Indianapolis *Daily Journal,* January 3, 1864; Terrell, *Report,* 1:71-74; *Official Records,* 3 series, 3:945.

[97] Morton to Provost Marshal General Fry, October 22, 1863, Assistant Adjutant General Townsend to Morton, October 23, 1863, and Morton to Generals Meade, Scofield, Burnside, and Grant, October 23, 1863, in Telegraphic Correspondence, 5:30, 34, 37-39.

[98] Holloway to Stanton, September 19, 1863, in Morton Letter Press Books, 3(September 1863-December 1866):7-8; Morton to Provost Marshal General Fry, October 7, 1863, in *Official Records,* 3 series, 3:865-66; Indianapolis *Daily Journal,* November 26, 1863, January 13, 1864; Terrell, *Report,* 1:29-31.

seeking to escape the draft.[99] In Indiana as elsewhere there was constant bickering between state officials and the War Department over alleged excessive quotas and over the failure to obtain the credits to which the state was supposedly entitled. Various localities complained that favoritism was being shown to others and that recruits were being credited to one district when they belonged to another.[100] Not until agents from Massachusetts and other eastern states began to enlist Negroes in Indiana for their own credit was local race prejudice sufficiently overcome to enable Hoosiers to raise a colored battalion of their own.[101]

Equally disturbing were the abuses which grew out of the system of bounty payments to volunteers. By the end of 1863 the Federal government was giving each new volunteer a bounty of $300 in several installments. Morton repeatedly urged that a larger portion of the money be paid in advance, because he thought it would further stimulate recruiting. The War Department made some concessions to him, but it insisted that large bounty payments in advance would only increase desertions.[102]

Indiana's state government never paid bounties, but many counties, townships, cities, and private groups provided varying amounts. In their desire to escape the draft some localities paid as much as $500 for a new

---

[99] Terrell, *Report*, 1:67-68.

[100] Holloway to Provost Marshal General Fry, September 3, 1863, in Telegraphic Correspondence, 16:302; Morton to U. S. Adjutant General Lorenzo Thomas, February 20, 1864, in *ibid.*, 5:140; Morton to Fry, February 1, 1864, in Morton Letter Press Books, 3 (September 1863-December 1866):83-88; Morton to Fry, January 11, February 29, 1864, in *Official Records,* 3 series, 4:24-25, 145; Indianapolis *Daily State Sentinel,* July 21, August 18, October 7, 1863; Terrell, *Report,* 1:51-53, 102-3.

[101] William H. Schlater to John T. Walker, May 28, 1863, in Morton Letter Press Books, 2(January-June 1863); Indianapolis *Daily Journal,* December 4, 1863; *Official Records,* 3 series, 3:1104; Terrell, *Report,* 1:79-81.

[102] Morton to Provost Marshal General Fry, September 22, 1863, and Fry to Morton, September 23, 29, 1863, in Telegraphic Correspondence, 5:5, 13; *Official Records,* 3 series, 3:831-32.

recruit and even sold bonds to raise money for that purpose. As a result volunteers were tempted to enlist in the places that gave the highest bounties. This practice caused great hardship in the poorer sections of the state which lost to other communities their manpower for filling their own quotas. Moreover, the inequality in local bounty payments produced resentment and discontent among the men in the field.[103]

These recruiting expedients and the provision of the conscription act which permitted draftees to furnish substitutes had still more sordid results. Substitute brokers established themselves in the river towns and collected Negroes, often by false inducements, to serve as substitutes in eastern states.[104] "Bounty jumping" was also common. "Volunteers," sometimes in collusion with brokers, would enlist in one township, collect the bounty, and then desert to repeat the process somewhere else. Strenuous efforts were made to apprehend these deserters. Some were sent to prison, a few were shot, and many more were manacled in squads and marched to the front in disgrace.[105]

Indiana's experiences in all these troublesome aspects of a wartime society were much like those of other states. The hardening of men by their intimate association with suffering and death, the lowering of moral standards, the intensity of partisanship in a period of swift social change, and the manifestation of war hysteria were inevitable results of the conflict. If any elements of "a more perfect civilization" were mixed in the "crucible of war," they are hard to find in the Hoosier records.

[103] Indianapolis *Daily Journal,* October 29, December 28, 1863; Terrell, *Report,* 1:64-67. During the war the various units of local government paid a total of $15,497,876.04 in bounties.
[104] Indianapolis *Daily State Sentinel,* August 24, 1864; *Official Records,* 3 series, 4:559-60; Terrell, *Report,* 1:70-71.
[105] Terrell, *Report,* 1:69-70, appendix, 285.

CHAPTER 10 — VOTING DOWN THE REBELLION

ON January 18, 1864, Governor Morton addressed a solemn and confidential letter to President Lincoln. Its apprehensive theme was embraced in the Governor's first blunt sentence: "Considerations of the most vital character demand that the war shall be substantially ended within the present year."[1] He was doubtful that the people would much longer support a war policy which gave no clear promise of immediate success.

More pertinent to Morton's calculations was the fact that the new year brought with it the prospect of state and national elections which would bring into review the policies of the Union party. With local Democrats waxing strong and bitter in their opposition to his extralegal financial measures and to the policies of the national administration, the Governor was far from optimistic about the outcome of the approaching campaign. Political success and the vindication of his official acts largely depended upon the triumph of the Union armies, a triumph which, in January, still appeared remote.

An added discouragement to the Union party was the serious split that developed within its own ranks. To a great extent the division was caused by the radical Repub-

[1] Morton to Lincoln, January 18, 1864, in Morton Letter Press Books, 3 (September 1863-December 1866) :73-75. For a similar letter addressed to Stanton, see *Official Records,* 3 series, 4:38-39.

(217)

licans' dissatisfaction with the moderate program of reconstruction which Lincoln had outlined the previous December. Others not counted among the radicals nursed the conviction that the administration's conduct of the war had been a failure and that new leadership was needed. These discontented groups found a willing champion in Secretary of Treasury Chase, a perpetual presidential candidate. By the beginning of 1864 treasury officials and the disaffected elements had launched a full-blown Chase movement in opposition to the renomination of Lincoln.

In Indiana numerous Republican politicians were either openly critical of the administration or noncommittal regarding their presidential preferences. During the past three years the Indianapolis *Journal* had often attacked Lincoln's conduct of the war, and on several occasions it made flattering comments about Chase's executive ability.[2] Morton had had many tiffs with Lincoln. Finding Chase ever ready to consult him in the dispensation of treasury patronage, he was more than generous in his praise of that cabinet officer.[3] When Chase visited Indianapolis in October, 1863, the Governor arranged an elaborate public reception for him. On that occasion Chase hinted that if he should become President, there would be a cabinet post for Morton. But the Governor was apparently too shrewd to commit himself.[4]

Some organs were outspoken in their opposition to Lincoln. The radical Indianapolis *Gazette* continued to

[2] Indianapolis *Daily Journal*, December 23, 1862, August 19, 1863.

[3] Donnal V. Smith, *Chase and Civil War Politics* (Columbus, Ohio, 1931), 77, 86. Julian observed that Chase was "amazingly ambitious," and that in his appointments "he seemed anxious to make fair weather with some of his old conservative foes. . . ." Julian, *Political Recollections*, 195.

[4] Indianapolis *Daily Journal* and *Daily State Sentinel*, October 15, 1863; Foulke, *Oliver P. Morton*, 1:251n. For a thorough treatment of the Chase movement in Indiana, see Winfred A. Harbison, "Indiana Republicans and the Re-election of President Lincoln," in *Indiana Magazine of History*, 34(1938):49-57.

express sympathy for the "persecuted" General Frémont whom Lincoln had removed from his western command. It deplored the "hasty" endorsement of Lincoln by conventions in various states.[5] The Indianapolis *Free Press*, mouthpiece of the radical German element, had long been denouncing the President, and early in 1864 a group of prominent Germans purchased it to support John C. Frémont's candidacy.[6] George W. Julian, still friendly toward Chase, diligently spread his own radical doctrines and made no secret of his hostility toward Lincoln's reconstruction policies. In January Julian was appointed to a national committee to organize and direct the Chase movement. But the radical congressman was not ready to identify himself so completely with the anti-Lincoln forces. Deciding to "let the presidential matter drift," he soon withdrew.[7] Meanwhile, a number of Indiana newspapers made an effort to launch a local Morton-for-president boom, but the Governor gave it no countenance.[8]

Yet Lincoln counted many firm supporters in Indiana, not only among Federal officeholders, but among the rank and file of the party. Numerous local meetings expressed confidence in the administration and in its policies. Besides, the opinions of the "War Democrats," whose presence was always featured at Union meetings, had to be considered. Any further concessions to Lincoln's radical critics were certain to encounter the opposition of this group. Actually the bulk of the local criticism of Lincoln was based upon dissatisfaction with his conduct of the war

[5] Indianapolis *Gazette,* March 26, 1863, February 9, 1864.
[6] Indianapolis *Daily State Sentinel,* February 11, 1864.
[7] Muncie *Delaware County Free Press,* quoted in *ibid.,* November 30, 1863; Julian, *Political Recollections,* 237-38; Clarke, *George W. Julian,* 250-51.
[8] Indianapolis *Daily Journal,* January 4, February 22, 1864; Indianapolis *Gazette,* January 21, February 20, 1864; Indianapolis *Daily State Sentinel,* December 7, 1863; Centreville *Indiana True Republican,* December 17, 1863. Some of Lincoln's opponents apparently tried to use Morton's name as a means of preventing the adoption of instructions for Lincoln at the state convention.

rather than with his conservatism. The Indiana Union party was still decidedly a conservative political organization.

Early in 1864 the Union state central committee called for a mass convention of "Unconditional Union men" to nominate a state ticket, a slate of presidential electors, and delegates to the national convention. The preliminary county conventions were all but unanimous in their choice of the party's gubernatorial candidate. Morton's friends saw to it that the delegates were properly instructed upon the question, while the Union press observed that there was an overwhelming demand for the renomination of the present incumbent.[9] Democrats protested that Morton was not eligible because of a provision in the state constitution which prohibited anyone from holding office as governor for more than four in any eight years. But Republicans simply pointed out that Morton had been elected lieutenant governor in 1860.[10]

On the question of the presidency the county meetings were less united. Lincoln's friends were determined to secure his endorsement at the state convention; his opponents wanted the delegates to go uninstructed. The vigorous actions of the Chase men at least kept the issue in doubt. Under the circumstances Morton believed that the convention could best serve the state party by taking no action at all upon the presidential question or upon controversial national issues. Such an arrangement would

[9] Indianapolis *Daily Journal,* January 1, 4, 5, 12, 21, 23, 25, 28, February 2, 15, 17, 18, 20, 22, 1864; Indianapolis *Gazette,* January 14, 1864.
[10] Indianapolis *Gazette,* January 5, 1864; Indianapolis *Daily State Sentinel,* January 7, 19, 26, 27, 1864; Indianapolis *Daily Journal,* January 5, 23, February 12, 1864. Though the wording of the state constitution was slightly ambiguous on this point, it is certain that Morton's nomination in 1864 at least violated its spirit. This article was definitely intended to prevent the same man from occupying the governorship for eight years in succession. Yet the Democrats failed to make an issue out of it during the campaign, and Morton's right to the office was not challenged.

have been quite satisfactory to the friends of Salmon P. Chase.[11]

On February 23 the delegates to the Union state convention assembled at the capital city. No sooner had a temporary organization been achieved than Cyrus M. Allen, Lincoln's fast friend, jumped upon the platform and proceeded to knock overboard the careful plans of the party managers. Allen introduced two resolutions. The first instructed the delegates to the national convention to vote for Lincoln, and the second proposed the nomination of Morton for governor by acclamation. The crowd responded with a tremendous howl of approval, and the resolutions were adopted without audible dissent. The opposition, unprepared for such action at that early stage, was caught completely off guard and had no opportunity for even a hearing. Allen was never counted among the Governor's friends, but his strategy of combining an endorsement of Lincoln with the inevitable nomination of Morton had the effect he anticipated. Thus the presidential issue was quickly settled, and the Chase men had to accept defeat before the convention had fairly begun.[12]

After the election of Joseph A. Wright as president of the meeting, Governor Morton came forward and read a long and carefully prepared speech which was subsequently printed and widely circulated as the campaign text of the Indiana Union party. The Governor made a thorough defense of his administration and traced the course of state affairs during the past year. He reviewed the conduct of the Democratic legislature and vindicated the action of the minority which he claimed had saved the state from revolution. Morton justified his financial policies by describing the disastrous consequences that might have resulted from the calling of a special session. His

---

[11] Foulke, *Oliver P. Morton*, 1:292n-93n; Smith, *Chase and Civil War Politics*, 111, 121-22.
[12] Indianapolis *Daily Journal, Gazette, Daily State Sentinel*, February 24, 1864.

attack upon the "disloyal" Democracy, avowed a friendly reporter, was "the most terrible indictment probably ever presented against any party."

When he turned to national issues, the Governor made no reference to either the presidential question or the fast-emerging problem of reconstruction. He chose instead to launch a withering attack upon the "Copperheads." Such men, he scornfully remarked, could only mourn the death of slavery and the resort to arbitrary arrests; but they had no tears for the sufferings of Union soldiers and southern Unionists who were exposed to the cruel and savage rebels. There could be no peace, he asserted, except by the sword. The real peace men were the soldiers who were crushing out the rebellion. After an eloquent tribute to Indiana's volunteers, he concluded defiantly: "Indiana has already made a large investment of her best blood in the cause of this Union, and will never consent to its dismemberment or to a dishonorable peace." Having thus again identified his party with the Union cause and with the spirit of patriotism, the "war governor" retired amid enthusiastic cheers from his admirers.[13]

The state platform embraced Allen's resolutions and proposed Andrew Johnson for the vice-presidency. It repeated the appeal for the suspension of partisanship until the rebellion was suppressed, affirmed a determination to make no compromise with traitors, and praised the conduct of the Union armies. The tariff, banking, reconstruction, and other mooted national issues were completely ignored. Concerning the current proposal for a constitutional amendment to abolish slavery, it merely favored "the destruction of everything which stands in the way of a permanent and perpetual peace." The nomina-

---

[13] Indianapolis *Daily Journal*, February 24, 1864. The Democrats were furious at Morton's attacks upon their loyalty. They called his slurs upon Democracy a weak apology for his usurpations. In April the Democratic state central committee issued a lengthy reply to the Governor's address. Indianapolis *Daily State Sentinel*, April 9, 11, 1864.

tions of candidates for various state offices gave adequate recognition to "War Democrats," as well as to the army. After selecting delegates to the national convention, state electors, and a new state central committee headed by Wright, the meeting adjourned amid pleas for harmony and unity behind the state ticket.[14]

The work of the state convention satisfied most Republicans and "War Democrats," but a few were critical and there was some disaffection. The Indianapolis *Journal* condemned Lincoln's friends for "rushing him into the field" so early. It doubted the wisdom of binding the state to Lincoln "before we know whether that is the best thing to be done," and insisted that it would have been better to have left the delegates uninstructed. Nevertheless, it deplored the continued feud between the friends of Chase and Lincoln and the persistent opposition of the radical Germans. The *Journal* warned that the rebellion was still strong and that the Democracy would triumph if the friends of the Union were divided among themselves.[15] Within a few weeks it had become reconciled to Lincoln's inevitable renomination and decided that any further opposition to him could be "little else but factious."[16]

But the radicals were not so easily conciliated. The Indianapolis *Gazette,* which became the chief Hoosier spokesman for Chase, deplored the tactics used by the friends of Lincoln at the convention and their refusal to give the opposition a chance to be heard. It insisted that the delegates were "boiling over with enthusiasm" for Morton and that any presidential candidate associated with his name at that time would have been endorsed.[17] Subsequently, when Lincoln's renomination appeared cer-

[14] Indianapolis *Daily Journal* and *Gazette,* February 24, 1864.
[15] Indianapolis *Daily Journal,* February 27, March 3, 4, 1864.
[16] *Ibid.,* March 10, 1864.
[17] Indianapolis *Gazette,* February 26, 1864.

tain, the *Gazette* gave him a reluctant endorsement but continued to demand a new cabinet of radical men.[18]

The radical Germans were even more recalcitrant. They openly refused to accept the action of the state convention regarding the presidency. Though they all favored Morton, many of them were not satisfied with the remainder of the state ticket which they believed had snubbed their group.[19] Republicans were frightened by reports that the Germans intended to scratch the rest of the Union ticket. And so in April, Gen. Nathan Kimball, the original Union candidate for lieutenant governor, suddenly declined his nomination, and the state central committee quickly selected Conrad Baker to replace him. Baker, it was understood, was satisfactory to the German element.[20]

Most Indiana radicals, like Julian, eventually decided to be cautious in their opposition to Lincoln and finally came to support him. But a few of them united with the disaffected Germans under the leadership of Major J. W. Gordon, a personal enemy of Morton, to foster antiadministration sentiment. In May they met at Indianapolis and selected delegates to a national convention of radicals which was to assemble at Cleveland.[21] On May 31 this convention nominated General Frémont for the presidency and adopted a platform which called for the complete abolition of slavery by constitutional amendment, demanded the confiscation of rebel property, and denounced Lincoln's interference with personal liberty.

A week later Indiana's Union party delegates went to Baltimore to aid in the renomination of Lincoln and in the nomination of Andrew Johnson for the vice-presi-

[18] Indianapolis *Gazette,* May 31, 1864.
[19] W. L. Stritter, Mount Vernon, to Morton, March 18, 1864, Chicago-Morton Collection; Indianapolis *Gazette,* April 18, 21, 1864.
[20] Indianapolis *Gazette,* April 26, 27, 1864; Indianapolis *Daily Journal,* April 11, 27, 1864.
[21] Indianapolis *Daily State Sentinel,* May 23, 24, 1864; Indianapolis *Daily Journal,* May 24, 1864.

dency. The national platform, which dodged the issues
of reconstruction and confiscation, was satisfactory enough
to Indiana's conservative Union politicians. It resembled
the state platform, except that it called slavery the chief
cause of the war and specifically demanded a constitutional amendment to abolish it. The action at Baltimore,
declared the *Journal,* was the "most fatal blow the rebellion" had yet received.[22]

At a time when Union men were depressed and their
cause was at a low ebb, Indiana's response to the President's long-expected renomination was far from enthusiastic. The Lincoln ratification meeting which assembled in
the State House yard on the evening of June 11 was a
small and somber affair. A number of speakers pictured
the nomination as the voice of the people and repeated
the maxim about not changing horses in the middle of
a stream. Governor Morton then delivered the principal
address. He described the Union party candidates and
platform as worthy of the support of all loyal men. Speaking to his German friends, Morton lauded their patriotism but attacked Frémont unsparingly. He pointed to
the General's strange letter of acceptance which declared
slavery to be dead and observed that if that were the case,
it must have been killed by Lincoln. Moreover, the Governor noted that Frémont had repudiated the confiscation
proposal and denounced Lincoln savagely. As a result
Frémont's letter was being read "with joy by his enemies
and with pain by his friends, and omitting one or two
sentences, there is nothing in it that might not have been
written and subscribed without inconsistency by Mr. Vallandigham."[23]

The Democratic press made the most of Morton's
denunciation of Frémont and frequently misquoted his
words to make it appear that he had criticized the radical
Germans themselves. The Governor hastily published a

[22] Indianapolis *Daily Journal,* June 11, 1864.
[23] *Ibid.,* June 13, 15, 1864; Indianapolis *Gazette,* June 13, 1864.

card vigorously denying any such attack and branding the Democratic reports as "unmitigated falsehoods." Nevertheless, some Germans were provoked at what he did say about Frémont, and the Indianapolis *Free Press* promptly removed Morton's name from its list of recommended candidates.[24]

Although Julian repudiated Frémont and gave his support to Lincoln,[25] his feud with Morton went on as usual. In 1864 the Governor's friends in the fifth district repeated their attempt of 1862 to prevent Julian's renomination for Congress. This time they rallied around General Sol Meredith, a close friend of Morton, whom the *Journal* had long portrayed as a dashing military hero. The ensuing conflict between the two factions was exceedingly violent. The Democrats were much amused by it, and they used it to expose the hollowness of Republican pretensions of nonpartisanship. Meredith accused Julian of being a Chase man and an enemy of Lincoln; Julian's friends called the General a "Copperhead" because of his opposition to emancipation and arming of Negroes.[26]

When Julian was victorious in the April primary election, the friends of Meredith vowed that he would continue to run as an independent, and the Richmond *Palladium* continued to print his name as the Union candidate.[27] Julian sought Lincoln's intervention, and the President had to threaten political reprisals before Meredith withdrew and the *Palladium* gave its radical foe a

---

[24] Indianapolis *Daily State Sentinel*, June 13, 17, 1864; Cincinnati *Enquirer*, quoted in *ibid.*, June 14, 1864; Indianapolis *Daily Journal*, June 14, 15, 1864; New Albany *Weekly Ledger*, June 22, 1864.

[25] Centreville *Indiana True Republican*, June 16, 1864.

[26] David P. Holloway, the commissioner of patents, J. F. Kibbey, Morton's former law partner, and W. S. T. Morton, the Governor's brother, led the opposition to Julian. Julian to Mrs. Laura Julian, March 29, 1864, Julian MSS.; Centreville *Indiana True Republican*, February 18, March 3, April 28, 1864; Indianapolis *Daily Journal*, April 5, 6, 1864; Indianapolis *Gazette*, March 26, 1864.

[27] Indianapolis *Daily Journal*, April 9, 14, 26, 28, 1864; Richmond *Broad Axe*, quoted in Indianapolis *Daily State Sentinel*, April 11, 1864.

reluctant endorsement.[28] All these evidences of disharmony within the Union party—in part a prelude to the conflict between radicals and conservatives over the issue of reconstruction—weakened its chances for success in the fall elections.

2

With Republicans thus torn internally, Governor Morton was doubly convinced that decisive military action must come during the summer of 1864. Early in the year he urged Stanton to raise immediately all the troops that would be needed to assure a victory. Recruiting would be easier, he suggested, while farmers were still unoccupied with their crops. Calls late in the spring or summer would be exceedingly disheartening.[29]

With this in mind the Governor energetically pushed the work of raising new regiments and filling the old. When Lincoln called for another 400,000 men, Morton once more declared that this would be the last call and that it would provide sufficient men to end the war that year.[30] Veteran re-enlistments and a considerable number of new volunteers soon filled the state's aggregate quota, although some local districts were in arrears. The War Department then proposed to execute a draft in those delinquent districts, but Morton entered a strenuous protest and issued a proclamation which noted that the state as a whole had furnished an excess above all calls. He made it clear that he would assume no responsibility for any ensuing draft. His curt explanation to the War Department was that he regarded it "inexpedient to draft in Indiana."[31] In consequence, no draft was made.

[28] Indianapolis *Daily Journal* and *Daily State Sentinel,* June 25, 1864; Lafayette *Argus,* quoted in Centreville *Indiana True Republican,* July 14, 1864; Julian, *Political Recollections,* 244-45.
[29] *Official Records,* 3 series, 4:38-39.
[30] Proclamation of General Carrington in Indianapolis *Daily Journal* and *Daily State Sentinel,* February 5, 1864.
[31] Indianapolis *Daily Journal,* April 16, 1864; Morton to Provost Marshal General Fry, March 3 and May 4, 1864, Morton to the People

In April the start of military campaigns and the urgent need for victory caused a movement in the West for the raising of a body of short-term troops. Morton and Governor John Brough of Ohio devised the project and ultimately called several other western governors to Indianapolis to discuss it with them. After considerable debate, during which Morton objected to proposals for a longer term of service, the governors agreed to raise 85,000 volunteers to serve for one hundred days. These men were to be mustered into United States service, they would receive no bounties, and they were not to be credited against any regular state quotas. On April 21, Lincoln and Stanton eagerly accepted the offer. Indiana's quota was to be 20,000 men.[32]

Despite every patriotic appeal, Morton's action in behalf of his state elicited little enthusiasm. Democrats were frankly critical and complained that, while Indiana's quotas were filled, eastern states were in arrears. Why then this further drain upon western agricultural labor merely to make up the deficiency of New England? They denounced the Governor's presumptuousness in making such a commitment for his state. They charged that his project was entirely a political move to give him "the dispensation of a few more commissions in order to help on with his re-election." Since the Governor had made sure that these troops would return before the elections, perhaps he intended to use them to intimidate voters at the polls. Morton's friends angrily replied that these dissenters were afraid of "the purifying effect of military service upon Copperhead feelings."[33]

of Indiana, March 15, 1864, and Fry to Morton, April 30, May 4, 1864, in *Official Records,* 3 series, 4:151, 182-85, 251, 260.

[32] Morton and Brough to governors of various western states, April 11, 1864, in Telegraphic Correspondence, 5:182; *Official Records,* 3 series, 4:237-39; Terrell, *Report,* 1:37-39. Governor Blair of Michigan was unable to attend the meeting because of ill health. Blair to Morton, April 14, 1864, AGO, Civil War Telegrams, Archives Division.

[33] Indianapolis *Daily State Sentinel,* April 25, 26, 29, 30, May 3, 4, 1864; New Albany *Weekly Ledger,* April 27, May 11, 18, 1864; Bluffton

But the hostility to the hundred-day call was not confined to the Democrats, for the *Sentinel* noted the "chilling Republican atmosphere" which greeted the proposal. Previous quotas had been a heavy drain upon Indiana's manpower and the remaining farm laborers were already busy in the fields. Hence many Republicans joined the Democrats in criticizing the project.[34] The *Journal* ultimately confessed that there was a general apathy and doubted that Indiana's quota would be filled. By the end of May the hundred-day movement had spent itself, with only eight regiments of 7,415 men having been recruited.[35] Morton and other Union party leaders were not encouraged by the result.

This failure was symptomatic of the general despondency which enveloped Indiana during the spring and early summer as the people sadly watched the progress of Union armies. There was not a glimmer of encouraging news to assure ultimate success. The terrible slaughter during Grant's Wilderness campaign in May culminated in the wearisome siege of Petersburg which apparently brought Federal troops no closer to the capture of Richmond. In the West Sherman's slow advance from Chattanooga at first did not seem to promise the decisive results for which the North prayed. In July a cavalry raid by Gen. Jubal A. Early again menaced Washington and threw its politicians into a panic. It was hardly surprising that many Hoosiers asked how long the futile bloodshed would continue and listened to the Democratic cry that the Lincoln administration was a failure.

With the Union party campaign already floundering,[36] its prospects were further impaired when the President,

---

Banner, quoted in Indianapolis *Daily Journal,* May 24, 1864; Fort Wayne *Times,* quoted in *ibid.,* May 25, 1864; Indianapolis *Gazette,* May 10 1864.

[34] Indianapolis *Daily State Sentinel,* May 2, 3, 1864; New Albany *Weekly Ledger,* May 11, 18, 1864.

[35] Indianapolis *Daily Journal,* May 3, 5, 7, 10, 31, 1864; Terrell, *Report* 1:38-39.

[36] Indianapolis *Daily Journal,* July 21, 1864; Hollister, *Schuyler Colfax,* 238.

on July 18, called for 500,000 more troops and gave Indiana another large quota to fill.[37] Democrats wailed about broken promises. Republicans did their best to conceal the huge Union losses and to explain the new call as the result of the need to replace veterans whose terms were about to expire.[38] But Governor Morton's worst fears had been realized. Gloomily he confessed that it would be impossible to raise the new levy by volunteering and that conscription would be necessary.[39] Since this inevitable draft would occur shortly before the state election, the Governor's party friends might well have despaired of the result.

3

Meanwhile, as Hoosiers became discouraged by the dismal war news, while radical Republicans grew ever more bitter toward Lincoln, and while Frémont remained in the field, Hoosier Democrats had bided their time. Now they looked forward to the October election with considerable confidence. After foregoing the custom of meeting on January 8, the Democratic state central committee fixed July 12 as the date for the state convention. Its call in February invited the support of all who favored the maintenance of the Union and opposed the "corrupt, destructive, and revolutionary abolition policy of the National and State Administrations."[40]

But Democratic leaders were soon troubled with their own factional disputes. They were particularly embarrassed by the war issue and were far from certain about what position the party would assume. The absence of Union military successes had given added strength to the peace men. Capitalizing upon the growth of peace senti-

---

[37] Indiana's quota under the new call was 25,662. *Official Records*, 3 series, 4:515-16; Terrell, *Report*, 1:48.

[38] Indianapolis *Daily Journal*, July 28, 1864.

[39] See Conrad Baker, assistant provost marshal, Indianapolis, to Provost Marshal General Fry, May 21, 1864, in *Official Records*, 3 series, 4:399.

[40] Indianapolis *Daily State Sentinel*, February 24, 1864.

ment, the small band of noisy extremists continued to embarrass the Democracy by their agitation and by their efforts to gain greater power in the party. Harrison H. Dodd, of Indianapolis, informed a local convention that there was but one word in his platform—*"peace!"*[41] Lambdin P. Milligan, of Huntington, demanded an immediate peace "without a separation of the agricultural States of the Union." This, he said, was the only way to prevent the people of the West from falling into "a state of pecuniary vassalage to the commercial and manufacturing interests of the East."[42] These men apparently preferred permanent disunion, or a separation from New England, to the continuance of a war which seemed to menace constitutional liberty and the foundations of agrarian rule.

A few of the more rabid peace men still further embarrassed their party by promoting secret Democratic societies. Among the most active participants in this exciting business were the conspiratorial Harrison H. Dodd, an Indianapolis printer; the aged Dr. William A. Bowles of French Lick Springs; Lambdin P. Milligan, "Copperhead" candidate for the gubernatorial nomination; John C. Walker, Democratic state agent in charge of Indiana's financial business in New York and violent personal enemy of Morton; Horace Heffren, an erratic politician from Washington County; and Andrew Humphreys, a leader of the peace men in Greene County.[43] Local secret organizations existed in Indiana as early as 1862, but they were short-lived and showed little evidence of central direction. Some members saw in them a defense against governmental tyranny and against the secret

[41] *Ibid.,* January 9, 1864.
[42] *Ibid.,* July 8, 1864.

[43] Indianapolis *Daily Journal,* August 22, 1862, July 8, September 15, October 18, 1863, June 20, 1864; Indianapolis *Daily State Sentinel,* July 23, August 18, 1862, June 25, 29, 1863, October 29, 1864; New Albany *Weekly Ledger,* October 16, 1861; Benn Pitman (ed.), *The Trials for Treason at Indianapolis . . .* (Cincinnati, 1865), *passim.*

organizations of Republicans; a few Democratic leaders found them useful in the circulation of party propaganda.[44]

In the fall of 1863 the Order of American Knights—subsequently called the Sons of Liberty—appeared in Indiana. With Dodd serving as the state grand commander, this society was better organized than the earlier groups. It had the same hierarchy of degrees and the same kind of fantastic rituals as its predecessors, and it professed similar objectives. While most Democratic leaders opposed the enterprise, a few joined it with the hope that it would aid them in the fall elections. The order was probably stronger in Indiana than in any other state of the Northwest, but even there its membership was unstable. At the height of its activity the grand secretary estimated its membership at 18,000, but he complained that few paid their dues. Doubtless the society attained its greatest proportions in the imaginative mind of "General" Dodd himself. On paper it had a military branch which was unknown to rank-and-file members. Actually this aspect of the society was an ephemeral thing which merely provided a few leaders with the title of major general. The ordinary members only deserved responsibility for the spreading of peace sentiment.[45] They knew nothing of the ambitious schemes of some of their leaders.

[44] Indianapolis *Daily State Sentinel,* March 13, 28, April 21, 23, June 19, July 22, August 5, November 23, 1863. See also Fesler, "Secret Political Societies," in *Indiana Magazine of History,* 14(1918):187-200, 213-14. Less reliable are Foulke, *Oliver P. Morton,* 1:376 ff. and Terrell, *Report,* 1:294 ff. Recent general accounts are George Fort Milton, *Abraham Lincoln and the Fifth Column* (New York, 1942) and Wood Gray, *The Hidden Civil War: The Story of the Copperheads* (New York, 1942).

[45] *Official Records,* 2 series, 7:627; Pitman (ed.), *Trials for Treason,* 80 ff.; Fesler, "Secret Political Societies," in *Indiana Magazine of History,* 14:187 ff.; Felix G. Stidger, *Treason History of the Order of Sons of Liberty* . . . (Chicago, 1903), 99, 182-83; Stidger to Capt. S. E. Jones, June 17, 1864, AGO files, Court Martial Records, National Archives, Washington, D. C.

But the followers of Dodd were not the representative men of the Hoosier Democracy. Almost invariably the local Democratic conventions which called for peace still insisted that any settlement must include a restoration of the Union. Few of them favored "peace at any price."[46] At the same time an influential group of Democratic leaders advised their friends that political success was possible only upon a war platform and warned them against allowing the peace faction to dictate to the rest of the party.[47] The New Albany *Ledger* still professed to see no road to peace except through the defeat of the Confederacy. The Dodd group, it maintained, was performing invaluable service for the Republicans, but "the man who is not willing to fight for the Union is not a Democrat."[48]

On July 12 the Democratic state convention assembled at Indianapolis. Immediately the moderates took control and, despite the complaints of the peace faction, conducted the meeting to their own satisfaction. After voting to refer all resolutions without debate to a special committee controlled by the moderates, the convention turned to the selection of candidates for state offices. Joseph E. McDonald, an accomplished jurist, a former attorney general, and a man of high personal integrity, was the overwhelming choice for governor and was easily nominated over Lambdin Milligan. David Turpie was chosen for lieutenant governor without opposition when Milligan withdrew in disgust.[49] The remainder of the ticket

[46] Indianapolis *Daily State Sentinel,* January 9, 11, 12, 19, June 6, 20, July 2, 6, 7, 1864.

[47] *Ibid.,* November 10, 21, 1863, January 9, 13, 16, April 19, June 18, 28, July 9, 1864; New Albany *Weekly Ledger,* December 9, 1863.

[48] New Albany *Weekly Ledger,* November 11, 18, 1863, March 23, July 6, 13, 1864.

[49] Turpie later declined the nomination and ran for Congress in the ninth district. The Democratic state central committee selected Gen. Mahlon D. Manson, a firm supporter of the war, to replace Turpie on the state ticket. Indianapolis *Daily State Sentinel,* August 13, 1864.

was filled by the renomination of the incumbent state officers.

In the afternoon McDonald addressed the convention with a speech which keynoted his subsequent campaign. He began with a critical review of Morton's policies and devious financial practices. If elected he promised that his oath to uphold the state and Federal constitutions would be "no idle pageant." McDonald then outlined his position upon the war and made a conscious effort to maintain the unity of his party. While opposing the war as it was then being prosecuted, he asserted that he was not aware that the Democrats had changed their position since 1862. And so, he explained, "I am for peace at the earliest practicable moment; but peace on the terms of the restoration of the Union under the Federal Constitution, with all its rights and guarantees to the several States North and South." Upon those principles he would welcome the support of Indiana's voters.

The party platform was another severe disappointment to the peace men. It evaded the war issue and merely stated vaguely that an adherence to the Constitution, to which the Democrats were pledged, necessarily implied "the restoration of liberty, and the rights of the States under the Constitution unimpaired," and that such adherence would "lead to an early and honorable peace." Other resolutions denounced Morton's usurpation of power, the violations of civil liberty, and the waste and corruption which had brought the nation "to the verge of bankruptcy and general ruin." The platform concluded with a long tribute to Indiana's soldiers and a promise to aid them and their families. The angry minority of "Copperheads" failed in an effort to amend the platform by inserting a straightforward peace resolution. After that the convention adjourned.[50]

[50] Indianapolis *Daily State Sentinel*, July 13, 14, 1864; Indianapolis *Daily Journal* and *Gazette*, July 13, 1864.

During the following weeks Indiana Democrats continued to air their differences in the press and at local meetings. But the moderates maintained their control of the party. By the time of the national convention which assembled at Chicago on August 29, they had made it clear that Gen. George B. McClellan was their choice for the presidential nomination. His selection was eminently satisfactory to the masses of Hoosier Democrats.

McClellan's subsequent letter of acceptance, which repudiated the "peace plank" in the national platform, was the final blow to the peace Democrats. The Indiana Democracy supported McClellan on his own terms with little dissent; the speeches of Hendricks, McDonald, and Dunham at the McClellan ratification meeting at Indianapolis, gave him an unqualified endorsement. References to the "peace plank" were notably scarce.[51] "The Democratic party is, most emphatically, the Union party of the country, and General McClellan is the true representative of its principles," exulted the New Albany *Ledger*.[52] McClellan was for peace, remarked the *Sentinel*, "but for peace upon the basis of Union. . . . Can more be conceded than this without consenting to a dissolution of the Union and the establishment of separate Confederacies?"[53] Thus, in 1864, the Hoosier Democracy remained basically an unconditional union party, and, to a large extent, a war party as well.[54]

[51] Indianapolis *Daily State Sentinel*, September 3, 19, 1864; New Albany *Weekly Ledger*, September 21, 1864.
[52] New Albany *Weekly Ledger*, September 14, 1864.
[53] Indianapolis *Daily State Sentinel*, September 10, 1864.
[54] The peace men did not conceal their disappointment, but the early plans of Vallandigham's friends to repudiate McClellan made little headway in Indiana. Voorhees publicly refused to co-operate with them and urged the consolidation of the Democracy behind McClellan. Terre Haute *Journal*, quoted in *ibid.*, September 14, 1864. J. M. Hanna, another prominent peace advocate, advised all Democrats to support McClellan as the only way to defeat Lincoln and protect civil liberty. *Ibid.*, September 21, 1864.

4

The state and national campaigns wore on without eliciting any real enthusiasm from a despairing people. With every indication that the war was indeed a failure, it was only the Hoosiers' intense devotion to the Union that prevented them from rushing headlong into the arms of the peace men. The prevailing gloom terrified the champions of the Union party, and they searched frantically for some means of bolstering their sinking cause.

Perhaps an appeal to Indiana's soldiers would have the desired effect. In the spring and early summer many state regiments came home to recruit or to be mustered out of the service at the expiration of their three-year enlistments. Governor Morton arranged for each of them a fine reception which usually served as a thinly disguised political rally.[55] The speeches of welcome and the responses of regimental officers generally introduced the politics of the day and subtly identified the cause of the soldiers with that of the Union party. Morton reviewed each regiment's history, extolled its achievements, and then slipped imperceptibly into a discussion of the issues being debated on the hustings. "We could rejoice," he proclaimed on one occasion, "and you could rejoice much more if you found all the people at home unanimous. It is not thus. There never was a war supported by all; there never was a cause in which all were united; and you will regret to find that there are those in Indiana who do not sympathize with you—who regret that you did not come home with your flags trailing in the dust. . . ."[56] Before these military receptions were

---

[55] Considerable correspondence dealing with arrangements for these receptions, and with the Governor's efforts to provide for the comfort of the regiments during their journey home, is in the Telegraphic Correspondence, vol. 5. For accounts of these receptions, see the files of the Indianapolis *Journal* and *Gazette*, February-July, 1864.

[56] Indianapolis *Daily Journal*, June 6, 1864.

concluded the Union party had presented its case to the army and to the citizens of the state.

At their regular political meetings Union orators merely elaborated upon the themes they had developed in the campaign of 1862. They urged loyal Democrats to abandon their party which had been seized by the "Copperheads," the men who had done "more to prolong this war than all the rebels in the South."[57] Not the tariff, not banking, but the preservation of the government was the one great issue before the people. The ballots of loyal men would have to sustain the armies in the field; a vote for the administration was a vote "squarely against secession and secession sympathy, and against the rebellion." The victory of the Union party, they said, was as important as a military victory, for the success of the Democracy would place the state in opposition to the government, cause its withdrawal from the war, and culminate in revolution in the Northwest.[58]

To carry this message to the Hoosiers the Union party conducted an unusually thorough canvass. Apparently the party had ample funds upon which to draw. Joseph Wright, D. S. Gooding, James Hughes, and other "War Democrats" instructed the Hoosier Democracy upon the issues and its duties in the crisis.[59] Army officers like Chaplain John H. Lozier, Gen. Alvin P. Hovey, and Col. Benjamin Harrison stumped the state and gave additional testimony to the unity of the soldiers behind Governor Morton and the Union party. A host of out-of-state speakers made their appearance at one time or another during the campaign, among them Andrew Johnson, Secretary Chase, Gen. John A. Logan of Illinois, and Gen. James A. Garfield of Ohio.[60] The Indiana

[57] *Ibid.*, January 22, February 25, 29, June 20, 22, 27, 1864.
[58] *Ibid.*, June 21, 24, 27, August 12, 18, 1864; Indianapolis *Gazette*, September 19, October 5, 1864.
[59] Indianapolis *Daily Journal*, April 4, August 29, September 1, 1864.
[60] *Ibid.*, August 16, September 16, 19, 29, October 7, 1864; Indianapolis *Gazette*, October 7, 8, 1864; Aurora *Commercial*, October 6, 1864.

Club, formed by Hoosier politicians in Washington, gave substantial aid in the form of money and loyal documents. The Union Leagues flooded the state with additional propaganda material.[61] Several eastern bankers appeared particularly interested in the success of Morton's campaign, and one of them vowed that "men of means should not let him lose . . . if it costs 50,000 dollars to win."[62]

The Democrats were equally hard at work. Hendricks, Voorhees, McDonald, and the state officers were tireless campaigners. The burden of their plea was that the Lincoln administration was a failure and that peace and reunion could come only through a Democratic victory. They elaborated upon their earlier protests against emancipation and Negro equality, against the subversion of the Constitution, and against the tariff, national banks, and other manifestations of economic revolution. They raged at the mounting national debt, the heavy load of taxes, the waste of blood and treasure, and the sacrifice of the interests of western farmers and laborers to those of the rich eastern bondholders.[63]

The two gubernatorial candidates sparked the campaigns of their respective parties. Late in July McDonald delivered his principal address at Greencastle, where he developed his convention speech into a thorough and critical review of Morton's policies.[64] A week later the Governor was at the same place to dissect his opponent's arguments and to lash out against the Democracy's equivocal position upon the war. He denounced the note of praise for the soldiers in the Democratic platform as

[61] Indianapolis *Daily Journal,* April 22, September 7, 1864.

[62] D. R. Martin, president, Ocean Bank of the City of New York, to Morton, September 30, 1864, AGO, Morton Correspondence, Archives Division; Martin to J. J. Brown, September 12, 1864, AGO, Civil War correspondence, Archives Division.

[63] Indianapolis *Daily State Sentinel,* March 17, 26, April 20, 27, May 19, June 22, July 28, August 17, September 1, 5, 26, 30, October 3, 7, 1864; New Albany *Weekly Ledger,* June 8, August 31, September 7, 14, 1864.

[64] Indianapolis *Daily State Sentinel,* July 22, 1864.

sheer hypocrisy; McDonald's real position, he claimed,
was shown by the fact that "every open and avowed
secessionist — every worshipper of Jeff Davis — every
Knight of the Golden Circle and Son of Liberty—every
Southern spy who is lurking through our borders is his
warm and earnest advocate."[65]

Upon the suggestion of McDonald, Morton agreed
to participate in a series of joint debates, the first to be
held at La Porte on August 10. During their encounters
McDonald continued to be evasive upon the war issue
as he strove to hold his party together. He spoke regularly
for an armistice and peace upon the basis of the
Union, but he was never quite clear how the South could
be persuaded to accept those terms. Morton pressed
McDonald relentlessly upon that point until the latter
ultimately declared that, compromise failing, he favored
a continued prosecution of the war for the Union.
Throughout the debates Morton always posed as the
busy executive who was fighting the obstructionism of
a mere politician.[66]

Despite the eloquent appeals of countless speakers, the
exhortations of the political press, and the heaps of campaign
literature, it was doubtful whether the citizens of
Indiana had any clear picture of the issues involved in
the contest. Most party leaders generally preferred to
appeal to popular prejudices, rather than to discuss
fundamental questions of national or state policy. Then
an amazing series of events on the eve of the election
separated the campaign from its last contacts with reality.

5

July and August passed, and still there were no decisive
military victories. Reports from discouraged Union party
politicians spoke glumly of impending defeat. And so,

[65] Indianapolis *Daily Journal*, July 28, 1864.
[66] For an account of these debates and summaries of the speeches, see
the files of the Indianapolis *Daily State Sentinel* and *Daily Journal* for
August and September, 1864. See also Foulke, *Oliver P. Morton*, 1:303 ff.

everything else failing, the friends of Governor Morton desperately revived their time-honored strategem and digressed upon the subject of domestic treason. This inflammatory device ultimately roused the electorate and rekindled the fires of partisan fervor. Republican political speakers and the party press soon returned to the familiar tales of a great Northwest conspiracy and expounded upon the necessity of voting against northern rebels who held the Democracy in their grip. Perhaps every Democrat was not a traitor, they said, but certain it was that every traitor was a Democrat.[67]

The evidences of Democratic disloyalty were apparently obvious enough for those who wished to find them. A decision by Judge S. E. Perkins holding military arrests to be illegal when the regular courts were open supposedly gave aid and comfort to the rebellion.[68] The sudden return of Vallandigham from Canada in June, at a time when General Morgan was again raiding Kentucky, might well have been the signal for a general revolt.[69] Above all, every crime, every riot, every local disturbance was paraded forth as an incipient "Copperhead" conspiracy. The ravings of Dodd and his coterie of extremists were exploited to the utmost; indeed the attention Dodd received in the Union press made him appear to be the very soul of the Democracy. "Jackson is dead," mourned the *Journal*, "but Dodd lives to go to Chicago."[70] Democrats angrily charged that "desperate political tricksters" were thus seeking to "hide their own iniquities," and that Morton was courting civil war in Indiana to serve his own purposes.[71]

---

[67] See especially Indianapolis *Daily Journal*, March 9, April 4, 7, 25, May 4, June 11, 20, 21, 22, 23, 24, 1864; Indianapolis *Gazette*, April 13, 1864.

[68] Indianapolis *Daily Journal*, February 3, 4, March 18, 1864.

[69] *Ibid.*, June 17, 21, 28, 1864.

[70] *Ibid.*, June 28, 1864.

[71] Indianapolis *Daily State Sentinel*, April 5, 25, May 3, 6, June 24,

The spread of the Sons of Liberty, primarily as a secret Democratic political club, provided additional material for the Union party's treason campaign. The most ludicrous aspect of this "secret" society was the fact that it was never able to conceal its secrets and proceedings, and that, so far from aiding the Democracy, its very existence was a source of infinite satisfaction to the Republicans. Governor Morton and the politically-minded General Carrington, who from July, 1863, until May, 1864, was on detached service in Indiana, and on May 23, was restored to the command of the District of Indiana, hired a score of detectives to investigate the Sons of Liberty and to make regular reports. These energetic spies went to work with an evident determination to discover the treason which they were being paid to find; but their reports offered no evidence of illegal or treasonable conduct by the society itself, other than the unfounded rumors that were circulating in the Union press. Knowing every move the Order made, Morton and Carrington had no reason to fear it as a menace to domestic peace. Instead, the Governor held the society "as a plaything in his hands," allowed it to grow, and "even coerce[d] it into his service."[72]

Carrington's ablest detective was Felix G. Stidger, an impoverished Kentuckian who had been abused by local guerrillas and was determined to "even up the score" with them and their sympathizers. In May, 1864, Stidger entered Carrington's service, made the necessary acquaintances, and got himself initiated into the Sons of Liberty in Kentucky. He soon won the confidence of

July 26, 28, August 3, 9, 1864; New Albany *Weekly Ledger,* June 22, 29, 1864.

[72] Foulke, *Oliver P. Morton,* 1:374. For accounts of the activities of these detectives, see bound volumes labeled Carrington Papers in Archives Division, Indiana State Library; Terrell, *Report,* 1:300; Pitman (ed.), *Trials for Treason,* 121; Stidger, *Treason History, passim; Official Records,* 2 series, 7:260-61, 3 series, 4:162-63; Foulke, *Oliver P. Morton,* 1:373-74, 405-7.

Judge Joshua F. Bullitt, the Kentucky commander, who secured his election as grand secretary of the state organization. Thereafter Stidger initiated neophytes into the order, established new local "castles," and kept the fees he collected as his compensation. Actually the Sons of Liberty had scarcely begun to organize in Kentucky before Stidger's appearance, and he almost deserved to be considered one of its founders. Since he was sent on frequent trips into Indiana, Stidger soon won the friendship of Dodd, Bowles, and other Hoosier leaders. Bowles was especially generous in divulging the plans of his confederates. Dodd once assured the detective that he was one of the few men he trusted completely. Meanwhile, Stidger made regular reports to Morton and Carrington keeping them informed of everything that transpired.[73]

In this way Carrington obtained possession of the secrets, rituals, constitution, and other written work of the order, which he edited and submitted to Morton in the form of an elaborate report. The Governor decided to hold back this material until later in the campaign and therefore delayed its publication until July 30 when it appeared in the Indianapolis *Journal*. At once the Union press portrayed the Sons of Liberty as the working part of the Democratic party. The Indianapolis *Gazette* drew the obvious political lesson implicit in the exposure: "A generous public may tolerate their presence so long as the public safety is not jeopardized thereby; but they must be vigilantly watched and debarred from all positions of trust and confidence."[74]

A few days later military authorities invaded Voorhees' former law office at Terre Haute and seized some pamphlets printed by the Order of American Knights,

---

[73] Stidger, *Treason History, passim;* Pitman (ed.), *Trials for Treason,* 111, 116; Foulke, *Oliver P. Morton,* 1:405n-6n; Milton, *Lincoln and the Fifth Column, passim.* Stidger's reports and much material on the Sons of Liberty are in the AGO, Court Martial Records, National Archives, Washington, D. C.

[74] Indianapolis *Gazette,* August 6, 22, 1864.

together with a large amount of the Congressman's
private correspondence. Letters of any political significance were subsequently printed by the Union press.
Angrily Voorhees denied any knowledge of the pamphlets, asserted that he had abandoned the office months
earlier, and explained that the owner had permitted him
to store his correspondence there. The result was an
exchange of abusive public letters between Voorhees and
Carrington whom the former branded as a "letter
thief."[75] But the political advantage was gained by Carrington's Union party friends.

At this critical juncture in the state campaign Grand
Commander Dodd plotted a mad conspiracy which, in
effect, forged the most potent weapon in the hands of
Governor Morton. Fearing to make known his fantastic
schemes even to the Sons of Liberty, Dodd and a few
cohorts devised a plan to free the rebel prisoners at
Camp Morton, to seize the arsenal, and to raise a general
insurrection. The ultimate objective was the formation
of a Northwest Confederacy, or possibly the joining of
the Northwest with the South. August 16 was fixed as
the date for the uprising.

When, on July 30, Judge Bullitt, one of Dodd's few
confidants, was arrested by military authorities at Louisville, Dodd immediately revealed the whole story of the
conspiracy to Stidger. On the night of August 2 Stidger
reported the plot to Morton and Carrington. The Governor's reaction was one of amazement that Dodd could
contemplate such an insane enterprise.[76] Yet Morton

[75] Indianapolis *Daily Journal,* August 6, 16, 22, 26, September 5, 1864;
Indianapolis *Daily State Sentinel,* August 9, 26, 1864. It was never proved
that Voorhees was a member of any secret society; Carrington later
confessed that he had no evidence to substantiate his charges. Carrington
to Governor J. Frank Hanly, March 9, 1907, typed copy in Carrington
Papers, folder labeled "Indiana in Civil War." See also Charles Roll,
*Colonel Dick Thompson. The Persistent Whig (Indiana Historical Col-
lections,* vol. 30, Indianapolis, 1948), 187-38.

[76] See account in Carrington Papers. See also Carrington to Assistant
Adjutant General Potter, Columbus, Ohio, August 9, 1864, in *Official*

and Carrington took no action to stop the conspirators, except to prepare the Legion and to take other military precautions against an emergency. This fact seemed to give considerable significance to a letter which Carrington later wrote to Stidger: ". . . we so fully knew their plans that they could make no public demonstration without getting caught in the act." It was this that caused Democrats to assert later that Morton would have allowed the insurrection to transpire to make political capital from it. Whatever the merits of that charge, certain it is that the judge advocate deviated from the facts when he asserted, at the subsequent treason trials, that only swift action by civil and military authorities prevented an uprising.[77]

Early in August Dodd described his plans to J. J. Bingham, editor of the Indianapolis *Sentinel* and chairman of the Democratic state central committee. He asked Bingham to call a party mass meeting at Indianapolis on August 16 to aid in the execution of the project. In astonishment Bingham flatly refused to co-operate with Dodd or to call the meeting. At the same time Michael C. Kerr, Democratic candidate for Congress in the second district, reported to Bingham that rumors of the conspiracy had leaked out in southern Indiana and that the farmers were in a panic. Appreciating the political capital that Dodd was furnishing the Republicans, these men related the story to McDonald and, on August 5, called a meeting of Democratic leaders. On that occasion they forced Dodd to promise to abandon the project. A week later prominent Indiana Democrats met again and exacted additional assurances from Dodd. As a result

---

Records, 1 series, 39:pt.2:236-38; Fesler, "Secret Political Societies," in *Indiana Magazine of History,* 14:243-44, 247-48, 285-86; Foulke, *Oliver P. Morton,* 1:400 ff.; Kenneth M. Stampp, "The Milligan Case and the Election of 1864 in Indiana," in *Mississippi Valley Historical Review,* 31(1944-45):48-50.

[77] Stampp, "The Milligan Case," in *op. cit.,* 31:49-50.

Voting Down the Rebellion 245

August 16 passed without an uprising, and the "great conspiracy" never passed beyond the bounds of mere talk.[78]

But if the leaders of the Democratic party believed that the Dodd conspiracy could be buried and forgotten, they reckoned without Morton. On August 20 the Governor received information that a quantity of arms had been shipped from New York to Dodd's printing establishment at Indianapolis. That night military authorities invaded the premises and seized a large amount of ammunition and thirty-two boxes labeled "tracts" which contained four hundred revolvers. They also found much of Dodd's private correspondence and material concerning the Sons of Liberty, including a list showing that several Democratic candidates for state offices were members.[79] The report of the raid, as well as the letters and additional information about the secret society, were immediately given sensational treatment in the Union press. "Let everyone stop and inquire where we are tending and what future is just before us," warned the *Journal*. "The signs of revolution have been visible about us for many months, and to-day we find ourselves standing upon its very brink."[80]

The citizens of Indianapolis flew into a perfect frenzy. On the night of August 22 there was a large and excited indignation meeting which caused no little alarm among the Democrats. Morton's speech was a triumphant vindication of his much-repeated charges of domestic treason. Dodd, he cried, was the mere tool of shrewder men, for the whole Democratic party was equally guilty of his crime. "It is all one thing to Jeff Davis whether we shall fall by means of a defeat at the coming elections or by the overthrow of the Union armies in the field."

---

[78] Stampp, "The Milligan Case," in *op. cit.*, 31:50; Fesler, "Secret Political Societies," in *Indiana Magazine of History*, 14:249-50.
[79] Stampp, "The Milligan Case," in *op. cit.*, 31:50-51.
[80] Indianapolis *Daily Journal*, August 22, 1864.

The Confederates knew that their last hope of success was to divide the people, and to get the Federal government into the hands of men who would at once concede them the victory.[81]

With this poignant text, Union party speakers carried the message of Democratic treason throughout the state and converted the wavering voters to their cause. Intense excitement supplanted the former apathy as loyal men were instructed in the need to vote down the rebellion at home. Democrats tried hard to brand the exposures as farces, and they denied that it was illegal to purchase arms. John C. Walker coolly claimed ownership of the confiscated revolvers and demanded their return. The Democratic candidates for state offices denied membership in any treasonable organization.[82] But the Union party had gained a tremendous advantage, and none understood the fact better than the Democratic leaders themselves. "The exposure of the Sons of Liberty is tearing the ranks of the Democracy all to flinders," rejoiced one of the Governor's secretaries. "McClellan stock is not quoted at all. McDonald stock is fast going down."[83]

Governor Morton had still another heavy blow prepared for his political foes. Late in August he decided that the leaders of the Sons of Liberty should be arrested at once and tried for treason before a military court. Carrington, however, was not ready to go that far, and he had his first serious disagreement with the bolder Morton. The General denied that he had authority to make the arrests and doubted the legality of military trials when the regular courts were open. But Morton feared delay and frankly asserted that an immediate trial

---

[81] Indianapolis *Daily Journal,* August 23, 24, 1864.

[82] *Ibid.,* August 25, 31, September 9, 1864; Indianapolis *Daily State Sentinel,* August 23-26, 30, 1864; New Albany *Weekly Ledger,* August 24, 31, 1864.

[83] W. H. H. Terrell to Gen. J. T. Wilder, September 6, 1864, Wilder MSS.

was "essential to the success of the National cause in the autumn elections." Hence he quickly obtained an order for Carrington's removal. On August 25 the Governor secured the appointment of Gen. Alvin P. Hovey, a political general from Indiana who was thoroughly in sympathy with his course.[84]

Early in September Hovey arrested Dodd and confined him in the Federal court building at Indianapolis. The commander then created a military commission of Indiana officers; Maj. Henry L. Burnett, judge advocate of the Department of the Ohio, took charge of the prosecution. J. W. Gordon and Martin M. Ray acted ably as Dodd's counsel.

The trial began on September 22. Dodd remained cool and confident until September 27 when Stidger took the stand to testify against him. Up to that point Dodd had no suspicion that he had revealed his plans to a government detective, and Stidger's appearance came as a profound shock.[85] For the next three days the intrepid detective presented his testimony as the government's chief witness. He related every detail of Dodd's contemplated insurrection and made a thorough exposure of the Sons of Liberty. Yet he neither offered clear evidence of an overt act on the part of the conspirators as required by the Constitution to prove treason, or proof that the secret society was implicated in any way. Stidger had no greater success in his efforts to demonstrate that the order was a conspiracy *per se*, which was one of the fundamental assumptions of the prosecution. In fact, he had to confess that he had no direct knowledge of the alleged military branch of the Sons of Liberty, and that he had never seen any of its members engage in military drill.[86]

[84] Stampp, "The Milligan Case," in *Mississippi Valley Historical Review*, 31:51-52. See also account in Carrington Papers; *Official Records*, 1 series, 39:pt. 2:303.
[85] Stampp, "The Milligan Case," in *op. cit.*, 31:52-53.
[86] Pitman (ed.), *Trials for Treason*, 19-37.

The scene which then ensued resembled *opéra bouffe* far more than a trial for treason. In the atmosphere of a political rally a host of detectives and renegade witnesses appeared to testify to the treasonable nature of the Sons of Liberty. But the best efforts of the judge advocate in the form of leading questions still failed to advance the "evidence" beyond mere rumors and hearsay reports. The counsel for the defense brought in evidence to show that in several cases questionable methods had been used to persuade men to testify. One witness confessed that a government detective had promised him relief from the draft if he would appear in the stand. Stidger himself, when first asked to testify against Dodd, suggested that in return he be "provided with a sufficiency to live hereafter in protection." The defense attacked Stidger unmercifully for his part in spreading the secret order and for accepting pay for initiating new members. The bias of the court reporter was apparent enough, for his reports gave little space to cross examinations, merely observing that "no additional facts were elucidated." The conscious effort to indict the whole Democratic party was illustrated in the following questions directed to a witness by the judge advocate:

"Q. Of what political faith were the majority of men comprising that organization [Sons of Liberty]?

"A. They were all Democrats.

"Q. State whether any other class of men were admitted, or was it *sine quo* [sic] *non* that a man must be a Democrat?

"A. I do not think that anyone would have got in unless he professed to be a Democrat."[87]

During the trial Hovey, Judge Advocate Burnett and Carrington (who did not publicize his opposition to military arrests after his removal) found time to address

---

[87] Pitman (ed.), *Trials for Treason, passim;* J. J. Eustis to Lt. Col. Thomas B. Farleigh, August 3, 1864, AGO, Court Martial Records, National Archives.

numerous Union party meetings. The Republican press printed full daily reports of the testimony and used it for political ends to the fullest extent. The Indianapolis *Journal* edited its reports and distorted the evidence to make the implications of treason appear more convincing. That all Sons of Liberty were traitors and that most Democrats were Sons of Liberty was the theme of its editorial comment.[88]

Early in the morning of October 7, a few days before the state election, Dodd performed one last service for the Union party: he escaped from his room in the government building. No precautions had been taken to guard against such an attempt, and unexplainable delays occurred before the alarm was sounded. Military authorities made no serious effort to capture Dodd, and he fled to Canada with little apparent difficulty. But the judge advocate and the Republican press could announce in triumph that Dodd's flight was the most conclusive proof of his guilt.[89]

Meanwhile, the other men suspected of being implicated in Dodd's conspiracy were arrested to undergo similar military trials. Chief among them were Bowles, Milligan, Andrew Humphreys, Stephen Horsey, Horace Heffren, and J. J. Bingham.[90] That the arrest of Bingham was primarily for its political effect was evident from the fact that no charges were ever preferred against him. The new trials did not begin until late October, but the citizens of Indiana had already been sufficiently instructed upon the disloyalty of the Hoosier Democracy.

---

[88] Stampp, "The Milligan Case," in *Mississippi Valley Historical Review*, 31:53-54. During September and October the columns of the Indianapolis *Daily Journal* and *Gazette* were filled with editorial comments upon the Dodd conspiracy, and reports of the political activities of Carrington, Hovey, and Burnett.

[89] Stampp, "The Milligan Case," in *op. cit.*, 31:55.

[90] *Ibid.*, 31:55-56. John C. Walker escaped arrest by a sudden trip to Canada. J. McMillan to Morton, September 27, 1864, Archives Division.

6

The exposure of the Sons of Liberty and the treason trials marked the beginning of a series of events which ultimately rescued the Union party from what had earlier appeared to be inevitable defeat. Sherman's capture of Atlanta early in September and Sheridan's successes in the Shenandoah Valley discredited the Democratic national platform's reference to the war as a failure. These encouraging victories were the occasions for joyous celebrations in Indiana. "The echo of every gun fell on Copperhead ears like the death knell of their hopes," exulted the *Journal*.[91] Finally the withdrawal of Frémont from the contest on September 22 made possible the consolidation of the Republican party, at least for the duration of the campaign.

Despite all these propitious events, Governor Morton was still worried about the prospects of his party. For example, the Governor and his friends were much concerned about the arrival in the state of groups of Southern refugees whom they feared might be settled in time to vote the Democratic ticket in October. Hence they begged the War Department and generals in the field to have these people returned to their homes and to send no more into Indiana.[92]

Union party leaders were also frightened because Indiana's quota under the President's last call for troops had not been filled by volunteers, and preparations were under way for the drafting of 12,000 men. Morton repeatedly requested that the draft be postponed until after the election. He made a special trip to Washington to explain that this was a political necessity. At last Indiana's Union politicians united in one final appeal

[91] Indianapolis *Daily Journal,* September 8, 21, 22, 1864.
[92] W. Gibson to Morton, September 26, 1864, Archives Division; Morton to Stanton, August 19, 1864, in Telegraphic Correspondence, 5:270, 272; *Official Records,* 3 series, 4:711-12.

in which they all but predicted defeat if the draft should be applied. But Lincoln and Stanton, having assurances from Sherman that the army would turn against the administration if the draft were postponed, refused to make the concession.[93] In consequence, the draft was executed shortly before the election. Republicans, in a perfect panic, tried to throw the full blame for the draft upon the Democrats. Morton and local military officials expected serious resistance, but there was little trouble.[94]

At the same time the Governor and other politicians were convinced that Indiana could only be saved for the Union party through the aid of a substantial soldier vote.[95] Since the state constitution prevented troops from voting in the field, the only possible expedient was to bring Indiana's men home for that purpose. Morton obtained early assurances that all the hundred-day volunteers would be returned before October, and, upon their arrival, he provided them with the usual flattering receptions.[96] Again he traveled to Washington to request that every soldier who could possibly be spared be furloughed in time for the October election. State leaders insisted that the votes of at least 15,000 soldiers were needed to insure a Union victory. Lincoln passed the suggestion on to General Sherman, pointing out that Indiana was the only state holding elections whose soldiers could not vote in the field. But the latter gave it a cold response. Angrily

---

[93] Stanton to Grant, September 11, 1864, in *Official Records,* 1 series, 42:pt.2:783-84; Sherman to Halleck, September 17, 1864, in *ibid.,* 1 series, 39:pt. 2:396; Stanton to Morton, September 18, 1864, in *ibid.,* 3 series, 4:732; Foulke, *Oliver P. Morton,* 1:366-70.

[94] Indianapolis *Daily Journal,* October 5, 1864; *Official Records,* 3 series, 4:725-26, 757-60; Terrell, *Report,* 1:48.

[95] J. V. Kelso to Morton, September 16, 1864, Chicago-Morton Collection; Indianapolis *Gazette,* July 9, 19, 20, 1864; Hollister, *Schuyler Colfax,* 238-39.

[96] Morton to Stanton, August 15, 1864, in Morton Letter Press Books, 3(September 1863-December 1866):111-12; Morton to Col. E. Shaw, September 14, 1864, in Telegraphic Correspondence, 13:234; Indianapolis *Daily Journal,* August 30, 1864.

the Indiana Republicans criticized the generals who failed to appreciate the political danger behind their lines.[97]

Failing in his attempts to obtain a general furlough of Indiana troops, Morton, as a last resort, secured permission to bring home the sick and wounded soldiers who were able to leave the army hospitals. Immediately he sent out special agents to collect them and made careful preparations for their comfort and entertainment upon their arrival.[98] As usual the Governor placed this work entirely in the hands of his special friends who made it clear to their charges that he alone was responsible for their furloughs and subsequent care.[99] In this manner nearly 9,000 disabled soldiers returned to the state in time to vote in October.[100]

As an added precaution Morton delayed the forwarding of new troops to the field. Secretary Stanton informed General Grant that it would be next to impossible to move soldiers out of Indiana until after the state election.[101] Many officers, as well as small bodies of troops located nearby, were also sent home to vote.[102] Soldiers thus gave vital aid to Morton in his campaign to defeat the rebellion with ballots.

7

On October 11, after a flurry of last-minute speeches and enthusiastic Union rallies, the Hoosiers went to the

---

[97] Lincoln to Sherman, September 19, 1864, in Nicolay and Hay (eds.), *Complete Works of Abraham Lincoln*, 10:225-26; Foulke, *Oliver P. Morton*, 1:366-69.

[98] Among the many communications regarding these arrangements, see especially Morton to Stanton, September 20, 1864; J. K. Barnes, Surgeon General, to Morton, September 24, 1864; and Morton to I. W. Montfort, September 27, 1864, in Telegraphic Correspondence, 5:284, 285, 13:246.

[99] R. W. Allen to Morton, October 2, 1864, in Telegraphic Correspondence, 13:267; Indianapolis *Daily Journal*, October 5, 1864.

[100] Morton to Stanton, October 14, 1864, in Telegraphic Correspondence, 5:306.

[101] *Official Records*, 1 series, 42:pt.2:783-84.

[102] Morton to General Hooker, and to General Burbridge, October 3, 1864, in Telegraphic Correspondence, 5:290, 292. Major O. Blake to Morton, October 17, 1864, Chicago-Morton Collection.

polls and gave their verdict in the state contest. The result surprised even the most optimistic Republicans: Morton and the rest of the Republican Union state ticket won by a more than 20,000 majority; the Union party regained control of the General Assembly; Union candidates were victorious in eight of the eleven Congressional districts.[103] Similar results in the October elections in Pennsylvania and Ohio foreshadowed the outcome of the national contest.

Despite the gloomy prospect, Democrats then made a desperate effort to save Indiana for McClellan. But the Union party campaigned just as strenuously to return Lincoln to the presidency. Shortly before the November elections the treason trials of Bowles, Humphreys, Heffren, Milligan and Horsey began and provided additional rich political material for the Republicans. The prosecution again tried to paint the Sons of Liberty as a conspiracy *per se* and to make the Order and the Democratic party appear synonymous.[104] Union party speakers toured the state and addressed the largest political meetings of the campaign. On October 14 Morton spoke at a great victory celebration in Indianapolis. The state triumph of his party, he asserted, "dealt the rebellion a staggering blow"; the re-election of Lincoln would virtually end the war.[105] On November 7, Indiana contributed to Lincoln's sweeping victory by giving him a 20,000 majority over McClellan. Republicanism was now firmly intrenched in both state and nation.

With the elections and political campaigning finally concluded, Indiana settled down to the business of aiding

---

[103] Indianapolis *Daily Journal,* October 19, 20, 29, November 7, 1864. Col. H. D. Washburn contested Voorhees' election in the seventh district, and the Republican Congress finally decided in favor of the former. William E. Niblack, of Vincennes, and Michael C. Kerr, of New Albany, were victorious Democrats.

[104] Stampp, "The Milligan Case," in *Mississippi Valley Historical Review,* 31:56; Foulke, *Oliver P. Morton,* 1:424.

[105] Indianapolis *Daily Journal,* October 15, 1864.

in the final suppression of the rebellion. Actually few fundamental issues had been decided by the recent political contest. It was the soldier vote, the late military victories, and the identification of the Union party with the cause of preserving the Union which gave an advantage to both Morton and Lincoln. The flimsy charges that Democrats were disloyal, the embarrassment that a few extreme peace men caused the Democracy, and the dramatization of the treason trials all had a pronounced effect upon Hoosier voters.[106] Basic state and national issues, such as the emerging problem of reconstruction, found little room in the appeals of the victorious party. It was probably inevitable that the settlement of such questions should have to wait until the Union armies were victorious and peace had been restored. Then the people would have time to reflect upon these less dramatic though equally vital matters.

[106] See Indianapolis *Daily Journal,* October 27, 1864, for an assertion that the Dodd conspiracy added 10,000 votes to the Union party majority.

THE PROBLEMS OF PEACE

CHAPTER 11

The last miles of the road to Appomattox were studded with fair promises of a victorious peace, and with grim warnings of the trouble that lay beyond. By the close of 1864 the end of the war was in sight, and Hoosiers waited expectantly for the surrender of the nearly exhausted Southerners. Grant's army, reinforced and well supplied, continued its inexorable siege of Petersburg and Richmond. The thin and ragged Confederate lines formed a feeble bulwark for a cause that was already lost. In December many Indiana regiments stood before Nashville with Gen. George H. Thomas and helped to destroy Gen. John B. Hood's invading army; others accompanied Sherman on his triumphant march from Atlanta to the sea. The year 1865 dawned with the bright prospect of a swift termination of the death and destruction which had plagued the nation during four long years of war.

The new year would also be an auspicious one for Governor Morton and Indiana Republicans. The legislature, scheduled to convene on January 5, would be controlled by the Republican Union party on all joint ballots. The lower house had a safe Union majority; the upper chamber was equally divided between the two parties, but Lieutenant Governor Conrad Baker would be entitled to cast the deciding vote in case of a tie.

Morton had little reason to doubt that his policies would be sustained, for his special friends expected to direct legislative proceedings.

In the Republican caucus on the night of January 4, John U. Pettit was easily nominated for speaker of the house over David C. Branham who had been allied with the Governor's party foes in southern Indiana. Party nominations for other legislative offices were equally satisfactory to Morton.[1] "We ought to be thankful we are not ambitious," John R. Cravens wrote consolingly to Branham. The strength of the Governor's political machine, he confessed, was overwhelming.[2]

On January 5, the Republicans had little difficulty in organizing the house and in electing all of their caucus nominees. In the senate the offices ultimately had to be divided between the two parties, which caused Republicans to complain somewhat lamely that Democrats thought only of party.[3] On the second day of the session Governor Morton stood before a joint meeting of the two houses and read his long and carefully prepared message. He presented a detailed account of Indiana's war history, its contribution to the Union cause, and its enterprises to aid the soldiers and their families. Once again Morton reviewed and defended his course since the meeting of the previous legislature and invited a thorough investigation of his expenditures during the past two years.[4] The address elicited long and loud applause from the Governor's legislative cronies and from a large audience of friendly citizens. Indeed, remarked the Indianapolis *Journal,* the scene was one

---

[1] Indianapolis *Daily State Sentinel,* January 5, 1865; Indianapolis *Daily Journal,* January 10, 1865.

[2] John R. Cravens to D. C. Branham, January 8, 1864 [1865], David C. Branham MSS., Indiana Division, Indiana State Library.

[3] Indianapolis *Daily Journal* and *Daily State Sentinel,* January 6, 1865.

[4] Indianapolis *Daily Journal* and *Daily State Sentinel,* January 7, 1865; Indiana *House Journal,* 1865, pp. 18-43.

"well calculated to excite emotions of gratitude and complacency in the breast of the Governor."⁵

After Morton's second inauguration on January 9, the legislature proceeded to the general business of the session. The majority lost no time in placing a cloak of legality about the Governor's past policies. W. H. H. Terrell submitted a complete report of the expenditures of the bureau of finance, and a joint legislative committee investigated its accounts and reported its books in order. At the same time the Military Auditing Committee approved Morton's operation of the state arsenal.⁶

Another important item on the legislative agenda was the reimbursement of those who had lent financial aid to the Governor. Amid violent Democratic criticism the majority passed a bill to repay the advances of Winslow, Lanier & Company with interest at seven per cent.⁷ A similar bill provided for repayment of the loans from various counties and private sources. Apparently, remarked the New Albany *Ledger,* Governor Morton believed that the chief duty of the legislature was to justify his official acts—"to legalize that which has been illegal and make lawful that which was unlawful."⁸

Besides routine tax and appropriation measures, the General Assembly considered several other questions of

---

⁵ Indianapolis *Daily Journal,* January 9, 1865.

⁶ Indiana *House Journal,* 1865, pp. 219-24, 375-80. Although all of the committee agreed as to the correctness of the books and vouchers, two of the members dissented from the recommendation of the majority report which would have put the legal stamp of approval on Governor Morton's creation of the bureau of finance and its activities. *Ibid.,* 245-46. The report of the arsenal is printed in *ibid.,* 499-514.

⁷ Indianapolis *Daily Journal,* January 17, 19, 20, 24, 25, 1865; *Laws of Indiana,* 1865, p. 77. On February 2 and 28, 1865, warrants were issued for payment to Winslow, Lanier & Company of $446,697.30 and $182,735.55 respectively, making a total of $629,432.85. Auditor's Register of Warrants, 1862-65, and Auditor's Ledger, 1862-65, in Archives Division, Indiana State Library. Morton estimated the amount paid by the company for the state to be about $575,000. Indiana *House Journal,* 1865, p. 40.

⁸ New Albany *Weekly Ledger,* March 8, 1865.

more than ordinary significance. It agreed to accept a general Congressional land grant, under the terms of the Morrill Act, for the establishment of a state agricultural college.[9] On February 13, after stormy debates and an unsuccessful attempt at a bolt by a few recalcitrant Democrats, the legislature ratified the then pending Thirteenth Amendment to the Federal Constitution. A large audience was present to witness Indiana's formal approval of national emancipation. The announcement of a favorable vote was greeted with cheers from the onlookers and with a roar of artillery from the State House yard.[10] Negro freedom was emerging from "the crucible of war."

As usual the General Assembly consumed a large portion of its time in futile partisan debates. This pursuit engaged the leaders of both parties who launched acrid attacks against the war records of their opponents. Because of the normal legislative procrastination the senate calendar was crowded in the last days of the session, and Democrats were able to block the passage of several measures which Morton had demanded. Chief among them was the so-called "Governor's Bill" which would have enabled him to pay the balance of Stanton's loan into the state treasury, and which would have forced the state to assume the financial obligation of the loan.[11] The failure to pass this bill delayed the settlement of this transaction with the Federal government for several years. But in most other respects the legislature had completely vindicated Morton's administration. The four war years had given him sufficient time to secure a firm hold upon the state Republican organization.

[9] Indianapolis *Daily Journal,* March 7, 1865; *Laws of Indiana,* 1865, pp. 106-11.
[10] Indianapolis *Daily Journal,* February 7, 12, 14, 1865.
[11] *Ibid.,* February 27, March 7, 1865; Indianapolis *Daily State Sentinel,* March 6, 1865; Indiana *House Journal,* 1865, pp. 350, 555, 672-73; Indiana *Senate Journal,* 1865, pp. 485, 510-14.

2

Meanwhile, during the closing months of the war, the Hoosiers were contributing their share of the reinforcements which strengthened the Union armies for the last blows against the Confederacy. In December, 1864, the President made a final call for 300,000 troops and gave Indiana another large quota to fill. The worst features of the recruiting system occurred in the response to this call, for each local district sought desperately to avoid another draft. They paid extravagant bounties and tried every device to secure credits regardless of how few men they might actually send into military service.[12] During the winter Morton made repeated efforts to have the draft postponed, and in February the legislature passed a resolution asking the War Department for still another delay.[13] But in March, Indiana had to endure a small draft to raise 2,424 additional men.[14]

The draft had scarcely been completed when military action virtually ceased. The fall of Richmond on April 2 presaged the end of Confederate resistance, and Hoosiers celebrated the event in statewide patriotic meetings.[15] Late in the night of April 9, the news of Lee's surrender at Appomattox reached Indianapolis. Instantly the sleeping city was awakened by the din of tolling bells and ceaseless rounds of artillery fire. Excited crowds poured into the streets, and parades, bonfires, and speechmaking continued until the early morning. The sudden release from the burden of war caused a mass delirium and obscured momentarily everything but the happy events

---

[12] Terrell, *Report*, 1:68.

[13] Morton to Stanton, February 3, 1865, and Morton to Lincoln, February 13, 1865, in *Official Records,* 3 series, 4:1098, 1169-70.

[14] Morton to Stanton, March 7, 10, 1865, and Stanton to Morton, March 7, 1865, in *ibid.*, 3 series, 4:1222, 1228; Indianapolis *Daily Journal,* March 13, 1865; Canup, "Conscription and Draft in Indiana," in *Indiana Magazine of History,* 10(June, 1914) :83.

[15] Indianapolis *Daily Journal,* April 4, 1865.

of the present.¹⁶ The War Department's prompt order that recruiting be stopped turned the people's thoughts to the question of how they could achieve a quick and orderly readjustment to peace and reunion.

But the general rejoicing ended abruptly when, early in the morning of April 15, the telegraph relayed the grim news of Lincoln's assassination. The profound and universal sadness produced by that event caused everyone to assume a gloomier attitude toward the problems of the future. In Indianapolis the flags of victory were now edged in black and lowered to half-mast; the hushed crowds which discussed the news made a sharp contrast with the boisterous merrymakers who had sauntered through the streets of the capital city a few days earlier. Business establishments were closed, and the Governor set aside April 19 as a day of mourning.

A public mass meeting which assembled in the State House square at noon of the same day reflected mingled feelings of grief and rage. The partisan hatreds engendered by the war found violent expression, and the charges of disloyalty lodged against the Democracy during the previous campaign again made an untimely appearance. Prayers, hymns, and reverent eulogies to the late President were grotesquely combined with bloodthirsty appeals for death to every traitor and cries that "the gallows has its uses in Indiana as elsewhere." When Hendricks came forward to speak there was a near riot, and Morton alone could silence the threats to kill Indiana's Democratic Senator.¹⁷ Democrats shared the sorrow of their political opponents but deplored the immediate attempt of some to turn Lincoln's death to political advantage.¹⁸

---

[16] Indianapolis *Daily Journal,* April 10, 1865; Indianapolis *Daily State Sentinel,* April 11, 1865.

[17] Indianapolis *Daily Journal* and *Daily State Sentinel,* April 17, 1865; Foulke, *Oliver P. Morton,* 1:438-39.

[18] Indianapolis *Daily State Sentinel,* April 18, 19, 1865; New Albany *Weekly Ledger,* April 19, 1865.

Lincoln's funeral train was scheduled to pass through Indianapolis en route to Springfield on April 30, and Governor Morton made elaborate preparations for the occasion. The capitol was gaudily decorated to receive the President's remains which were to lie in state in the rotunda throughout the day. The principal streets and business establishments of the capital city were draped in black. When the funeral cortege, which was escorted from Richmond by the state's representatives, arrived at Indianapolis, a dismal procession escorted the coffin through a drenching rain to the State House. Thousands of curious spectators from Indiana and adjoining states filed past the coffin until late at night. Then the remains were returned to the waiting train to resume the journey to Springfield.[19]

In the turmoil which followed Lincoln's assassination Indiana Republicans did not neglect to make known their complete confidence in Andrew Johnson, the new President. On the morning of April 15 Morton telegraphed an assurance to Johnson that he would cordially support the new administration.[20] The public meeting held on the same day passed a similar resolution. A few days later the Governor headed a delegation of local politicians who visited Johnson to offer additional testimonials of their faith in him. On that occasion Morton, to the intense annoyance of Julian and the Indiana radicals, read a carefully prepared paper outlining and defending a conservative program of reconstruction.[21] Julian and the other radicals, who regarded Lincoln's death as a "godsend,"

[19] Indianapolis *Daily Journal* and *Daily State Sentinel*, May 1, 1865; Terrell, *Report*, 1:387; Cottman, "Lincoln in Indianapolis," in *Indiana Magazine of History*, 24(1928):11, 14.
[20] Morton to Johnson, April 15, 1865, in *Official Records*, 1 series, 49:pt. 2:359.
[21] Julian to Mrs. Julian, April 21, 1865, Julian MSS.; Richmond *Indiana True Republican*, May 11, 1865; extracts from Julian's MS. Journal, printed in *Indiana Magazine of History*, 11(1915):337; Foulke, *Oliver P. Morton*, 1:440-42.

had already begun a contest with the conservatives for control of the new President.²² The campaign truce between the two factions had long since ceased, and the lines were clearly drawn for a new struggle for party domination.

A year later Morton would regret these and other conservative utterances made in the months of indecision following the war. By the spring of 1866 he had come to realize that the radicals were the real power in his party, and he opportunistically joined them in repudiating Johnson's plan of reconstruction. After he entered the Senate in 1867 Morton soon became a leader of the radicals and a dominant figure in the Grant administration. There was cruel irony in the fact that Morton ultimately took the command of the Indiana radicals away from Julian. Needless to say, he never absorbed any of the idealism that Julian had given to the radical cause. By 1870 Morton's control of the state machine was great enough to enable him finally to prevent Julian's renomination for Congress. Morton thus squared accounts with his most persistent and penetrating critic.

3

In May, although military operations had ended, the question of the final disposal of the principals in the treason trials of 1864 still remained unsettled. The previous December the military court had found Bowles, Milligan, Horsey, and Humphreys guilty of the various charges brought against them. The first three were sentenced to be hanged, the last to be imprisoned at hard labor for the duration of the war. But with Lincoln's approval, General Hovey commuted Humphreys' sentence to detention within the limits of two townships in Greene County.²³

---

²² Julian to Mrs. Julian, April 17, 27, 1865, Julian MSS.; extracts from Julian's MS. Journal in *op. cit.*, 11(1915):334-36; Richmond *Indiana True Republican*, April 20, 27, 1865; Julian, *Political Recollections*, 255.

²³ Indianapolis *Daily State Sentinel*, January 2, 1865; Indianapolis

Hoosier interest in the case had been declining ever since the elections the previous fall. Then early in 1865 a strong local movement developed to persuade Lincoln to grant executive clemency to these victims of military rule. Friends of the prisoners raised money for the cause; prominent Democrats, aided by several Republicans, traveled to Washington to make a direct appeal to the President.[24] At first Morton gave the plea for commutation no support, and Lane, Colfax, and Julian went to Lincoln with the demand that the prisoners be executed.[25] Nevertheless, those who urged mercy seemed to have influenced the administration, for Lincoln had fixed no date for the executions up to the time of his assassination.[26]

After Lincoln's death, while the general excitement was at its height, President Johnson decided to carry out the original sentences and ordered the executions to take place on May 19.[27] But as the excitement cooled, there was increasing opposition to this severe penalty, and many members of both parties urged the President to reverse his decision. They flooded the Governor with letters asking him to use his influence with Johnson.[28] At this juncture Judge David Davis of the United States Supreme Court appeared in Indianapolis and had a conference with Morton. Apparently he convinced the Governor that, since the regular courts had been open and undisturbed,

---

Daily Journal, January 3, 1865; Nicolay and Hay (eds.), *Complete Works of Abraham Lincoln,* 10:338; *Official Records,* 2 series, 8:10, 11, 548.

[24] David Kilgore to Morton, January 5, 1865, AGO, Morton Correspondence, Archives Division; Indianapolis *Daily Journal,* January 5, 27, 1865; Indianapolis *Daily State Sentinel,* January 28, 1865.

[25] Indianapolis *Daily Journal,* February 8, 1865.

[26] Indianapolis *Daily State Sentinel,* May 9, 1865.

[27] *Official Records,* 2 series, 8:548-49.

[28] See letters of J. C. Lutz, May 11, 1865, Silas F. Miller, May 12, 1865, and Alexander McPheeters, May 22, 1865, to Morton, Archives Division; D. O. Dailey, Huntington, to Morton, May 9, 1865, and Johnson to Morton [n.d.], AGO, Civil War Telegrams, Archives Division; Indianapolis *Daily Journal,* May 12, 15, 1865; New Albany *Weekly Ledger,* May 17, 1865.

the military commission which tried the prisoners had been illegal. In any event Morton now changed his position and suddenly determined that Indiana should not be selected as the first state for the performance of military executions. Hence he wrote to Johnson and strongly recommended the commutation of the original sentences to life imprisonment. The Governor sent additional letters to the President through Mrs. Milligan and through several political friends.[29] The Indianapolis *Journal* suggested that, in view of the questionable legality of the military commission, the cases be retried in the Federal courts.[30]

The first results of the Governor's efforts to save the prisoners was the commutation of Horsey's sentence of life imprisonment and the postponement of the date for the execution of Bowles and Milligan to June 2.[31] Finally, on May 30, the sentences of the last two were also commuted to life imprisonment, and the prisoners were promptly sent to the penitentiary at Columbus, Ohio.[32]

A year later, just as their case was being taken to the Supreme Court, the prisoners were pardoned by Johnson. But the Court ruled that the regular courts had been open at the time of the trial and that the military commission had therefore been illegal.[33] Subsequently Milligan won a suit against the members of the military court for damages resulting from his illegal imprisonment. The jury awarded him the trivial sum of $5.00.[34] But the Milligan

[29] Morton to Johnson, May 13, 22, 1865, in Telegraphic Correspondence, 6:10; Morton Letter Press Books, 6(March 1865-June 1866); Cincinnati *Enquirer*, quoted in Indianapolis *Daily State Sentinel*, May 20, 1865; Terrell, *Report*, 1:314; Foulke, *Oliver P. Morton*, 1:427-31.

[30] Indianapolis *Daily Journal*, May 15, 17, 1865.

[31] *Official Records*, 2 series, 8:587.

[32] R. Mussey, Washington, D. C., to Morton, May 31, 1865, AGO, Civil War Telegrams, Archives Division; *Official Records*, 2 series, 8:637; Indianapolis *Daily State Sentinel*, June 1, 1865; Indianapolis *Daily Journal*, June 2, 1865.

[33] *Ex parte* Milligan, 4 *Wallace*, 2(1866).

[34] Foulke, *Oliver P. Morton*, 1:431-32.

case became a judicial bulwark in defense of American civil rights.

4

Early in June, 1865, the first Hoosier troops began to return to be mustered out of Federal service. Having planned another series of colorful receptions for the Indiana regiments, Governor Morton earnestly protested against a War Department arrangement by which the soldiers could break ranks in Washington and go home individually. The Governor won his point, and the local troops were forced to make a final appearance at Indianapolis in full regimental organization.[35]

When they arrived at the capital, the veterans received flattering attention from state politicians and local citizens. Each new group was fed and entertained and then marched to the State House. There Morton, the "soldiers' friend," had his last words with the men whom he had called to serve in the Union armies. Again the Governor gave a brief historical sketch of the achievements of each regiment, lauded its personal sacrifices, and reminded the men again that some had remained at home to injure the Union cause. The responses of regimental officers often turned to political topics; a few of them demanded that Morton be the Union party candidate for President in 1868. Benjamin Harrison served formal notice that the veterans intended to be heard in postwar politics, and that they would spurn any politician who had been "lukewarm in the good cause."[36]

Following these ceremonies the "boys in blue" returned to their homes and to civilian life. Doubtless they observed little that had changed during their absence, for

---

[35] Morton to T. M. Vincent, May 12, 1865; Morton to Stanton, May 23, 1865, in Telegraphic Correspondence, 6:12, 16; W. H. DeMott to Morton, May 25, 1865, Chicago-Morton Collection; Indianapolis *Daily Journal*, May 22, 1865.

[36] Indianapolis *Daily Journal*, June 12, 17, 27, 1865; Foulke, *Oliver P. Morton*, 1:445-46.

the transformation of Hoosier society was too subtle to be quickly comprehended. Nor could the effects of army life upon Indiana's 180,000 veterans be more readily discerned.[37] Yet, while this civilian army melted away with surprising speed, few of the men could forget the experiences which had formed the greatest adventure of their lives. Soon the ex-soldiers united again to play their expected role in state and national politics. From their ranks, with the aid of the politicians who courted them, emerged the Grand Army of the Republic. Shortly the countless "soldiers' friends" had become equally ardent friends of the veterans.

5

The warm spring days of 1865 found the citizens of Indiana uneasy in their thoughts of the future. Military force had restored the Union, but four years of war had left its mark upon the nation. The perplexing problems of reconstruction were now added to the venerable issues of prewar politics. A few shrewd men already realized that a new political and economic crisis might be as serious as the one through which the country had just passed.[38]

The recent civil conflict had dealt a staggering blow to the Hoosier Democracy and to its Jacksonian principles. Republicans rejoiced at the triumph of their economic doctrines and gloated over the political ruin of their foes. Democrats observed bitterly that the dominant party had fought them as ardently as it had fought the rebels, and had used the war as a device to rule the country.[39] Republicans celebrated the death of state sovereignty and the "miserable and demogogical" dogmas of the Virginia and Kentucky Resolutions. Democrats mourned that free-

---

[37] The total number of troops furnished by Indiana for all terms of service was 208,367. The number who were killed in action or died of disease was 24,416. Terrell, *Report*, 1:106, appendix, 5-6.

[38] Indianapolis *Daily Journal*, March 21, 1865.

[39] Indianapolis *Daily State Sentinel*, November 18, 1864, April 8, 1865; Indianapolis *Daily Journal*, May 4, 1865.

dom itself was dying.⁴⁰ The Indianapolis *Sentinel* doubted that the nation would ever go back to the Constitution, for it was easier "after a lapse from truth to add fresh heresies than to return to the old standard of orthodoxy." The national banks, the huge public debt, the circulation of large quantities of paper money would form the basis for "a new school of political economy where the axioms of the science, as formerly taught . . . [would] be reckoned on the list of exploded errors."⁴¹

But Indiana Democrats did not long encumber their cause with a nostalgic yearning for things that had passed. The leaders of these western agrarians were soon busy resurrecting their party in order to re-engage their foes and to make themselves felt in the new nation. They quickly confessed that slavery was dead and warned that Democrats should not "tie the corpse around their necks." Instead they preferred to face the living issues of national reconstruction.⁴²

What these issues would be did not long remain in doubt. The *Sentinel* reminded its readers that the war had left the tariff question unsettled and that in this respect the interests of the West and South were still identical. Western Republicans, it affirmed, were the mere tools of New England, and tariff reduction could be the program by which the Democracy would rescue the nation from "a great manufacturing aristocracy."⁴³ Other party leaders saw in the growing indignation of western farmers against the railroad monopolies another problem demanding a solution.⁴⁴ Finally, there were already cries of pro-

---

⁴⁰ Indianapolis *Daily Journal*, May 29, 1865. See speech of Voorhees in *Congressional Globe*, 38 Congress, 1 session, appendix, 71 ff.

⁴¹ Indianapolis *Daily State Sentinel*, May 12, 1865.

⁴² *Ibid.*, December 9, 1864, February 9, 1865; New Albany *Weekly Ledger*, November 23, December 7, 1864, April 19, 1865. See also speech of Voorhees in *Congressional Globe*, 38 Congress, 2 session, 180.

⁴³ Indianapolis *Daily State Sentinel*, February 18, March 2, June 6, 1865.

⁴⁴ New Albany *Weekly Ledger*, December 21, 1864, January 4, 1865; Indianapolis *Daily Journal*, December 30, 1864, January 4, 1865.

test against the national banking system which enriched a few men but failed to meet the West's constant need for additional capital.⁴⁵

The *Sentinel* confidently predicted that the present attempt of New England to be "overseers of the whole nation" would be as odious to the West as the past attempt of the South had been. Hence, it prophesied, the western states, with their identity of interests, would soon make themselves a power in the land. "And they will make that power felt in impressing their policy upon the nation."⁴⁶ The roots of western insurgency were already deep in the soil of Indiana. In 1872 and 1876 the Democrats would capitalize on agrarian discontent with the new order to capture the governorship; in the latter election they would, for the first time since 1856, win the state's presidential electoral votes. From their ranks would come the leaders of the Granger and Populist movements.

But the triumphant Republicans, heirs to the Whig tradition, were equally prepared for the future and ready to meet this new threat from their irrepressible foes. The Indianapolis *Journal* noted with satisfaction that war and Republican rule had brought to the Northwest an unprecedented degree of material well-being. Indiana, it observed, was a region "of unabated prosperity."⁴⁷ Accordingly, in the spring of 1865 Indiana's political rulers surveyed the Hoosier scene and pronounced it good.

⁴⁵ Indianapolis *Daily State Sentinel,* November 4, 15, December 15, 16, 1864, February 25, 1865.
⁴⁶ *Ibid.,* January 5, 1864.
⁴⁷ Indianapolis *Daily Journal,* November 9, 1864, June 14, 1865.

BIBLIOGRAPHY

BIBLIOGRAPHY

MANUSCRIPTS

Edward B. Allen MSS. Thirty-six items covering the years 1854-64. Indiana Division, Indiana State Library.

David C. Branham MSS. Ten items covering the years 1859-65. Indiana Division, Indiana State Library.

Henry B. Carrington MSS. One folder covering the years 1862-65, five letter books, and a series of manuscript accounts of his service while commanding the District of Indiana. Archives Division, Indiana State Library.

George F. Chittenden MSS. Four folders covering the years 1860-65. Indiana Division, Indiana State Library.

John Coburn MSS. One box containing a few items relating to the Civil War period. Indiana Division, Indiana State Library.

Schuyler Colfax MSS. Twenty-nine letters covering the Civil War period. Indiana Division, Indiana State Library.

Court Martial Records, Adjutant General's Office. Material relating to the Sons of Liberty and Indiana treason trials. National Archives, Washington, D. C.

Lucius C. Embree MSS. Two folders and one letter book covering the Civil War period. Indiana Division, Indiana State Library.

Henry K. English MSS. Items relating to the organization of the Indiana Union clubs. Indiana Division, Indiana State Library.

William H. English Collection. Two folders covering the years 1858-65. Indiana Historical Society Library.

Calvin Fletcher Papers and Diary. Letters to Calvin Fletcher, 1861-62, and Diary for April-May, 1861. Indiana Historical Society Library.

William Dudley Foulke MSS. Contain five Morton letters for the Civil War period. Indiana Division, Indiana State Library.

William S. Garber, "Concerning the Quarrel between Oliver P. Morton, Governor, and Michael C. Garber, Editor" (Indianapolis, 1927), unpublished article in Indiana State Library.

Allen Hamilton MSS. Two boxes covering the Civil War period. Indiana Division, Indiana State Library.

Milo S. Hascall MS. Autobiography (1865). A brief account of his life and services while commanding the District of Indiana. Archives Division, Indiana State Library.

Indiana. Adjutant General's Office, Civil War Telegrams. A collection of telegrams sent and received by the executive department during the Civil War. Archives Division, Indiana State Library.

———, Letter Books (1861-68). Eleven volumes covering the terms of Adjutant Generals Lazarus Noble and W. H. H. Terrell. Archives Division, Indiana State Library.

———, General Correspondence. A collection of miscellaneous letters which came to the office of the adjutant general during the Civil War period. Archives Division, Indiana State Library.

———, Morton Correspondence. One folder of letters received by Morton which were filed in Adjutant General's Office. Archives Division, Indiana State Library.

Indiana. Auditor of State. Ledger, 1862-65, and Register of Warrants, 1862-65. Two volumes in Archives Division, Indiana State Library.

Indiana. Bureau of Finance. Accounts, monthly statements, and reports for the years 1863-65. Archives Division, Indiana State Library.

George W. Julian MSS. Nine folders covering the Civil War period. Indiana Division, Indiana State Library.

Vallette Miller MSS. Seventy-five items relating especially to the election of 1860 and the Constitutional Union party. Indiana Division, Indiana State Library.

Oliver P. Morton MSS. Eighteen dispatch books containing copies of telegrams sent and received; nine letter press books of letters sent by Morton and his secretaries. Archives Division, Indiana State Library.

———, One drawer containing the Chicago-Morton Collection, in Archives Division. Letters received by Morton during the Civil War period. They were taken to Chicago by William R. Holloway, Morton's Civil War secretary, but were later returned to the state as official records. Archives Division.

———, One folder of Morton correspondence covering the Civil War period, in Executive Office file. Archives Division.

———, One folder of Morton correspondence and twenty-four photostats of original letters in Butler University Library and the Henry County Historical Society. Indiana Division, Indiana State Library.

New England Loyal Publications Society MSS. A few items dealing with the propaganda activities of this society in Indiana. Boston Public Library; photostats in possession of Professor Frank Freidel, Vassar College.

Daniel D. Pratt MSS. Ten boxes covering the Civil War period. Indiana Division, Indiana State Library.

Benjamin Spooner MSS. Fifty-eight photostats of letters covering the years 1862-64. The originals were in possession of Mrs. Frank Hutchinson, Lawrenceburg, in 1934.

Richard W. Thompson MSS. One folder covering the years 1855-65. Indiana Division, Indiana State Library.

John T. Wilder MSS. Two folders covering the Civil War period. Indiana Division, Indiana State Library.

BOOKS, ARTICLES, AND PRINTED RECORDS

Bailey, Louis J., "Caleb Blood Smith," in *Indiana Magazine of History,* 29(1933):213-39.

Baringer, William E., *A House Dividing: Lincoln as President Elect* (Abraham Lincoln Association, Springfield, 1945).

————, *Lincoln's Rise to Power* (Boston, 1937).

Beale, Howard K. (ed.), *The Diary of Edward Bates 1859-1866* (American Historical Association *Annual Report,* 1930, vol. 4 [Washington, D. C., 1933]).

Benton, Elbert J., *Movement for Peace without a Victory during the Civil War* (Western Reserve Historical Society *Collections,* No. 99, Cleveland, 1918).

Bogardus, Frank S., "Daniel W. Voorhees," in *Indiana Magazine of History,* 27(1931):91-103.

Boyer, Margrette, "Morgan's Raid in Indiana," in *Indiana Magazine of History,* 8(1912):149-65.

Brand, Carl F., "History of the Know Nothing Party in Indiana," in *Indiana Magazine of History,* 18(1922):47-81, 177-206, 266-306.

Bright, Jesse D., Letters of, to William H. English, in *Indiana Magazine of History,* 30(1934):370-92.

Canup, Charles F., "Conscription and Draft in Indiana during the Civil War," in *Indiana Magazine of History,* 10(June, 1914):70-83.

Carman, Harry J., and Luthin, Reinhard H., *Lincoln and the Patronage* (Columbia University Press, 1943).

Carpenter, Francis B., *The Inner Life of Abraham Lincoln. Six Months at the White House* (Boston, 1883).

Clarke, Grace Julian, "'The Burnt District,'" in *Indiana Magazine of History,* 27(1931):119-24.

————, *George W. Julian* (Indiana Historical Collection, vol. 11, Indianapolis, 1923).

———— (ed.), "George W. Julian's Journal—The Assassination of Lincoln," in *Indiana Magazine of History,* 11(1915):324-37.

Cochran, William C., "The Dream of a Northwestern Confederacy," in the State Historical Society of Wisconsin *Proceedings,* 1916 (Madison, 1917), 213-53.

Cole, Arthur C., *The Irrepressible Conflict, 1850-1865 (A History of American Life,* vol. 7, New York, 1934).

Cottman, George S., "James F. D. Lanier," in *Indiana Magazine of History,* 22(1926):194-202.

————, "Lincoln in Indianapolis," in *Indiana Magazine of History,* 24(1928):1-14.

Coulter, E. Merton, "Commercial Intercourse with the Confederacy in the Mississippi Valley, 1861-1865," in *Mississippi Valley Historical Review,* 5(1918-19):377-95.

――――, "Effects of Secession upon the Commerce of the Mississippi Valley," in *Mississippi Valley Historical Review*, 3(1916-17):275-300.

Crenshaw, Ollinger, "The Knights of the Golden Circle: The Career of George Bickley," in *American Historical Review*, 47(1941-42):23-50.

Davis, John G., series of letters to, in *Indiana Magazine of History*, 24(1928):201-13.

Dictionary of American Biography (20 vols. and index. New York, 1928-36).

Dodd, William E., "The Fight for the Northwest, 1860," in *American Historical Review*, 16(1910-11):774-88.

Dorpalen, Andreas, "The German Element and the Issues of the Civil War," in *Mississippi Valley Historical Review*, 29(1942-43):55-76.

Dudley, Harold M., "The Election of 1864," in *Mississippi Valley Historical Review*, 18(1931-32):500-18.

Duncan, H. C., "James Hughes," in *Indiana Magazine of History*, 5(1909):85-98.

Dunn, Jacob P., *Indiana; a Redemption from Slavery* (*American Commonwealths*, rev. ed., Boston and New York, 1905).

Ellis, E. W. H., "Autobiography of a Noted Pioneer," in *Indiana Magazine of History*, 10(March, 1914):63-73.

Esarey, Logan, *A History of Indiana* (2 vols. 3d ed., Fort Wayne, 1924).

――――, *State Banking in Indiana, 1814-1873* (Indiana University Studies, No. 15, Bloomington, 1912).

Facts for the People by a Citizen of Indiana (Indianapolis, 1862).

Fesler, Mayo, "Secret Political Societies in the North during the Civil War," in *Indiana Magazine of History*, 14(1918):133-286.

Fite, Emerson D., *The Presidential Campaign of 1860* (New York, 1911).

――――, *Social and Industrial Conditions in the North during the Civil War* (New York, 1910).

Foulke, William Dudley, *Life of Oliver P. Morton, Including His Important Speeches* (2 vols., Indianapolis, 1899).

French, William M. (ed.), *Life, Speeches, State Papers and Public Services of Gov. Oliver P. Morton* (Cincinnati, 1864).

Gephart, William F., *Transportation and Industrial Development in the Middle West* (Columbia University Studies in History, Economics, and Public Law, vol. 34, no. 1, New York, 1909).

Gibson, Charles, "Edward Bates," in *Missouri Historical Society Collections*, 2(1900):52-56.

Gray, Wood, *The Hidden Civil War. The Story of the Copperheads* (New York, 1942).

Grayston, Florence L., "Lambdin P. Milligan—A Knight of the Golden Circle," in *Indiana Magazine of History*, 43(1947):379-91.

Gresham, Matilda, *Life of Walter Quintin Gresham 1832-1895* (2 vols., Chicago, 1919).

Halstead, Murat, *Caucuses of 1860: A History of the National Political Conventions of the Current Presidential Campaign* . . . (Columbus, Ohio, 1860).

Harbison, Winfred A., "The Elections of 1862 as a Vote of Want of Confidence in President Lincoln," in *Papers* of the Michigan Academy of Science, Arts and Letters, 14(1931):499-513.

————, "Indiana Republicans and the Re-election of President Lincoln," in *Indiana Magazine of History*, 34(1938):42-64.

————, "Lincoln and Indiana Republicans, 1861-1862," in *Indiana Magazine of History*, 33(1937):277-303.

Hesseltine, William B., *Lincoln and the War Governors* (New York, 1948).

Holcombe, John W., and Skinner, Hubert M., *Life and Public Services of Thomas A. Hendricks* (Indianapolis, 1886).

Holland, Cecil, *Morgan and His Raiders* . . . (New York, 1942).

Holliday, John H., *Indianapolis and the Civil War* (Indiana Historical Society *Publications*, vol. 4, no. 9, Indianapolis, 1911).

Hollister, Ovando J., *Life of Schuyler Colfax* (New York and London, 1886).

Hubbart, Henry C., *The Older Middle West, 1840-1880* . . . (New York, 1936).

————, "'Pro-Southern' Influences in the Free West, 1840-1865," in *Mississippi Valley Historical Review*, 20 (1933-34):45-62.

Indiana General Assembly. *Brevier Legislative Reports*, compiled by Ariel and William H. Drapier, vols. 4 (1861), 5(spec. sess. 1861), 6 (1863).

————, *Documentary Journal*, 1861-65.

————, *House Journal*, 1857, 1861-65.

————, *Laws of Indiana*, 1861-65.

————, *Report of the Committee on Public Expenditures of the Expenses of the Executive Department of the State of Indiana* (Indianapolis, 1867).

————, *Senate Journal*, 1861-65.

Indiana Supreme Court, *The War Power of the President* [Indianapolis, 1863].

————, *Reports*, vol. 20.

Jackson, Adah, "Glimpses of Civil War Newburgh . . .," in *Indiana Magazine of History*, 41(1945):167-84.

Jordan, Henry D., "Daniel Wolsey Voorhees," in *Mississippi Valley Historical Review*, 6(1919-20):532-55.

Julian, George W., *Political Recollections, 1840-1872* (Chicago, 1884).

————, *Speeches on Political Questions.* . . . (New York, 1872).

Kenworthy, Leonard S., *The Tall Sycamore of the Wabash. Daniel Wolsey Voorhees* (Boston, 1936).

Kettleborough, Charles, *Constitution Making in Indiana* (3 vols., *Indiana Historical Collections*, vols. 1, 2, 17, Indianapolis, 1916, 1930).

—————, "Indiana on the Eve of the Civil War," in *Proceedings of the Tenth Annual Meeting of the Ohio Valley Historical Association* (Indiana Historical Society *Publications,* vol. 6, no. 1, n.d.), 137-89.

Kohlmeier, Albert L., *The Old Northwest as the Keystone of the Arch of American Federal Union* . . . (Bloomington, Ind., 1938).

Leopold, Richard W., *Robert Dale Owen. A Biography* (Harvard Historical *Studies,* vol. 45, 1940).

Lippincott, Isaac, *A History of Manufactures in the Ohio Valley to the Year 1860* . . . (Chicago, 1914).

Luthin, Reinhard, "The Democratic Split during Buchanan's Administration," in *Pennsylvania History,* 11(1944):13-35.

—————, *The First Lincoln Campaign* (Harvard University Press, 1944).

—————, "Indiana and Lincoln's Rise to the Presidency," in *Indiana Magazine of History,* 38(1942):385-405.

—————, "Organizing the Republican Party in the 'Border-Slave' Regions: Edward Bates's Presidential Candidacy in 1860," in *Missouri Historical Review,* 38(1943-44):138-61.

—————, *See also* Carman, Harry J.

McClure, Alexander K., *Abraham Lincoln and Men of War Times* (Philadelphia, 1892).

McCormack, Thomas J., *Memoirs of Gustave Koerner 1809-1896* . . . (2 vols., Cedar Rapids, Iowa, 1909).

Meneely, Alexander H., *The War Department, 1861. A Study in Mobilization and Administration* (Columbia University *Studies in History, Economics and Public Law,* No. 300, New York, 1928).

[Merrill, Catharine], *The Soldier of Indiana in the War for the Union* (Merrill and Co., Indianapolis, 1864).

Milton, George Fort, *Abraham Lincoln and the Fifth Column* (New York, 1942).

Monks, Leander J., Esarey, Logan, and Shockley, Ernest V. (eds.), *Courts and Lawyers of Indiana* (3 vols., Indianapolis, 1916).

Morton, Oliver P., *Emigration to the United States of North America. Indiana as a Home for Emigrants* (Indianapolis, 1864).

Murphy, Charles B., *The Political Career of Jesse D. Bright* (Indiana Historical Society *Publications,* vol. 10, no. 3, Indianapolis, 1931).

Murphy, Maurice, "Some Features of the History of Parke County," in *Indiana Magazine of History,* 12(1916):144-57.

Nichols, Roy F., *The Disruption of American Democracy* (New York, 1948).

Nicolay, John G., and Hay, John, *Abraham Lincoln. A History* (10 vols., New York, 1890).

——— (eds.), *Complete Works of Abraham Lincoln* (12 vols., New York, c. 1894, 1905).

Perkins, Howard C., *Northern Editorials on Secession* (2 vols., New York, 1942).

Pitman, Benn (ed.), *The Trials for Treason at Indianapolis* . . . (Cincinnati, 1865).

Randall, James G., *The Civil War and Reconstruction* (Boston and New York, 1937).

———, *Constitutional Problems under Lincoln* (New York, 1926).

———, *Lincoln the President. Springfield to Gettysburg.* (2 vols., New York, 1945).

Report on the Indiana Stock Frauds Made by the Committee of the New York Stock Exchange (New York, 1862).

Rhodes, James F., *History of the United States from the Compromise of 1850* (7 vols., New York, 1896-1919).

Roll, Charles, *Colonel Dick Thompson. The Persistent Whig* (Indiana Historical Collections, vol. 30, Indianapolis, 1948).

———, "Indiana's Part in the Nomination of Abraham Lincoln for President in 1860," in *Indiana Magazine of History*, 25(1929):1-13.

Scribner, Theodore T., *see* Stevenson, David.

Scrugham, Mary, *The Peaceable Americans of 1860-1861. A Study in Public Opinion* (Columbia University *Studies in History, Economics, and Public Law*, vol. 96, no. 3, New York, 1921).

Seeds, Russel M., *History of the Republican Party of Indiana* (Indianapolis, 1899).

Shannon, Fred A., *The Organization and Administration of the Union Army, 1861-1865* (2 vols., Cleveland, 1928).

———, "State Rights and the Union Army," in *Mississippi Valley Historical Review*, 12(1925-26):51-71.

Sharp, Walter R., "Henry S. Lane and the Formation of the Republican Party in Indiana," in *Mississippi Valley Historical Review*, 7(1920-21):93-112.

Smith, Donnal V., *Chase and Civil War Politics* (Columbus, Ohio, 1931).

———, "The Influence of the Foreign-Born of the Northwest in the Election of 1860," in *Mississippi Valley Historical Review*, 19(1932-33):192-204.

———, "Salmon P. Chase and the Election of 1860," in *Ohio Archaeological and Historical Quarterly*, 39(1930):515-607, 769-844.

Smith, Edward C., *The Borderland in the Civil War* (New York, 1927).

Smith, Theodore C., *The Liberty and Free Soil Parties in the Northwest* (Harvard Historical *Studies*, vol. 6, New York, 1897).

Smith, Willard H., "The Colfax-Turpie Congressional Campaigns, 1862-1866," in *Indiana Magazine of History*, 38(1942):123-42.

———, "Schuyler Colfax and the Political Upheaval of 1854-1855," in *Mississippi Valley Historical Review,* 28(1941-42):383-98.

Snepp, Daniel W., *Evansville's Channels of Trade and the Secession Movement 1850-1865* (Indiana Historical Society *Publications,* vol. 8, no. 7, Indianapolis, 1928).

Stampp, Kenneth M., "The Impact of the Civil War upon Hoosier Society," in *Indiana Magazine of History,* 38(1942):1-16.

———, "Kentucky's Influence upon Indiana in the Crisis of 1861," in *Indiana Magazine of History,* 39(1943):263-76.

———, "Letters from the Washington Peace Conference of 1861," in *Journal of Southern History,* 9(1943):395-403.

———, "Lincoln and the Strategy of Defense in the Crisis of 1861," in *Journal of Southern History,* 11(1945):297-323.

———, "The Milligan Case and the Election of 1864 in Indiana," in *Mississippi Valley Historical Review,* 31(1944-45):41-58.

Stevenson, David, and Scribner, Theodore T., *Indiana's Roll of Honor* (2 vols., Indianapolis, 1864, 1866).

Stidger, Felix G., *Treason History of the Order of Sons of Liberty . . .* (Chicago, 1903).

Stillé, Charles J., *History of the United States Sanitary Commission . . .* (Philadelphia, 1866).

Sulgrove, Berry R., *History of Indianapolis and Marion County* (Philadelphia, 1884).

Sutherland, James, *Biographical Sketches of the Members of the Forty-first General Assembly . . .* (Indianapolis, 1861).

Taylor, Charles W., *Biographical Sketches and Review of the Bench and Bar of Indiana . . .* (Indianapolis, 1895).

Terrell, W. H. H., *Report of the Adjutant General of Indiana* (8 vols., Indianapolis, 1869).

Tracy, Gilbert A. (ed.), *Uncollected Letters of Abraham Lincoln* (Boston and New York, 1917).

Trissal, Francis M., *Public Men of Indiana. A Political History from 1860 to 1890* (2 vols., Hammond, Ind., 1922).

Turpie, David, *Sketches of My Own Times* (Indianapolis, 1903).

Tyner, Martha A., "Walter Q. Gresham," in *Indiana Magazine of History,* 29(1933):297-338.

United States Census. *Manufactures of the United States in 1860; Compiled from . . . the Eighth Census . . .* (Washington, D. C., 1865).

———, *Population of the United States in 1860; Compiled from . . . the Eighth Census . . .* (Washington, D. C., 1864).

United States Congress, *Congressional Globe,* 37 Congress, 1 and 2 sessions; 38 Congress, 1 and 2 sessions.

Voorhees, Charles S., *Speeches of Daniel W. Voorhees of Indiana . . .* (Cincinnati, 1875).

Voorhees, Daniel W., *Forty Years of Oratory . . . Lectures, Addresses and Speeches* (2 vols., Indianapolis, 1898).

Walker, Charles M., *Sketch of the Life, Character, and Public Services of Oliver P. Morton* (Indianapolis, 1878).

Wallace, Lew. *Lew Wallace. An Autobiography* (2 vols., New York, 1907).

The War of the Rebellion: A Compilation of the Official Records of the Union and Confederate Armies (4 series, 70 vols., Washington, D. C., 1880-1901).

Weeden, William B., *War Government, Federal and State in Massachusetts, New York, Pennsylvania and Indiana 1861-1865* (Boston and New York, 1906).

Williams, T. Harry, *Lincoln and the Radicals* (Madison, Wis., 1941).

Winslow, Hattie L., and Moore, Joseph R. H., *Camp Morton, 1861-1865. Indianapolis Prison Camp* (Indiana Historical Society *Publications*, vol. 13, no. 3, Indianapolis, 1940).

Winther, Oscar O., "The Soldier Vote in the Election of 1864," in *New York History*, 25(1944):440-58.

Wish, Harvey (ed.), "Civil War Letters and Dispatches," in *Indiana Magazine of History*, 33(1937):62-74.

Woodburn, James A., "Henry Smith Lane," in *Indiana Magazine of History*, 27(1931):279-87.

———, "Party Politics in Indiana during the Civil War," in American Historical Association *Annual Report*, 1902, vol. 1:225-51.

Woollen, William W., *Biographical and Historical Sketches of Early Indiana* (Indianapolis, 1883).

Zimmerman, Charles, "The Origin and Rise of the Republican Party in Indiana," in *Indiana Magazine of History*, 13(1917):211-69, 349-412.

NEWSPAPERS

Aurora *Commercial*. Incomplete file, 1859-65.

Aurora *Standard and Press*. 1856-57.

Centreville *Indiana True Democrat*. 1850-52.

Centreville *Indiana True Republican*. 1858-65. (Moved to Richmond in January, 1865.)

Chicago *Press & Tribune*. 1860-61.

Cincinnati *Daily Commercial*. Incomplete file, 1860-61.

Evansville *Weekly Gazette*. 1861-64.

Fort Wayne *Standard*. 1854-55.

Indianapolis *Chapman's Chanticleer*. 1853-54.

Indianapolis *Daily Atlas*. August 1859-March 1860.

Indianapolis *Daily Journal.* 1860-65.
Indianapolis *Daily State Sentinel.* 1854-65.
Indianapolis *Gazette.* Incomplete file, 1862-64.
Indianapolis *Indiana American.* 1858-60.
Indianapolis *Indiana Free Democrat.* Incomplete file, 1853-54.
Indianapolis *Indiana Republican.* November 1854-September 1855.
Indianapolis *Locomotive.* 1854-60.
Indianapolis *Old Line Guard.* July 1860-November 1860.
La Porte *Times.* 1858-60.
Madison *Courier.* 1861.
New Albany *Tribune.* February 28, 1860.
New Albany *Weekly Ledger.* 1854-65.
Richmond *Jeffersonian.* 1854-57.
Richmond *Palladium.* February 16, 1860.
South Bend *St. Joseph Valley Register.* Incomplete file, 1854-64.
Vincennes *Gazette.* 1854-58.

INDEX

Abolition, weakness of movement in Indiana, 9, 22, 26, 32, 33, 144, 145-46; advocates of, oppose conciliation of South, 58-59; opposed as aim of Civil War, 81, 92-93, 129, 135, 137; causes split in Union party, 145; by Constitutional amendment, 222, 224, 225, 258. *See also* Emancipation; Slavery.

Agricultural college, land grant for, accepted, 258.

Agriculture, and tariff policy, 4-7, 43-44, 56, 139, 267; vs. industry, 10; predominance in Indiana's economy in 1850's, 11-12; flourishes during Civil War, 190; political issue following war, 267-68.

Allen, Cyrus M., 37, 75, 84, 221.

American party (Know - Nothing party), and tariff, 6; Whig element in, 10; fuses with Republican party, 22, 23; members desert Republican state convention (1860), 29-30; join Constitutional Union party, 35-36.

Anderson, Maj. Robert, commander at Fort Sumter, 71.

Anti-Nebraska Democrats, 6.

Antislavery movement, *see* Abolition.

Appomattox, surrender at, 255, 259.

Appropriations, *see* Finances, state.

Arkansas, 64.

Arms and ammunition, *see* Army, Union, arms, supplies, and equipment for.

Army, Confederate, *see* Civil War, campaigns and battles.

Army, Union, administration of, *see* War Department;
arms, supplies, and equipment for: Morton seeks information on, 69; difficulties encountered in obtaining, 104, 106-12; competition among states and Federal government over, 109-10;
calls for troops, 71, 78, 100, 104, 142, 143, 144, 213, 214, 227, 228, 230, 250, 259;
quotas and enlistments: (1861), 71, 105; (1862), 143 - 44; (1864), 228, 229, 230, 250, 259; disputes over, 215;
volunteers: throng to Indianapolis, 72; excess of, following first calls, 74, 77-78, 102-3, 104; wavering policy of War Department in recruiting of, 77-78, 103, 104-5, 106, 107, 133, 143; recruiting lags, 106, 143-44, 163, 227, 228, 229; regimental uniforms, 109n-10n; inducements offered for, 213-15, 215-16, 259;
financing of, state appropriation for, 76; used to make political capital, 86-88, 89-91, 173-75, 236-37, 265-66;
commissions: politicians seek, 88; how made, 89-91; state jealousies over Federal appointments, 122;
sick and wounded, care for, 123-26, 180;
draft: upon state militia (1862), 144, 155-56; national conscription system adopted, 202-3; substitute system under, 216; in 1864, pp. 250-51; in 1865, p. 259;
decline in morale, 163, 187-88;

Army Union (Cont.)
deserters, 163, 164, 215, 216; rallies to Morton's support against alleged disloyalty, 172-73; sends memorials and resolutions to General Assembly, 173-75; Negroes in, 215; Indiana soldiers returned home to vote, 251-52; recruiting stopped, 260; number of Indiana veterans, 266; total troops furnished by Indiana, 266n; total of Indianans killed, 266n. *See also* Civil War, campaigns and battles; Indiana Legion; Militia, state; Ohio, Department of the.

Army of the Potomac, 133.

Arsenal, state, 108-9, 180; report, 257; Federal, established at Indianapolis, 109.

Atlanta (Ga.), capture of, 250.

Baker, Conrad, 224, 255.

Baltimore (Md.), scene of Constitutional Union convention (1860), 36; of Union party convention (1864), 224-25.

Banks and banking, political issue in Indiana, 7-8, 189-90, 222, 237, 238, 267-68; effect of secession on, 54, 189; new system of Federal banks created, 189-90, 267-68. *See also* First National **Bank** of Indianapolis; State banks.

Bates, Edward, candidate for president, 6n, 28-29, 34, 35-36, 36-37, 38.

Battle of Pogue's Run, 201.

Bell, John, presidential candidate, 36, 42; votes received in Indiana, 48n.

Bigger, Finley, 15.

Bingham, J. J., editor Indianapolis *Sentinel,* 17, *see also* Indianapolis *Sentinel;* refuses to co-operate with Dodd's conspiracy, 244; arrested, 249.

Bingham, Lucius, 84.

Blackford County (Ind.), resistance to draft in, 156.

Blair, Austin, governor of Michigan, 228n.

Blair, Frank, 38, 46.

Bonds, state, issuance and sale of, 76-77; frauds in, 77; payment of interest on, 181-84; profiteering in, 188.

Borderland, composition of, 13; interests of, as influence on Indiana politics, 22; effect of secession on, 52, 54-55; defense of, 153. *See also* Southern Indiana.

Bosworth, Dr. R., 89n.

Bounty payments, for volunteers, 215-16, 259.

Bowles, Dr. William A., "peace" advocate, 231, 242; arrested and tried for treason, 249, 253; sentenced to hang, 262; pardoned, 264.

Bowling Green (Ky.), seized by Confederate army, 115, 118.

Bragg, Gen. Braxton, 152, 153, 205, 213.

Brandenburg (Ky.), 205.

Branham, David C., 256.

Breckinridge, John C., presidential candidate, 41-42; votes received in Indiana, 48n.

Bright, Jesse D., 130, 167; dominates Democratic politics in Indiana, 15-16; hatred of Stephen A. Douglas, 16, 41-42; repudiated by Douglas Democrats, 16-17, 18; loses control of party in Indiana, 19-21; supports Breckinridge, 41-42; expelled from U. S. Senate, 97-98.

Britt, Matthew L., state treasurer, 182.

Brough, John, governor of Ohio, 228.

Brown, John, raid into Virginia, 25.

Buchanan, James, administration attacked and defended, 16, 20, 25.
Buell, Gen. Don Carlos, commander of Army of the Ohio in Kentucky campaign, 153, 154; feud with Morton, 154; removed from command, 159-60.
Bullitt, Joshua F., Kentucky commander, Sons of Liberty, 242, 243.
Bull Run, Battle of (1861), 93, 104.
Burnett, Maj. Henry L., prosecutor in trial of leaders of Sons of Liberty, 247, 248.
Burnside, Gen. Ambrose E., commander of Department of the Ohio, 197, 198, 202, 204, 207, 210.

California, 64-65.
Cambridge City (Ind.), 159.
Cameron, Simon, presidential candidate, 37; secretary of war, criticism of, and incompetency as administrator, 101-3, 119; accused of neglecting Indiana, 107; approval of continuance of state arsenal sought, 109; replaced by Stanton, 120.
Camp Dick Robinson, 114.
Camp Morton, 71, 77, 111, 167.
Campaigns, political, 1860, pp. 31-34, 42-46; 1862, pp. 137 ff.; 1864, pp. 223-24, 225-26, 236 ff.
Carrington, Gen. Henry B., commander of military district of Indiana, 197-98; aids in building up Indiana Legion, 205; arrested for intoxication and failure to pursue Morgan's raiders, 209; aids recruiting, 213; helps expose Sons of Liberty and Dodd's conspiracy, 241 ff.; refuses to arrest leaders, 246-47; addresses Union meetings, 248.
Chancellorsville, Battle of, 213.
Chapman, Joseph W., 19.
Chase, Salmon P., presidential candidate, (1860), 35; (1864), 218, 219, 220, 221, 223; speaks in Indiana, 46, 237; secretary of the treasury, 181, 190.
Chicago (Ill.), scene of Republican convention (1860), 34.
Chicago *Times,* suppression of, 197.
Chickamauga, Battle of, 213.
Cincinnati (Ohio), 114; threatened by Confederate attack, 152, 153.
Civil liberties, suspension of, in Maryland, 92; loss of, during war, 131, 141-42, 197-98, 198-99, 200, 201-2, 224, 234; decision on military arrests and trials of civilians, 240, 264-65.
Civil War, commencement of hostilities, 70; aims of, debated and defined, 81-82, 92-93, 96, 97, 129, 131, 134, 135, 137, 140, 145-46, 191-92, 234;
campaigns and battles: Bull Run (1861), 93, 104; in Kentucky (1861), 115, 118; fall of Forts Henry and Donelson, 123, 125, 133; Shiloh, 133; McClellan's failure at Richmond, 142; Manassas (1862), 142; raids into southern Indiana, 150-51, 205-10; Kentucky (1863), 152-55; Vicksburg, 162; Fredericksburg, 162; Murfreesboro, 162, 167; defeats and victories in 1863, pp. 212-13; Wilderness campaign and siege of Petersburg, 229; Early's raid against Washington, 229; capture of Atlanta, 250; siege of Petersburg and Richmond, 255; fall of Nashville, 255; Sherman's march to the sea, 255; fall of Richmond and collapse of the Confederacy, 259;
effect of, on economic conditions, 78-79, 139-40, 189-91, 238, 267-68; and civil liberties, 92-93, 94, 131, 197-98, 198-99, 200, 224, 234;

Civil War (Cont.)
effect on Hoosier society, 186 ff., 194, 195, 196, 216, 266. *See also* Defense, state; Army, Union.

Clay, Cassius M., 37, 46.

Clay, Henry, influence on Indiana politics, 4, 6, 14, 34.

Cleveland (Ohio), 224.

Colfax, Schuyler, 22, 25, 35, 36, 37, 142, 143, 146, 263; political tiff with Morton, 88; agent to obtain arms, 107; elected to Congress (1862), 156n.

Columbia City *News*, on Hascall's Order No. 9, p. 199.

Columbus (Ky.), seized by Confederate army, 115.

Commerce, *see* Industry and commerce.

Commissary department, state, criticism of, 110-11.

Compromise of 1850, p. 9.

Confederacy, The, *see* South, The.

Confiscation of rebel property, acts for, 146; favored by radicals, 224.

Conner, A. H., 192.

Conscription, *see* Draft.

Constitution of Indiana, carries clause preventing emigration of Negroes into state, 9; grants suffrage to foreign born, 9; forbids soldiers voting in field, 251.

Constitution of the United States, question of amending to meet secession crisis, 64, 65; maintenance of supremacy of as aim of Civil War, 82, 96, 129, 131, 134, 234; Thirteenth Amendment, 258.

Constitutional Union party, 35-36, 48.

"Copperheads," 195, 208, 211, 222, 234, 237, 240, 250.

Corinth (Tenn.), 133, 174.

Corwin, Thomas, of Ohio, 46.

Corydon (Ind), raided by Morgan's cavalry, 206.

Cravens, James A., elected to Congress, 47n; proposes formation of state of Jackson, 56; on tariff, 93; loyalty of, 152, 210.

Cravens, John R., political antagonist of Morton, 84, 85, 256.

Crittenden, John J., compromise resolutions, 53, 55, 63; resolution on war aims, 82, 131, 137, 145, 191.

Curtin, Andrew G., 39, 40n, 212.

Davidson, A. H., 35.

Davis, David, 39, 264.

Davis, Jefferson, president of the Confederacy, 159, 195; letter from Bright, 97-98.

Davis, Gen. Jefferson C., kills Gen. Nelson, 155.

Davis, John G., peace Democrat, 130.

Dawson, John W., 23.

Dearborn County (Ind.), Republican convention endorses popular sovereignty, 26.

Defense of state, state appropriations for, 76; burden of, falls on Southern Indiana, 80; of Ohio River "front," 113, 114, 115-16, 118; against Confederate invasion of Kentucky, 153; Federal funds for, 181; increased after Hines's cavalry raid, 205; during Morgan's Raid, 205 ff. *See also* Indiana Legion, Militia, state.

Defrees, John D., 22, 24, 25; founder of Indianapolis *Atlas*, 6n; at Chicago convention, 36, 38-39.

De Hart, Richard P., 75n.

Democratic party and Democrats, fosters sectional feeling against New England and the East, 3, 12, 33, 54, 193; victories in Indiana down to 1860, p. 4n; wins emigrant vote, 9;

Index

Democratic party and Democrats (Cont.) stand on: industry vs. agriculture issue, 10; homestead bill, 3n, 43; tariff, 4-5, 6, 43-44, 54, 93, 132, 139-40, 172, 238, 267; state and national banks, 7, 8, 190, 238, 267-68; slavery, 9, 42-43, 44; popular sovereignty and Dred Scott decision, 20; states' rights, 80, 191, 203; abolition, 135; emancipation, 131, 238; river vs. railroad transportation, 132, 144, 171, 189; Republican financial policies, 139-40, 171, 190, 238, 267, 268; domination of, by Jesse D. Bright, 15-16; split between Bright and Douglas factions, 16-18, 19, 20, 21, 41-42; state convention and platform, 1860, pp. 19-21; loses members to Republican party over Kansas-Nebraska bill, 22; campaign, 1860, pp. 33ff., 42ff., national conventions, 1860, pp. 41-42; defeated in elections, 46-47, 47-48; probes disunity in Republican party, 50; role during secession crisis, 53-54, 54-55; accusations of disloyalty and treason against, 61, 63, 94, 130, 136, 148-49, 151, 158-59, 162-63, 164-65, 167, 170-71, 172, 175, 192, 194 ff., 222, 238-39, 240 ff.; in General Assembly, 1861, pp. 62, 63-64, 66-67; support Washington peace conference, 63-64; bolt Assembly to prevent passage of certain acts, 66-67; reaction to Fort Sumter, 72; loyalty proclaimed, 72, 151-52, 157, 165-66, 175-76, 240; in General Assembly, special session, 1861, pp. 75-76; deplore economic changes caused by Civil War, 78-79, 139-40, 189-90, 238, 267-68; war aims, 81-82, 92-93, 129, 131-32, 135, 140, 145-46, 191, 234; accuse Morton of making purely political military appointments, 90; protest loss of civil liberties, 92, 131, 140-42, 191, 197, 198-99, 201-2; to act as loyal opposition party, 92-93, 94, 128-29, 210; "War Democrats" join Union party, 95, 96, 134; attack Wright's appointment to the Senate, 98; 1862 convention and platform, 129-33; sectional split, 129-30; "peace" element and societies in, 130-31, 162-63, 169-70, 230-32, 233, 235, 241, *see also* Sons of Liberty; campaign, 1862, pp. 137 ff.; "War Democrats" return to, 138-39; and draft, 156, 203, 204, 251; victory and celebration, 1862, pp. 156-57, 158-59; in General Assembly, 1863, pp. 166 ff.; reaction to Morton's extralegal administration (1863-65), 179-85, 217; mass convention at Indianapolis, 199-200; reaction to Morgan's Raid, 208, 209-10; protest eligibility of Morton for governorship, 220; criticize quotas and recruiting, 228, 230; state convention and platform, 1864, pp. 230, 233-34; national convention, 235; campaign, 236, 238-39; defeated in elections, 253, 254; in General Assembly, 1865, pp. 255, 256, 257, 258; prevent passage of "Governor's Bill," 258; and Lincoln's assassination, 260; effect of Civil War on principles of, 266; revival among western

Democratic party and Democrats (Cont.)
agrarians, 267, 268. *See also*
"War Democrats."
Dennison, William, governor of Ohio, 117n, 122.
Deserters, from Union army, 163, 164, 215, 216.
Develin, Lafe, 41n.
Disloyalty, *see* Treason and disloyalty.
Dodd, Harrison H., peace advocate, 166, 231; grand commander, Sons of Liberty, 232, 240, 242; plans Northwest Conspiracy, 243, 244; office raided, 245; arrest, trial, and escape, 247-49.
Douglas, Stephen A., political enmity with Jesse D. Bright, 16, 41-42; in 1860 campaign, 33, 41, 45; nominated for president, 41; votes received in Indiana, 48n; proclaims support of administration at opening of war, 73.
Draft, 133; upon state militia (1862), 144, 155-56; system of national conscription adopted, 202-3; opposition and resistance to, 203, 204, 213, 214-15; substitute system under, 216; War Department proposal for, 1864, denounced by Morton, 227; necessity of acknowledged, 230; held in 1864, pp. 250-51; in 1865, p. 259.
Dred Scott decision, 20.
Dueling, resolution outlawing, 62n.
Dumont, Ebenezer, joins Union party, 95, 96; elected to Congress, 156n.
Dunham, Cyrus L., 19, 88, 95, 210, 235.
Dunn, William M., 52-53, 145.

Early, Gen. Jubal A., 229.
East, The, *see* New England and the East.
Economic conditions, in Indiana in the 1850's, 3-4, 10-13; effect of Civil War on, 78-79, 139-40, 189-91, 238, 267-68. *See also* Agriculture; Banking; Finances, state; Industry and Commerce; State Banks; Tariff.
Edgerton, Joseph K., 199.
Ekin, Capt. James A., U. S. quartermaster for Indiana, 120.
Elections, 1854, p. 22; 1856, p. 24; 1858, p. 24; 1860, pp. 14, 43, 46-47, 47-48; 1862, pp. 156-57; 1863, p. 212; 1864, pp. 252-53, 253-54.
Emancipation, emerges as political issue, 129; compensated, proposed for District of Columbia, 146; increase of sentiment in favor of, 146-47; Lincoln issues proclamation of, 147, 162; reaction to, 147-48, 163.
English, William H., 131n; warns "War Democrats," 138; heads First National Bank, 190.
Evansville (Ind.), 12, 118.
Everett, Edward, vice-presidential candidate, Constitutional Union ticket, 36, 42.

Feagler, Henry, 62n.
Federal government, conflicts with states, 102, 109-10, 113-16, 116 ff.; strengthened by Civil War, 140, 191, 203, 266-67. *See also* Lincoln, Abraham; Army, Union; War Department.
Felonies Act, 78.
Fillmore, Millard, 23, 24.
Finances, state, crisis in, caused by secession, 61-62, 79-80; legislative auditing committee created, 76, 84-85; appropriations and provisions for defense, 76, 77, 107 ff., 181; suffer from weak credit standing, 77; Assembly fails to pass appropriation bill, 178, 179; taken over by Morton, 180-84; move given legal sanction by Assembly, 257; profiteer-

ing and swindling, 188; settlement of loan from Federal government, 258. *See also* Bonds; State Banks.
First National Bank of Indianapolis, 190.
Fitch, Graham N., 88.
Fletcher, Calvin, 150; agent to secure arms, 107.
Fletcher, Miles J., killed in accident, 150.
Fort Donelson, fall of, 123, 125, 133.
Fort Henry, fall of, 123, 125, 133.
Fort Sumter, fired upon, 70; falls, 71, 100.
Fort Wayne (Ind.), 50; riot at, 196n.
Fort Wayne *Sentinel*, 202-3.
Fredericksburg (Va.), 162.
Free-Soil party, fuses with Republican party, 22; enraged by Republican concessions to Know-Nothingism, 23; denounces Defrees' popular sovereignty stand, 25.
Frémont, Gen. John Charles, presidential candidate, 1856, 23; commander of western army, reinforcements for, 104, 123; attacked by Morton, 225-26; presidential candidate (1864), 219, 224; withdraws from contest, 250.

Garber, Michael C., political antagonist of Morton, 84, 85, 90.
Garfield, Gen. James A., 237.
General Assembly, 1861, pp. 61-67; 1861 special session, 75-80, 80-81; investigates commissary department, 111; 1863 session, 166-77 *passim;* fails to pass appropriation bills, 178, 179; receives memorials and resolutions from soldiers, 173-75; 1865 session, 255-58; asks draft be postponed, 259.

General Military Agency of Indiana, distributes sanitary stores, 124.
Germans, as political issue, 9-10; oppose Bates as presidential nominee, 37, 38; Republicans bid for votes of, 29, 45, 224, 225-26; swing to Republicans in 1860, p. 48; favor Frémont for president in 1864, pp. 219, 224; refuse to support Morton, 226.
Gettysburg, Battle, 213.
Giddings, Joshua R., 40-41, 46, 50.
Gooding, D. S., 237.
Gordon, Maj. J. W., 224; counsel for Dodd, 247.
Governors, state, power wielded by, in raising army, 100; conflicts with Federal administration, 102, 110, 114, 117; contract for army supplies in open market, 107; jealousy among, 121; join to aid recruiting, 143, 228.
"Governor's Bill," 258.
Granger movement, 268.
Grand Army of the Republic, 266.
Grant, Gen. U. S., 115, 123, 125, 161, 213, 229, 252, 255.
Greeley, Horace, 39, 40n, 51.
Greencastle (Ind.), 238.
Gresham, Walter Q., 51, 84, 88.

Habeas corpus, suspension of writ of, 92, 141.
Hamill, Samuel R., 200.
Hamilton (Ohio), 209.
Hamilton, Allen, 95.
Hammond, Abram A., governor, 8n.
Hanna, Bayless W., 169, 177.
Hannaman, William, director, Indiana Sanitary Commission, 124.
Harrison (Ohio), on route of Morgan's Raid, 209.
Harrison, Benjamin, 88, 237, 265.
Harrison, William Henry, 4n.
Hartford Convention, 136.

Hascall, Gen. Milo S., commander of District of Indiana, 198-202; commands troops to pursue Morgan's raiders, 209.

Hassaurek, Frederick, of Cincinnati, 45.

Heffren, Horace, state representative, 63, 65, 75; challenged by G. C. Moody, 62n-63n; participates in Democratic secret societies, 231; arrested and tried for treason, 249, 253.

Helper, Hinton R., *Impending Crisis*, 32.

Hendricks, Thomas A., 99; joins Douglas faction, 17; nominated for governor (1860), 19-20, 21; bargain with Turpie, 28n; campaign, 33, 43; proclaims loyalty to Union and support of war, 72, 152; accused of disloyalty, 149, 156, 164; addresses 1862 Democratic convention, 131-32; addresses Democratic victory jubilee, 159; elected to U. S. Senate, 168; at Democratic mass meeting (1863), 201; urges submission to draft, 204; supports McClellan for president, 235; in 1864 campaign, 238; addresses mass meeting upon Lincoln's death, 260.

Hines, Capt. Thomas H., cavalry raid into southern Indiana, 205.

Hobson, Gen. Edward H., 207, 209.

Holloway, William R., private secretary to Morton, 83, 87; on military appointments, 91n.

Holman, William S., 42, 57, 95, 134n, 139, 152, 210; elected to Congress, 47n.

Homestead bill, as political issue, 3, 26, 29, 33, 43.

Hood, Gen. John B., 255.

Hopkins, Milton B., 134.

Hord, Oscar B., attorney general, 181-82.

Horsey, Stephen, arrested and tried for treason, 249, 253; sentenced to hang, 262; commutation of sentence and pardon, 264.

Hovey, Gen. Alvin P., 237; commander of District of Indiana, arrests leaders of Sons of Liberty, 247, 248.

Hudson, Robert N., joins army, 88; agent to obtain arms, 107.

Hughes, James, 95, 237.

Humphreys, Andrew, participates in Democratic secret societies, 231-32; arrested and tried for treason, 249, 253; sentenced, 262.

Illinois, division of, to form state of Jackson, proposed, 56; protests number of Indiana brigadier generals, 122.

Immigrants, as political issue in Indiana, 9-10. *See also* Germans; Irish.

Impending Crisis, by Hinton R. Helper, mentioned, 32.

Indiana, elements of population, 2, 12n; divergent elements and interests in, on eve of Civil War, 2, 4 ff., 13-14; proposals concerning alliance with the South, 56; division to form state of Jackson, proposed, 56; proposals of reapportionment of, defeated, 66, 176, 177; collapse of constitutional government, 179-84; organized into subordinate military district, 197; threatened with martial law, 198; combined with Michigan to form military district, 202; reaction to Morgan's Raid, 206-8; disloyalty in, *see* Sons of Liberty, Treason and disloyalty; recruiting in, quotas, etc., *see* Army, Union. *See also*, Defense, state; Finances, state; Northern Indiana; Sectionalism: Southern Indiana.

Index

Indiana Club, formed in Washington, D. C., 237-38.

Indiana Legion, creation of, 80; called out upon Confederate invasion of Kentucky, 153; funds for procured from Federal government, 181; traps Hines's cavalry company, 205; in Morgan's Raid, 206, 207, 208.

Indiana Sanitary Commission, 124-25, 126.

Indianapolis (Ind.), 50; Lincoln visits, 67-68; effect of opening of Civil War on, 70-71, 74; volunteers arrive at, 71-72; during Morgan's Raid, 207-8; reaction to Dodd's conspiracy, 245; to Lee's surrender, 259-60; to Lincoln's assassination, 260, 261.

Indianapolis *American*, 36.

Indianapolis *Atlas,* 6n.

Indianapolis fairgrounds, transformed into Camp Morton, 71.

Indianapolis *Free Press,* 219.

Indianapolis *Gazette,* 145, 165, 218, 223-24, 242.

Indianapolis *Journal,* on need for capital investment in Indiana, 3-4; on expansion of industry, 11; on victory as "duty" of Republican party, 34-35; suggests Abraham Lincoln as president, 37; on Lincoln's nomination, 40; on slavery as issue in 1860 campaign, 44; opposes coercion of seceded states, 51; proposes compromises on secession, 52; becomes less comprising toward South, 61; attacks *Sentinel* for sympathizing with treason, 73; proclaims Indiana loyal, 73; on Morton as "soldiers' friend," 87; accuses Democrats of treason, 94; pleads for Union party, 95; on Wright's appointment to Senate, 98; on rebel invasion of Kentucky, 115; on movement of Indiana troops to Kentucky front, 118; attacks administration's prosecution of war, 119, 161; blames McClellan for military reverses, 142; opposes tampering with slavery, 145-46; defends emancipation proclamation, 148; demands removal of Gen. Buell, 154; attacks Gen. Nelson, 154; on Democratic victory in 1862, p. 157; on alleged Democratic conspiracy, 165; on state finances, 180; on changing commercial conditions, 189; on prosperity during Civil War, 191; on war aims, 192; on Union campaign and election of 1864, pp. 218, 223, 225; publishes exposé of Sons of Liberty, 242; on Dodd conspiracy, 245; on treason trials, 249, 264; on military victories, 250; on Morton's message to the Assembly, 1865, p. 257; on well-being in Indiana following war, 268.

Indianapolis *Locomotive,* 45.

Indianapolis National Guard, 70.

Indianapolis *Old Line Guard,* 42.

Indianapolis *Sentinel,* on tariff, 5; becomes organ of Douglas Democrats, 17; on Bright's visit to Indianapolis, 18; on disunity in Republican party, 22-23, 50; on possible dissolution of Union, 56n; on Morton's stand against secession, 60; reaction to Fort Sumter, 72; accused of sympathizing with treason, 72-73, 94; on use of army as political steppingstone, 88; attacks Republican "no-party" scheme, 92, 138; on Governor's military appointments, 90; on Wright's appointment to Senate, 98; on Republican criticism of their own administration, 119, 130; on military arrests, 141; on emancipation proclamation, 147; on New England and the war, 166; on opening of 1863 Assembly, 167; on

Indianapolis Sentinel (Cont.)
Morton's "dictatorship," 184-85; on new national banking system, 190; on "military rule" in Indiana, 197, 202; loyalty of, 211; on effect of Civil War on Freedom, 267; on western insurgency against New England, 268.

Industry and commerce, plea for capital for, 3-4; expansion of, 10-11; effect of secession on, 50, 53-54, 78-79, 132; revival of, 133, 189, 190, 191, 267-68.

Irish, as political issue, 9-10.

Jackson, state of, proposed, 56.
Jackson, Andrew, lingering influence on Indiana politics, 4, 131, 133, 136, 167; defeat of Democracy of, 14, 189, 190, 266-68.
Jackson, Gen. Thomas Jonathan (Stonewall), 142.
Jefferson, Thomas, 10.
Jeffersonville (Ind.), 114; Lane-Hendricks debate at, 33.
Johnson, Andrew, 33; vice-presidential candidate, 222; nomination, 224; speaks in Indiana, 237; succeeds to presidency, 261, 262; pardons Indianans convicted of treason, 263-64.
Jones, James G., 88.
Julian, George W., 29, 45, 46, 94; attacks conservative Republicans on slavery issue, 22, 23, 58, 83, 147; attacks fusionist policies of Republicans, 25, 26; on tariff, 6; joins Republican party, 22; favors nomination of Salmon P. Chase, 35; gives support to Lincoln, 40; proclaims Indiana loyal, 73; breaks with Morton, 83-84; seeks dismissal of Caleb B. Smith, 84n; criticizes Morton's military appointments, 90; regards Union party as too conservative, 135; favors emancipation, 147; elected to Congress, 1862, p. 156n; supports Lincoln, 219, 224, 226; feud with Morton, 226-27; opposes Johnson's conservative reconstruction program, 261; supplanted by Morton as leader of the radicals, 262; seeks execution of Indianans convicted of treason, 263.

Kansas, and Lecompton Constitution, 16; admission of, 29.
Kentucky, efforts to maintain neutrality, 112-13, 115; campaign in (1861), 118, (1862), 152-55; Morgan's Raid in (1864), 240.
Kerr, Michael C., 244, 253n.
Kilgore, David, 53.
Kimball, Gen. Nathan, 224.
Knights of the Golden Circle, 149-50, 165; exposé of, 151; rumors of plots to convert Democratic mass meeting into uprising, 199; accused of aiding Morgan's raiders, 209.
Know-Nothing party, *see* American party.
Koerner, Gustave, warns against Bates's nomination, 38.

Lane, Henry S., joins Republican party, 22; deal with Morton over gubernatorial nomination, 27-28; campaign for governor, 31-33, 43; and presidential nomination (1860), 36, 37, 39-40; election as governor, 47; offers compromise on slavery extension, 52; elected to U. S. Senate, 61; at Union rally, 96; opposes abolition, 145; seeks execution of Indianans convicted of treason, 263.
Lane, Gen. Joseph, 20.
Lanier, James F. D., helps Indiana finance Civil War, 76. *See also* Winslow, Lanier & Company.
La Porte (Ind.), 239.
Law, John, 47n.
Lecompton Constitution, 16.

Lee, Gen. Robert E., surrender, 259.

Lincoln, Abraham, 161, 169, 170, 181; candidacy and nomination of, 37, 40; campaign clubs, 45; votes received in Indiana (1860), 48n; silence on secession crisis attacked by Democrats, 53; and question of compromise with, or coercion of, South, 58; proclaims inviolability of Union in speech at Indianapolis, 67-68; attempt to provision Fort Sumter precipitates Civil War, 70; calls for troops, 71, 78, 100, 104, 142, 143, 144, 213, 214, 227, 228, 230, 250, 259; ignores Morton's request for military appointment, 89; suspension of civil liberties criticized, 92-93, 141, 170; conflicts with Governor Morton and other state officials, 102, 114, 115, 116 ff.; discourages overrecruiting, 105; Kentucky policy, 113-15, 116, 118; criticized for lack of interest in army, 118-19; and emancipation, 146, 147, 162; Morton addresses on subject of ending war in 1864, p. 217; moderate reconstruction program, 218; Republican criticism of administration, 218, 219-20; 1864 campaign and re-election, 221, 224, 225, 253; intercedes in Julian's behalf, 226-27; refuses to postpone draft, 250-51; commutes Humphreys' sentence, 262; pardon sought for Indianans convicted of treason, 263; assassination, 260; lies in state in Indianapolis, 261.

Logan, Gen. John A., 237.

Louisville (Ky.), 78, 79, 155; threatened by Confederate attack, 152, 153.

Lowry, Robert, 19.

Loyal Leagues, 193.

Lozier, John H., 237.

McClellan, Gen. George B., 113, 114; to direct secret service organization, 117n; organizes Army of the Potomac, 133; failure at Richmond, 142; nominated for president, 235, 246; defeated in election, 253.

McClernand, John A., 161.

McCulloch, Hugh, 8.

McDonald, Joseph E., Democratic nominee for governor (1864), 233, 234, 238, 239, 244, 246; supports McClellan for president, 235.

McLean, John, 36, 37.

McMullen, Rev. J. W. T., 29.

Magoffin, Beriah, governor of Kentucky, 113.

Manson, Mahlon D., blamed for defeat at Richmond (Ky.), 154; nominee for lieutenant governor, 233n.

Mansur, Isaiah, director commissary department, 111.

Maryland, suspension of civil rights in, 92.

Meigs, Montgomery C., quartermaster general, 110.

Memphis (Tenn.), 133.

Meredith, Sol, 88, 226-27.

Michigan, fails to send delegates to Washington peace conference, 64; combined with Indiana to form military district, 202.

Military arrests, 141-42, 197, 200, 202, 246-47; declared illegal if civil courts open, 240, 263-64.

Military Auditing Committee, 257.

Militia, state, bills for reorganization of, defeated, 66, 176-77; act for reorganization of passed, 80; tenders services to Governor, 70; draft on, 144, 155-56; called out during Morgan's Raid, 207.

Milligan, Lambdin P., peace advocate, 231; loses gubernatorial nomination, 233; arrested and

Milligan, Lambdin P. (Cont.)
tried for treason, 249, 253; sentenced to hang, 262; pardon, 264; sues military court for damages, 264-65.
Milroy, Gen. Robert H., 146, 173.
Minnesota, 64.
Mississippi River, importance to Indiana's economy, 12; importance of keeping open, 57, 96, 122-23, 160-61; opened by fall of Vicksburg, 213.
Missouri Compromise, 22, 52.
Montgomery, Maj. Alexander, U.S. quartermaster of Indiana, 119-20.
Moody, G. C., challenges Horace Heffren to duel, 62n-63n.
Moral standards, affected by Civil War, 187-89, 216.
Morgan, Gen. John Hunt, raid into Indiana, 205-10; into Kentucky (1864), 240.
Morgan County (Ind.), arrest of deserters in, 164.
Morrill Act, for land-grant colleges, 258.
Morrill tariff, 54.
Morton, Oliver P., candidate for governor, 1856, 6n; joins Republican party, 22; favors abandoning slavery as party issue and adopting issue of imperialism, 25; deal with Lane over gubernatorial nomination, 27-28; campaign for lieutenant governor, 31-33; opposes Seward's nomination, 36; inaugurated as governor, 61; personality and ambition, 59, 82-83; assumes leadership of Republican party, 59-60, 82-83; takes stand against compromise with South, 60-61; and Washington peace conference, 63, 64, 65; welcomes Lincoln to Indianapolis, 67; denounces treason and makes preparation for war, 68-69; calls special session of Assembly, 74-75;

and army: pledges troops to enforce law, 70; tenders men for Federal service, 71; works to raise and equip troops, 71, 101, 102, 103, 104-5, 106 ff., 142-43, 143-44, 161, 213-14, 227, 228; proposes creation of "President's Legion," 105; *see also* Indiana Legion, State militia; clashes with inefficiency in Federal administration, 70, 101, 103, 104, 107, 116-21; calls for submergence of partisanship, 75; sells state bonds, 76; receives certain powers in reorganization of militia, 80; organizes and assumes leadership of Union party, 83; breaks with Julian, 83-84; involved in sectional struggle for control of party, 84-85; ignores legislative auditing committee, 85; answer to Republican antagonists, 85-86; uses soldiers for political capital, 86-87, 88, 123-24, 172-73, 174, 228, 236-37, 265, 266-67; seeks military appointment, 89; relations with Lincoln, 89, 102, 114, 115, 116 ff., 217, 218; uses power to make military appointments to serve political ends, 89-91; invited to Union rally, 96; appoints Joseph A. Wright to succeed Bright in Senate, 98; establishes state arsenal, 108-9; urges investigation of state quartermaster department, 112; efforts to defend Ohio River "front," 113-15, 152; offers advice and criticism on prosecution of war, 113-16, 116-21, 160-61, 217;

clashes with United States officials and army officers: Major Montgomery, U. S. quartermaster of Indiana, 119-20; General Ripley, 108-9, 120; Col. Simonson, 120; Secretary of War Stanton, 120-21; Generals Buell and Nelson, 154-55, 159-60; asks for Hascall's removal, 202; jealousy and suspicion of other states, 121-22; opposed by radical element in Union party, 135; presides at 1862 Union convention, 136; approves emancipation proclamation, 148; plot to kill, alleged by Republicans, 150; alleges disloyalty in Indiana, 151, 163-64, 167, 172, 173, 205, 208, 222, 238-39; criticized for sending raw recruits into Kentucky campaign, 153; and draft: opposes and delays, 155, 227, 250-51, 259; warns against resistance to, 204; resignation suggested following elections in 1862, p. 158; works to open Mississippi River, 160-61; relations with General Assembly, 1863, p. 168-70; becomes virtual dictator of Indiana, 179-84; confesses Southern Indiana most loyal part of state, 210; protests frequent military arrests, 198; activities during Morgan's Raid, 206-7, 207-8, 208-9; relations with Salmon P. Chase over presidential nomination, 218; presidential boom for, 219; candidate for governor, 1864, eligibility questioned, 220; nomination for governor and campaign, 221-22, 225-26, 238-39; addresses Lincoln's ratification meeting, 225; feud with Julian, 226-27; extralegal administration denounced by Democrats, 234; supported by eastern banking interests, 238; uses exposé of Sons of Liberty and Dodd conspiracy to make political capital, 241 ff.; brings about arrest of leaders of Sons of Liberty, 246-47; checks southern refugee emigration into Indiana, 250; works to obtain soldier vote, 251-52; addresses Union party victory rally, 253; success of political machine, 255-56; message to Assembly, 1865, pp. 256-57; extralegal administration approved by Assembly, 257; honors Lincoln upon his death, 261; relations with President Johnson, 261, 262; assumes leadership of radical Republicans, 262; works to obtain pardon for Indianans convicted of treason, 263-64.

Murfreesboro (Tenn.), 162, 167, 174.

National Leagues, 193.
Negroes, number in Indiana (1860), 2; attitude toward in Indiana, 9; enlisted in army, 215. *See also* Abolition; Emancipation; Slavery; Thirteenth Amendment.
Nelson, Gen. William, feud with Morton and General Davis, and death, 154-55.
New Albany (Ind.), 12.
New Albany *Ledger,* shows prosouthern, antieastern sentiment, 12; on disunity in Republican party, 50; proposes alliance of Indiana with South, 56; on possible effect of closing Mississippi River, 57; attacks Republican "no-party" scheme, 92; on fear of long war, 93; becomes mouthpiece of "War Democrats," 95-96; opposes Democratic call for 1862 convention, 130; and Union party, 134n, 135; on opening Mississippi River, 144; denounces emancipation proclamation and supports Democratic party, 147; loyalty, 211; favors prosecution of war, 233; on McClellan's nomination, 235; on legalization of Morton's extralegal administration, 257.
Newburgh (Ind.), rebel raid, 150-51.

New England and the East, prejudice against, in Indiana, 3, 12, 33, 54, 93, 132, 144, 189, 228, 231, 238, 267, 268; accused of profiting from war, 166.
New England Loyal Publications Society, 192.
New Orleans (La.), 79.
New York (N. Y.), Indiana bonds sold in, 76, 77.
New York *Herald*, 87n.
New York Loyal Publications Society, 192.
New York *Tribune*, quoted, 40n, 51.
Niblack, William E., 253n.
Northern Indiana, cleavage between southern and, 13, 22, 54, 78-79; wins political power from southern section, 80, 84-85.
Northwest, Old, social and economic conditions in the 1850's, 1-2.
Northwest Confederacy, proposal of, 56; denounced by Morton, 136.
Northwest conspiracy, 240, 243.

Ohio, Department of the, highhanded conduct of officers of, 196 ff.
Ohio, State of, contribution to Indiana's population, 12; Morgan's raiders enter, 209.
Ohio River, importance of, in Indiana's economy, 12, 13; unifying force in borderland, 13; as "front" in Civil War, 113, 114.
Order of American Knights, 232, 242. *See also* Sons of Liberty.
Orth, Godlove S., joins Republican party, 22; elected to Congress, 156n.
Owen, Robert Dale, commissioner to procure arms for Indiana, 107-8, 110; works for continuance of state arsenal, 109; serves as liaison agent between state and Federal government, 116; advocates emancipation, 146-47.

Packard, M. A. O., 62n.

Paducah (Ky.), 115.
Panic of 1837, p. 7.
Panic of 1857, pp. 10, 43, 54.
Peace advocates, in Democratic party, 130-31, 162-63, 169-70, 230-32, 233, 234, 235.
Pendleton, George H., 159.
People's party, *see* Republican party.
Perkins, Judge S. E., decision concerning legality of military arrests, 240.
Perryville (Ky.), battle of, 155.
Petersburg (Va.), siege of, 229, 255.
Pettit, John, of Kansas, 18.
Pettit, John U., 256.
Philips, J. E., 73n.
Piatt, Donn, 160n.
Pierce, Franklin, 16.
Plymouth *Democrat*, editor arrested under Hascall's Order No. 9, p. 199.
Pogue's Run, Battle of, 201.
Popular sovereignty, 17, 24-25, 26, 41.
Population, elements in Indiana, 2, 12n.
Populist movement, 268.
Porter, Albert G., 96.
"President's Legion," proposed, 105.
Profiteering, 188-89.
Pugh, George, of Ohio, 45.

Quartermaster department, **state**, criticism of, 110, 111-12. *See also* Army, Union.
Quotas, *see* Army, Union.

"Rail Maulers," 45, 60.
Railroads, vs. river transportation, 12-13, 56, 79, 132, 144, 171, 189; accident on, described as treasonable plot, 150; thrive during Civil War, 190-91; prejudice against, 267. *See also* Transcontinental railroad.
Ray, Martin M., on war aims, 81; joins Union party, 95; invited to

Union rally, 96; addresses Union party convention, 136-37; returns to Democratic fold, 147-48; counsel for Dodd, 247.

Reapportionment, bill for, defeated, 66, 176, 177.

Reconstruction, as political issue, 217-18, 222, 225, 261-62, 266.

Recruiting, *see* Army, Union: volunteers.

Republican party and Republicans, stand on: homestead bill, 3, 26, 29, 33, 43; tariff, 5-6, 43-44, 54, 139; state and national banks, 7, 8; slavery and abolition, 9, 22, 29, 43, 44, 52-53, 58-59, 145, 222, 223; coercion or compromise of seceded states, 50-53, 57-58, 58-59; Washington peace conference, 64, 65;

as a fusion party, 10, 21-22, 22-23, 24; platform and victory (1854), 22; national organization founded, 23; struggles to find unifying issues, 24-25, 25-26; state platform and defeat (1856), 23; adopts conservative platform (1858), 24; state convention and platform (1860), 27-30; make bids for German votes, 29, 45, 224, 225-26; campaign, 31 ff., 42 ff.; national convention, 34-41; split between conservatives and radicals, 35, 36, 41; victory in 1860, pp. 46-47, 47-48; disunity and factionalism among, 50-53, 62-63, 83-86, 91, 224; Morton assumes leadership of, 59-60, 82-83; in General Assembly, 1861, pp. 62-63, 64, 65, 66-67; in special session, 1861, pp. 75-76; define war aims, 81, 82, 97, 134, 137, 145, 192, 237; makes political capital out of soldiers, 87-88, 172-73, 174, 236-37, 266-67; anti-Morton faction criticizes military appointments, 90; sincerity of "no-party" plea belied, 92; organize "no-party" Union party, 94-95; attack 1862 partisan Democratic state convention, 130; financial policy and extravagance attacked, 139-40, 238, 267, 268; prosecution of war deplored by Democrats, 140; charged with intimidation of political enemies, 141; split over slavery, 145; spread tales of treason and Democratic disloyalty, 148-49, 149-51, 158-59, 163-65, 167, 170-71, 172, 194-96, 204-5, 212, 240 ff.; and draft, 156, 203, 204; in General Assembly (1863), 168 ff.; hold Union meetings to counteract "disloyal" Democratic activities, 172; bolt Assembly to prevent passage of Democratic-sponsored legislation, 177-79; trend toward stronger central government under, 191; organize secret societies for disseminating Union propaganda, 193; at Democratic mass meeting (1863), 201; victories in 1863 elections, 212; reaction to Morgan's Raid, 209-10; antiadministration Chase movement in, 218; make concessions to Germans, 224; radical element nominates Frémont for President, 224; makes political capital out of treason trials, 248-49; withdrawal of Frémont as candidate, 250; blame Democrats for draft, 251; triumph, 1864, p. 253; make political capital out of Lincoln's assassination, 260; split over reconstruction policy, 261-62; triumph of principles of, following Civil War, 266-68. *See also* Union party.

Richmond (Ky.), Union defeat at, 154.

Richmond (Va.), siege of, 255, 259.

Richmond (Ind.) *Palladium,* 10-11, 226.

Ripley, Gen. James W., head of Federal ordnance department, opposes operation of state arsenal, 108-9; feud with Morton, 120.

Ristine, Joseph, state auditor, 181-82, 183n, 184.

Robinson, John L., United States marshal, 18, 21.

Rockport (Ind.), 34, 164.

Rosecrans, Gen. William S., commander of Army of the Ohio, 160, 167, 174.

Rushville *Jacksonian,* 18.

Salem (Ind.), on route of Morgan's Raid, 207.

Salineville (Ohio), 209.

Sanitary Commission, *see* Indiana Sanitary Commission; United States Sanitary Commission.

Schurz, Carl, warns against Bates's nomination, 38; aids Republican campaign in Indiana, 45.

Scott, Winfield, General-in-chief of the Army, 114.

Scottsburg (Ind.), on route of Morgan's Raid, 207.

Secession, of South Carolina and Gulf States, 49; reaction to, in Indiana, 49-50; effect on business, 50-51, 53-54, 189-90; political effect of, 50 ff., 237; compromises offered on, 52-53, 54-55; attitude of borderland on, 54-55; increase in favor of coercion against, 57-58; Morton takes stand against, 60-61; Lincoln defines attitude on, 67.

Secrest, Henry, 136.

Secret service organization, to operate in South, 117n.

Secret societies, 136, 149-50, 163, 192-93, 231-32. *See also* Knights of the Golden Circle; Order of American Knights; Sons of Liberty; Union clubs.

Sectionalism, as political issue, 3; evidenced in attitudes toward the tariff, 5, 43-44, 56, 93, 139-40; increased by secession movement, 52, 56; weakened by opening of Civil War, 72; shift of political power from southern to northern Indiana, 80; evidenced in Republican factionalism, 84-85; in difficulties between state and Federal governments, 121; between East and West during Civil War, 122-23; evidenced in split in Democratic party, 129-30; in Union party, 135. *See also* New England and the East; Northern Indiana; Southern Indiana.

Seward, William H., 49; presidential candidate, 35, 36, 39, 40; secretary of state, 119, 143.

Seymour, Horatio, governor of New York, 169.

Sheridan, Gen. Philip H., 250.

Sherman, Gen. William Tecumseh, 123, 213, 229; opposes postponement of draft, 250; capture of Atlanta, 250; march to the sea, 255.

Shiloh, Battle of, 133.

Shipbuilding, 12.

Simonson, Col. John S., U. S. mustering officer at Indianapolis, 120.

Six Regiments bill, 77, 84, 102; attacked by southern Indiana Republicans, 84, 85.

Slavery, as issue in party alignments (1856-1860), 6; attitude toward, in Indiana, in the 1850's, p. 9; in 1862, pp. 145-46; in 1860 campaign, 25-26, 29, 32, 33, 40-41, 43, 44; and secession crisis, 52-53, 58-59; exclusion from territories, 146; constitutional amendment to abolish, 222, 224, 225, 258. *See also* Abolition; Emancipation; and under Democratic party and Democrats and

Republican party and Republicans

Smith, Caleb B., strong protectionist, 6; joins Republican party, 22; in Republican campaign (1860), 32; attitude toward abolition and emancipation, 32, 147; wins promise of cabinet position, 39; rejoices over Lincoln's nomination, 40; secretary of the interior, dismissal sought by Julian, 84n; aid sought in enlisting volunteers, 103.

Smith, G. Clay, 80n.

Smith, Gen. Kirby, launches Kentucky campaign, 152.

Social conditions, of Old Northwest in 1850's, 1-2; in Indiana in 1850's, 2-3; altered by Civil War, 186 ff., 216, 266.

Soldiers, *see* Army, Union.

Soldiers' families, provision for, 76, 187.

"Soldiers' friends," 86-87, 123-24, 173, 174, 265, 266.

Soldiers' vote, Union party works to win, 250-51.

Sons of Liberty, 232; exposé of, 241-49; arrest of leaders and trials, 246-49, 262-65; Republicans make political capital of, 253.

South, The, commercial relations with Indiana, 11-12, 13, 54-55, 56-57, 79, 96, 132; secession of, 49; conciliation or coercion of, becomes political issue, 50 ff., 57, 68; subjugation of, as aim of Civil War, 81, 82, 131, 140; refugees from, 250.

South Bend (Ind.), 50.

South Carolina, secedes from Union, 49.

Southern Indiana, cleavage between northern and, 13, 22, 54, 78-79; suffers economic crisis at outbreak of Civil War, 78-79; loses political power to northern section, 80, 184-85; thrown into panic by Kentucky's neutrality, 113-14; defense of, 113, 114, 115-16, 118, 153; raids into, 150-51, 205-10; loyalty of, 210.

Spencer County (Ind.), Republican convention, 26.

Stanton, Edwin M., secretary of war, 120, 143, 181, 258; feuds with Morton, 121; criticizes Hascall's conduct, 202; refuses to postpone draft, 250-51; co-operates in getting soldiers' vote, 252.

State agricultural college, land grant for accepted, 258.

State banks, 7-8; expansion of, discussed, 61-62; effect of Civil War on, 189-90.

States, conflict with Federal government, 109-10, 113-16, 116 ff., 227; jealousy among, 121; sovereignty of, in raising army, 100; in caring for sick and wounded, 123-26. *See also* States' rights.

States' rights, as issue in Civil War, 82; affected by Civil War, 191, 266; suffer by national conscription measure, 203.

Stidger, Felix G., aids in exposing Sons of Liberty, 241 ff., 247, 248.

Stone, Asahel, succeeds as director of state commissary department, 111.

Stover, D. C., state agent, 77.

Strong Bands, 193.

Sturm, Capt. Herman, directs state arsenal, 108, 109.

Sumner, Charles, 44, 50.

Surgeons, army, qualifications of questioned, 89-90.

Tanner, Gordon, 19.

Tariff, 4-7, 26, 43-44, 56, 93, 132, 139-40, 172, 189, 222, 237, 238, 267-68; Morrill Act, 54.

Temperance, advocates of, join Republican party, 22.
Terre Haute (Ind.), 164; Republican campaign opened in, 31-32.
Terrell, William H. H., adjutant general, on General Ripley, 109; on disloyalty in Democratic Assembly, 173; director of bureau of finance, 181; financial secretary, report, 257.
Thirteenth Amendment, ratified by General Assembly, 258.
Thomas, Gen. George H., 255.
Thompson, Richard W., 36, 96.
Tod, David, governor of Ohio, 209; invited to Union rally, 96.
Transcontinental railroad, advocated, 26, 29.
Treason and disloyalty, accusations of, hurled by Indiana legislators, 62; Assembly passes act defining and providing penalty for, 78; societies organized for, alleged, 136, 149-50, 163, 192-93; accusations of, hurled against Democrats, for political purposes, 94, 148-51, 164-65, 170-71, 172, 175, 194, 208-9, 212, 240 ff.; report of U. S. District Court on, 151; Democrats refute accusations, 157; cries of, evidence of war hysteria, 194, 212; General Burnside's general order concerning, 197; Hascall's Order No. 9, pp. 198-99, 200, 202; efforts to find evidence in Indiana fails, 241, 247, 248; trials for, 247-49, 253, 262, 263-64. *See also* Knights of the Golden Circle; Sons of Liberty.
Treasury, Department of, acts to check trade with Confederate states, 79.
Trials for treason, 247-49, 253, 262, 263-64.
Turpie, David, candidate for lieutenant governor, 1860, pp. 28n, 33; 1864, p. 233; elected to U. S. Senate, 168.

Underwood, John C., of Virginia, 46.
Union, The, inviolability of, proclaimed by Lincoln, 68; by Morton, 68-69; Indiana's loyalty to, proclaimed, 72, 73; preservation of, as aim of Civil War, 81, 82, 92, 93, 129, 131, 134, 235.
Union clubs, for dissemination of Union propaganda, 192-93.
Union League, 192, 238.
Union meetings, strive for conciliation with South, 55, 63; denounced by radicals, 61.
Union party, product of Morton's political efforts, 83; formation of, 95; formulates policy, 134; "War Democrats" join, 95, 96, 134, 135; calls meeting in Indianapolis, 96-97; attacks Democratic partisan activities, 134; 1862 convention and platform, 134-37; split between radicals and conservatives, 134-35, 218-27; campaigns, 137 ff.; called hypocritical by *Sentinel*, 138; loses support of "War Democrats," 138; torn by slavery issue, 145; loses strength following issue of emancipation proclamation, 147-48; resorts to tales of rebel barbarism and Democratic disloyalty, 148-49; loses strength by Confederate campaign into Kentucky, 155; defeated in 1862 election, 156-57; split over reconstruction policies, 217-18; 1864 convention and platform, 220-24; national convention and platform, 224-25; campaign, 236-38, 238-39, 239-40; uses Sons of Liberty and Dodd conspiracy as political capital, 240 ff.; revives during treason trials, 249-50; requests draft be postponed, 250; works to obtain soldier vote, 251-52; vic-

torious in 1864, pp. 252-53, 253-54. *See also* Republican party.

United States District Court, submits report on disloyalty in Indiana, 151.

United States Senate, expels Jesse D. Bright, 97-98.

United States Surgeon General, protests interference of Indiana Sanitary Commission, 125.

Vajen, J. H., director of state quartermaster department, 111-12.

Vallandigham, Clement L., 45, 159, 197, 210, 212, 225, 235n, 240.

Vanderburgh County (Ind.), Republican convention, 26.

Vernon (Ind.), on route of Morgan's Raid, 207.

Versailles (Ind.), on route of Morgan's Raid, 207.

Vicksburg (Miss.), 161, 162; fall of, 213.

Vincennes *Gazette*, 6n.

Virginia, calls Washington peace conference, 63-64.

Volunteers, *see* Army, Union.

Voorhees, Daniel W., 47n, 99; sketch of, 211; fosters sectional pride against New England, 3n; accused of being disunionist, 46; takes stand against coercion of seceded states, 55; proclaims loyalty and support of war, 72, 152, 235n; accused of disloyalty, 149, 156, 164, 196, 243; threatened by Indiana soldiers, 164; attacks Hascall's Order No. 9, p. 200; urges submission to draft, 204; in 1864 campaign, 238; loses Congressional election, 253n.

Walker, John C., 19; state agent, 183; participates in Democratic secret societies, 231, 246.

Wallace, Lew, Douglas Democrat, 19; appointed adjutant general, 71; joins army, 88; joins Union party, 95; aids recruiting, 143; commands defense of Cincinnati, 153; relieved of command, 154; heads investigation of Buell's Kentucky campaign, 160n; on increasing desertions, 163.

War Democrats, join Union party, 95, 96, 134, 136, 137-38; return to Democratic party, 138-39, 147, 148; participate in 1864 Union party campaign, 223, 237.

War Department, incompetency of, 101-2, 104, 106, 107; wavering recruiting policy, 77-78, 102, 103, 104-5, 133, 143; conflicts with state governments, 110, 113-16, 116 ff., 227; assumes Indiana's military debts, 180; gives Morton funds for state defense, 181; approves Morton's plan for aiding recruiting, 214, 228; makes bounty payments to volunteers, 215-16, 259; orders cessation to recruiting, 260. *See also* Army, Union; Draft.

Warrick County (Ind.), Republican convention, 26.

Washburn, Col. H. D., 253n.

Washington peace conference, 63-65.

Welles, Gideon, secretary of the navy, 119.

Whig party, in Indiana, 4; and tariff issue, 4, 6; bids for immigrant votes, 9; decline of, and absorption into American party, 9-10; fusion with and influence on Republican party, 22, 32-33, 34, 36; elements of, join Constitutional Union party, 36.

"Wide Awakes," 45.

Wilder, Col. John T., 173.

Wilderness campaign, 229.

Willard, Ashbel P., 18, 19, 45n.

Willcox, Gen. Orlando B., commander District of Michigan and Indiana, 202, 209.
Wilson, Henry, 50.
Winslow, James, 182.
Winslow, Lanier & Company, 76, 182-83, 184, 257.
Wisconsin, 64.
Women of Indiana, help care for sick and wounded, 124.

Wright, Gen. Horatio G., 197.
Wright, Joseph A., governor of Indiana, 8n, 12-13; member of Union party, 96, 136, 221, 233, 237; appointed to United States Senate, 98; attacked for opposing emancipation, 147.

Yates, Richard, governor of Illinois, 160.